1001 QUESTIONS ANSWERED ABOUT THE MINERAL KINGDOM

Richard M. Pearl

DOVER PUBLICATIONS, INC.
New York

Dedicated to Mignon

Published in Canada by General Publishing Company, Ltd., 30 Lesmill Road, Don Mills, Toronto, Ontario.

Published in the United Kingdom by Constable and Company, Ltd., 3 The Lanchesters, 162–164 Fulham Palace Road, London W6 9ER.

Bibliographical Note

This Dover edition, first printed in 1995, is a slightly altered republication of the 1968 revised edition of the work originally published by Dodd, Mead & Company, New York, in 1959. In the Dover edition, a Publisher's Note has been added; eight black-and-white photos that appeared in the original are omitted; the list of mineral magazines (Question 976) has been updated; and the former color frontispiece now appears on the inside front cover.

Library of Congress Cataloging-in-Publication Data

Pearl, Richard Maxwell, 1913–
   1001 questions answered about the mineral kingdom / Richard M. Pearl.
      p.   cm.
   "A slightly altered republication of the revised edition (1968) of the work originally published by Dodd, Mead & Company, New York, in 1959. For the Dover edition, a Note has been added, eight black-and-white photos which appeared in the original have not been included, and the list of mineral magazines (Question 976) has been updated"—T.p. verso.
   Includes bibliographical references (p.   –) and index.
   ISBN 0-486-28711-4 (pbk.)
   1. Minerals—Miscellanea. I. Title.
QE365.P33   1995
549—dc20   95-6204
                                                    CIP

Manufactured in the United States of America
Dover Publications, Inc., 31 East 2nd Street, Mineola, N.Y. 11501

PUBLISHER'S NOTE, 1995

In 1959 and 1968 when this work was originally published and revised, the harmful effects caused by exposure to asbestos (Question 137) and radon gas (Question 649) were not known. Since that time, however, both substances have been proven to be dangerous carcinogens. Asbestos is no longer used where it may come in contact with the public (i.e. as fireproof insulation), and radon gas, which has been found to form concentrations in buildings due to natural seepage from some mineral deposits, has forced the evacuation of numerous people when detected.

PREFACE

The products of the Mineral Kingdom are among the most familiar substances with which we come in contact in our daily lives. And yet the average person knows less about them than about almost any other element of his environment. This book has been written to make clear the answers to 1001 questions pertaining to the Mineral Kingdom—its scientific, industrial and commercial, cultural, and hobby aspects—all of which are found within the borders of this fascinating realm of nature.

The dedication of this book to my wife reflects my indebtedness to her for full participation in all phases of its preparation.

CONTENTS

THE MINERAL KINGDOM

From the Old Stone Age and the New Stone Age man moved cautiously through the Bronze Age into the Age of Iron. In a very real sense we still live in the Age of Iron, or more truthfully, the Age of Steel. Ahead seems to loom the still-nebulous Atomic Age, characterized perhaps by the utilization of the nuclear power of uranium, perhaps of thorium, possibly of hydrogen—we surely know not what. Eugene Ayers has called ours the Age of Fossil Fuels and there is strong evidence to prove the point. It has been said that, in the Second World War, as in the First, the "Allied cause floated to victory upon a wave of oil"; and only in those nations endowed by nature with an abundance of good coal has the Industrial Revolution flourished most mightily.

The animal, vegetable, and mineral kingdoms were first so classified in 1691 as separate realms or provinces of nature. The Mineral Kingdom includes not only the true minerals as defined on page 1, but also the rocks of the earth's crust, in which the minerals occur, as well as those intriguing rocks known as meteorites, which come to us from beyond our own planet. Within these rocks are found the native metals, natural alloys, and mineral compounds, both metallic and nonmetallic; some are mineral resources of present importance, while the significance of the others lies in the future. Mineral resources also include the fossil fuels—coal, petroleum, and their related substances—and the indispensable liquid, water. Soil, equally essential to life on earth, is almost a mineral resource, resulting, as it does, from the physical and chemical break-down of rock.

These subjects and many others are discussed in the following chapters, which are designed to answer the 1001 questions most often asked about the Mineral Kingdom and man's relation to it.

I. MINERALS AND CRYSTALS

Introduction. Because they make up most of what we call rocks, the individual minerals are the starting point for any worthwhile survey of the Mineral Kingdom. These are the chemical substances, homogeneous and with compositions ranging within fixed limits, that are formed in nature by inorganic processes. They include such familiar things as water and ice, such remarkable things as diamonds and liquid mercury or quicksilver, and things with such odd names as coquimbite and pseudowollastonite. We study them for their own characteristic properties and as the principal constituents of the large-scale bodies called rocks. Crystals, with their smooth surfaces and lustrous faces, are, as Abbé Haüy said in 1817, "the flowers of the minerals" and represent the interesting and attractive ways in which minerals tend to grow, if given room enough and time enough. On this planet Earth there seems to have been plenty of both. Minerals and crystals are scientific substances, economic substances, aesthetic and hobby substances, or all of these, depending upon the circumstances and your concern with them.

1. Why do mineral names end in *ite*? The familiar ending ite, used with most mineral names, goes back to ancient times. In the forms of *ites* and *itis* it was added by the Greeks, and later by the Romans, to ordinary words that denoted qualities, uses, constituents, or localities of minerals and rocks. Thus, *siderites* (now siderite) was made from the word for iron because the mineral contains iron; *haematites* (now hematite) was made from the word for blood because of the red color of the mineral when powdered. All the present kinds of mineral names, except names for persons, were used in classical days.

The ending *lite* is assumed to have come from the French suffix *lithe*, derived in turn from *lithos*, the Greek word for stone. In mineral names, however, it may merely stand for *ite*, with the letter *l* added for ease in speaking.

Other terminations have been used less extensively, though they include some of the most attractive-sounding mineral names. The ending *ine* appears in olivine, tourmaline, and nepheline; *ane*, in cymophane; *ase*, in dioptase, euclase, and orthoclase; *yre*, in dipyre;

ote, in epidote and glaucodote; *ole,* in amphibole; *aste,* in pleonaste; *age,* in diallage; *ime,* in analcime and xenotime; *ome,* in harmatome; and *ore,* in chlinochlore, diaspore, and pyrochlore.

2. How are minerals named?   Most newly named minerals are christened by the mineralogist who first describes them in print. The law of priority is applicable to mineral names and is superseded only when the original name is proved to have been incorrect or inadequate. The Mineralogical Society of America has a Committee on Nomenclature and Classification of Minerals which recommends rules to be followed in naming minerals.

Some of the most common mineral names are so old that their origin is unknown or doubtful. These include quartz, zircon, beryl, galena, cinnabar, gypsum, corundum, and tourmaline.

The first modern mineral to be named for a person was prehnite, which in 1790 was named by Werner (see Question 13) after Colonel von Prehn, who had brought the first specimen to Europe from the Cape of Good Hope where he had found it. This method of naming minerals has now become the most widely favored one.

In 1837 James D. Dana published the first edition of his *System of Mineralogy,* in which he applied a multiple Latin name to minerals, similar to the names used in botany and zoology. By 1850, however, when the third edition was published, he had rejected his entire nomenclature.

3. Who have been honored with mineral names?   Since the first such name was applied to prehnite (see Question 2), hundreds of scientists, rulers, philanthropists, mineral collectors, and other persons have had their names perpetuated in the names of minerals. There are too many to record here and any list would necessarily be incomplete. Outside the geologic field, however, a few of especial interest may be worth noting, as follows: Willemite, for William I, king of the Netherlands; goethite, for Johann Wolfgang Goethe, German poet who was an ardent mineral enthusiast; stephanite, for the Archduke Stephan of Austria; uvarovite, for Count Uvarov, a Russian statesman; and alexandrite, for Alexander II of Russia.

4. Which mineral names commemorate localities?   There are so many minerals in this category that a mere list would be voluminous

They range from the supposed occurrence of amazonstone near the Amazon River to the discovery of altaite in the Altai Mountains of Asia. Vesuvianite from Mount Vesuvius, labradorite from Labrador, thulite from the old name for Norway, turquois from Turkey (where it was marketed), alaskaite from the Alaska mine in Colorado, cubanite from Cuba, kernite from Kern County in California, aragonite from a former kingdom in Spain—these are only a few typical ones.

5. Which mineral names deal with occurrences?   Apart from their geographic localities, a number of minerals have been named because of their occurrence or their mineral or rock associations. Thus, emplectite is from the Greek "entwined" because it is found so intimately with quartz. On the other hand, monazite was coined from the Greek "to be solitary," though principally because of its rarity. Realgar is from the Arabic "powder of the mine" because it came from a silver mine. Perhaps the worst blunder in naming any mineral was in regard to pyroxene, which comes from the Greek "fire" and "stranger" because it was believed not to occur in igneous rocks (see Chapter II). No mineral is more characteristic of these rocks, and high temperature ones, at that!

6. Which mineral names come from mythology?   Scandinavian, Roman, and Greek mythology have furnished names for minerals. From the north country come aegerite, after Aegir, god of the sea, and thorite, after Thor, god of thunder. Roman myths have provided martite, after Mars, god of war, because of its red streak; neptunite, after Neptunus, god of the sea; and mercury, after Mercurius, messenger of the gods, because of its volatile and quick-moving nature ("quicksilver"). From Greece have come the names castorite and pollucite, after the twins Castor and Pollux, and tantalite, after Tantalus, with whom we associate the word tantalize—this mineral proved very difficult to dissolve in acid.

7. Which mineral names refer to their chemistry?   Of the large number of minerals whose names have reference to their chemical composition or chemical relationships, one of the more interesting is aenigmatite, which comes from the Greek "riddle" because its nature was puzzling to the chemist who analyzed it. No less candid is thaumasite, derived from the Greek "to be surprised" because of its unexpected composition. Xenotime is from the Greek "vain" and "honor" because it proved to contain yttrium, which had been mistaken for a new element. Another mineral name of Greek origin is dyscrasite, from "bad mixture" because it contains antimony, an element not highly regarded among metallurgists. Anhydrite, meaning without water, was so called because it contains no water, in contrast to gypsum, which is otherwise like it in composition.

8. Which mineral names pertain to their use?   Among the mineral names of this kind is nephrite, one of the two types of true jade (see Question 734), which was employed as a remedy for kidney disease. Pyrolusite is from the Greek "fire" and "to wash" because it removes the color due to iron impurities in molten glass. Muscovite, the white mica, was originally Muscovy glass, so called because it served for window panes in Muscovy, or ancient Russia. Amethyst, the purple variety of quartz, comes to us from the Greek "not drunken" because it was used to prevent intoxication. Chrysocolla means "gold glue" in Greek because it, or something like it, was used to solder gold. Similarly, orpiment means "gold paint" because it was used as a golden-yellow pigment. Owing to its use in pencils, graphite gets its name from the Greek *graphein,* "to write."

9. Which mineral names describe color?   Albite, an important kind of feldspar, is from the Latin word for "white," while leucite comes from the Greek word of the same meaning. In contrast, melaconite is derived from the Greek "black dust" because of its powdery black color, and psilomelane is from "smooth" and "black" in the same language. Rhodonite and rhodochrosite both come from the Greek word for "rose," as does the flower rhododendron. Its yellow color gave rise to the name for grossularite, a subspecies of garnet (see Question 723), which is from the Latin botanical name for gooseberry. Celestite is from the Latin "heavenly" because of the blue color of the first specimen that was found. Lazulite, because of its blue color, is distantly named from the Arabic "heaven," and the quite similar name azurite is from the Persian for "blue."

10. Which mineral names indicate other properties?   Besides color, various other properties have helped to give minerals their names. Magnetism and electricity, for instance: whereas magnetite indicates the strong attractive power of this mineral, analcime comes from the Greek word for "weak" because of its feeble electrical effects. Pertaining to specific gravity (see Question 88) is the name barite from the Greek "heavy." Cleavage (see Question 93) is represented, among other minerals, by euclase, which means "to break well" in Greek. Hardness (see Question 87) is best indicated by the name diamond, from the Greek "invincible" because it was believed to be indestructible, although, owing to its perfect cleavage, this is an entirely erroneous idea. Fusibility (see Question 100) is referred to especially clearly by fluorite, derived from the Latin "to flow" because it melts easily. The luster of stilbite is described in its name, which comes from the Greek "to glitter."

11. Who were the pioneer mineralogists? The earliest works that had a significant bearing upon the development of mineralogy were the writings of the Greek philosopher Aristotle (384–322 B.C.), the Greek philosopher and scientist Theophrastus, who died about 287 B.C., and Pliny the Elder (Gaius Plinius Secundus, 23–79 A.D.), who died while trying to observe the eruption of Vesuvius. During the rest of Roman times and the Dark and Middle Ages, mineralogy was kept barely alive through the numerous "lapidaries" and encyclopedias that began to appear after Pliny.

In modern times, but prior to the 19th century, the principal investigations were conducted and published by the following men: Georgius Agricola (1494–1555) (see Question 12); Carolus Linnaeus (1707–1778), the great Swedish botanist, also known as Carl von Linné; Baron Axel Fredric Cronstedt (1722–1765), the Swedish mineralogist and chemist who in 1751 first isolated nickel in an impure state and who introduced the use of the blowpipe: Abraham Gottlob Werner (1750–1817) (see Question 13); Torbern Olof Bergman (1735–1784), the Swedish chemist and physicist, who first obtained pure nickel; Martin Heinrich Klaproth (1743–1817), the German chemist who discovered uranium, titanium, and zirconium; and Jean Baptiste Louis Romé de Lisle (1736–1790), the French crystallographer.

12. Who was Agricola? After long centuries marked by little more progress in the study of the earth than had been made by Roman naturalists such as Pliny and Lucretius, mineralogy and geology were literally reborn overnight with the Saxon physician, chemist, and diplomat, Georgius Agricola, whose German name was Georg Bauer. Living from 1494 to 1555, he wrote a remarkably complete and authoritative treatise on mining, metallurgy, and minerals, which was published in 1556 under the title *De Re Metallica*. (Herbert Hoover and his wife produced a scholarly English translation of this Latin classic in 1912.) This book had been preceded in 1530 by Agricola's *Bermannus* and in 1546 by his *De Natura Fossilium*—"fossils" in those days included anything dug from the earth, and in this sense it referred to minerals; his was the first textbook of mineralogy in the modern meaning. Agricola proposed the first mineral classification based upon observed physical properties. With Agricola's trailblazing work the way was opened for the science of mineralogy, which was elucidated in relatively modern terms by Werner, though more than two centuries later.

13. What was Werner's unique contribution to mineralogy?   The name of Abraham Gottlob Werner seems to be best known among students of the earth sciences for his misguided influence in delaying the advance of geology by his insistence upon wrong fundamental concepts of the origin of rocks and metals. He must have been an inspiring teacher at the Freiberg Mining Academy, because students flocked to him from all parts of Europe and returned to their homes to promulgate his opinions. Nevertheless Werner deserves ample credit for his successful attempts at mineral classification and for a chemical understanding of numerous old and new minerals. He may well be called the father of scientific and systematized mineralogy. A silicate mineral, wernerite, is named after him.

14. What is the Dana system?   Based upon the relatively new science of *crystal chemistry,* as determined by X-ray studies and chemical analyses, the Dana system is the classification of minerals most used by professional mineralogists in North America. It is descended from the original classification proposed in 1868 by James D. Dana (not the original one of 1837, see Question 2) and later revised by his son, Edward S. Dana. Both men were professors at Yale University. The current revision (the seventh edition) is largely the work of Charles Palache, Harry Berman, and Clifford Frondel, all of Harvard University; three of the volumes are in print but the ones on the silicates remain unfinished. The Dana system begins with the native elements, first the most metallic, which is gold. Each mineral is assigned a number, using a flexible decimal code whereby new minerals can be added without disturbing the rest. The numbers used in the sixth edition are widely used in museum and private collections, but the new sequence has not been as much favored.

15. How are minerals classified? A chemical classification is most suitable for understanding minerals. The relatively new science of crystal chemistry combines the chemical composition and the atomic structure in classifying minerals, but it requires a knowledge of both subjects.

The simplest chemistry of minerals is that of the native elements, and the most complex is that of the silicates. Although the *chemical classes* of minerals may be subdivided in great detail, the usual ones include the following: elements, sulfides, tellurides, arsenides, sulfosalts, oxides, hydroxides, halides, carbonates, nitrates, borates, sulfates, chromates, phosphates, vanadates, arsenates, tungstates, molybdates, uranates, and silicates.

Each of these chemical classes, based upon the principal chemical composition, is further subdivided into *families* or *types,* which are based on a decreasing ratio of positive to negative ions or electrostatically charged atoms. Families may be divided into *groups,* which are usually minerals of closely similar structure, or minerals whose chemical composition or physical properties are close enough so that they are best described together. *Series* are minerals that show a continuous variation in properties with a changing chemical composition. *Species* are either major members of a series or else independent minerals not belonging to a series. *Varieties* are usually chemical deviations from the composition of a species, but they may be physical or genetic variations significant enough to give them their own names.

16. Can two minerals have the same composition? More than one mineral having the same chemical composition may exist in nature, but to be unlike, each must have a different atomic structure. Diamond and graphite both consist solely of carbon, but, as their physical properties readily suggest, the atoms are arranged differently in the two minerals. Pyrite and marcasite, likewise, have the same composition, both being iron sulfide, FeS_2, but they occur in different crystal systems and their structures are not the same. Calcite and aragonite are both calcium carbonate, $CaCo_3$ (see Question 31). Such pairs of minerals are said to be *dimorphous*. Three minerals— kyanite, andalusite, and sillimanite—all share the same chemical formula, Al_2SiO_5. These are *trimorphous*. The general term, to cover all instances, is *polymorphism*.

17. What are native metals?   These are metallic elements that occur by themselves in nature, hence as minerals. Five are of especial interest and importance. Native gold has been the mineral par excellence in the minds of man since primitive times. Native silver is not as familiar but it is not a rare mineral, especially in the Western Hemisphere. Native platinum is somewhat restricted in its occurrence, and is always alloyed with other metals of the platinum group (see Question 408). Native copper is abundant in the Keweenaw Peninsula of northern Michigan and is found in small quantities in other copper districts. Native iron is chiefly confined to meteorites, though some exists on Disco Island, on the west coast of Greenland. Besides these, the native metals include lead, mercury, tantalum, tellurium, and tin, all of which are rare. Solid solutions of gold and silver, called electrum, and of silver and mercury, called amalgam, are also regarded as native metals. Native arsenic, antimony, and bismuth, though they look metallic, are classed by chemists as semi-metals.

18. What is a halfbreed?   This curious name is applied to the masses of native copper and native silver that occur, not only in association but in combination, in the great copper deposits of northern Michigan (see Question 421). The Keweenaw Peninsula is the most important locality in the world for native copper; native silver is common enough but is always found in small pieces. When a halfbreed tarnishes, both metals may look alike, but when newly cleaned, the two gleam side by side in their strikingly contrasting colors.

19. What are the native nonmetals?   Sulfur and carbon are elements that occur as minerals, and are the important native nonmetals. Native selenium and tellurium are also found as minerals, though rarely. Readily recognized by its yellow color, sulfur is found in three different forms of crystals and as masses, some of which are of huge size, especially the bodies associated with anhydrite, gypsum, and calcite in the cap rock of salt domes (see Question 20).

Carbon as a mineral is known either as graphite or as diamond, both having the same chemical composition, though the atoms are arranged differently enough to produce two minerals about as unlike as possible. Graphite is soft enough to be used as the "lead" in lead pencils; diamond is the hardest of all minerals. Graphite is black and may look dull or earthy; the brilliant appearance of diamond is well known. Graphite is flexible in thin sheets; diamond is brittle, but both show cleavage, though in unlike directions.

20. Which is the most common native element? The composition of the interior of the earth is unknown, although it may very well consist of a core of iron or an iron-nickel alloy, surrounded by a shell or mantle of silicate minerals, perhaps containing some elements in a metallic state. Above and around these zones is the outer

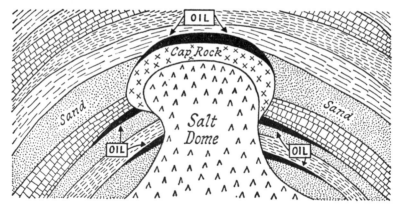

Typical salt dome

zone known as the earth's crust, and within this crust the most abundant native element is sulfur. Sulfur is found, indeed, around the craters of volcanoes, in sulfur-bearing waters such as hot springs, and in beds of sulfate minerals, especially gypsum, as well as in veins associated with sulfides of various metals. The enormous bodies of sulfur, however, that occur in the cap rock of so-called salt domes make sulfur undeniably the most abundant of all the elements that are obtained in native form by man.

The salt domes, which are situated within the near-surface rocks of the Gulf Coast in Texas, Louisiana, and Mexico, and beneath the water of the Gulf of Mexico, as well as in other countries (Germany, Spain, Rumania, Iran), are of various sizes and shapes and of great thickness. A typical North American salt dome is a plug of rock salt and anhydrite that has been forced into the overlying strata; it is generally topped with a caprock of anhydrite, gypsum, and cavernous limestone, in the cavities of which is found the sulfur. Boling Dome, in Texas, is estimated to contain 40 million tons of native sulfur.

21. Why are sulfur crystals fragile?   Because they are so low in heat conductivity, crystals of sulfur expand on the outside when warmed, leaving the interior unchanged. This can result in the destruction of a fine crystal by disintegration. In fact, a sulfur crystal can be heard to crack if held in the hand close to the ear.

22. What is plumbago?   This is an old name for graphite, related in origin to the term black lead, which has also been applied to the same mineral.

23. What are the sulfides?   Including most of the ore minerals, the sulfides are an important class of minerals composed of sulfur combined with a metal or semi-metal. Among the more important and interesting of the sulfides are argentite, chalcocite, bornite, galena, sphalerite, chalcopyrite, cinnabar, pyrite, and marcasite. With them are often grouped for convenience the selenides, tellurides (see Question 380), arsenides, and antimonides, which are chemically rather similar.

24. What is mispickel?   This odd name, an old German word of unknown origin, is a synonym for arsenopyrite, which is an iron arsenide-sulfide ($FeAsS$), the most common mineral containing arsenic. Several notable localities for arsenopyrite are in Germany, in the silver mines of that country.

25. What is a sulfosalt?   The chemical class known as sulfosalt embraces a number of important minerals which are double sulfides, in which a semimetal, such as antimony or arsenic, takes the place of a metal in the formula. Thus enargite, whose formula is Cu_3AsS_4, might be regarded as a sulfide of copper and a sulfide of arsenic—hence a sulfosalt. Tetrahedrite and tennantite, pyrargyrite and proustite, and jamesonite are other major representatives of this class.

26. What is feather ore? The plumelike or featherlike metallic minerals known as feather ore fall into two groups, brittle or flexible. The brittle ones are varieties of jamesonite. The flexible ones may be zinkenite or plumosite or boulangerite or meneghinite. All of these are lead-antimony sulfides, or so-called sulfosalts (see Question 25).

27. How are the oxides classified? A simple classification of the oxide minerals divides them into anhydrous and hydrous groups, but a more elaborate arrangement might include simple oxides, multiple oxides, oxides containing hydroxyl (the combination expressed as OH), and hydroxides. An even further break-down is possible, depending upon the precision desired. Some of the important minerals in this class include corundum, hematite, magnetite, cassiterite, goethite or limonite (see Question 521), and bauxite.

28. What are the halides? The halides—not to be confused with the mineral halite, which is one of them—are compounds of metals and the halogen ("salt-former") elements, which are fluorine, chlorine, bromine, and iodine. The most familiar of these are halite and fluorite.

29. What is salt? Common table salt is known to the chemist as sodium chloride and to the mineralogist as halite, from the Greek *hals,* meaning "salt." To the scientist, however, the term salt applies to any of the class of compounds that is derived from acids by replacement of the hydrogen by a metal. Unless this general chemical usage is implied, the word salt is usually taken to mean halite or sodium chloride. The source of the mineral is rock salt (see Question 311).

30. What is remarkable about cryolite? When the Norsemen first visited the west coast of Greenland they found the Eskimos using pieces of a heavy white stone to anchor their native craft. When sunk in the water, this strange stone became practically invisible. Today we know the substance as the mineral cryolite—and Greenland is still the chief, and indeed virtually the only, source of supply. Cryolite—

its name means frost-stone—has almost the same light-bending power or index of refraction (see Question 674) as water. Therefore, light goes through it and into water with almost no deviation in direction, and so the mineral is nearly invisible when immersed. The Greenland deposit, now depleted, was a huge one; the raw material that was quarried there was shipped to Copenhagen, Denmark, for processing for its eventual use as an insecticide and in the aluminum industry.

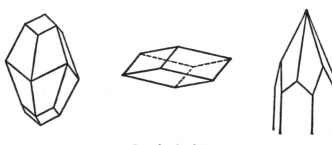

Crystals of calcite

31. Which are the carbonate minerals?   Three main groups of carbonate minerals are usually distinguished. The calcite group, the members of which belong to the hexagonal crystal system (see Question 120), includes calcite, dolomite, magnesite, siderite, rhodochrosite, and smithsonite. In composition they grade more or less into one another, and some of the mixtures have been given special names. They have excellent rhombohedral cleavage.

The aragonite group crystallizes in the orthorhombic system and includes aragonite, strontianite, witherite, and cerussite. Their cleavage is rectangular.

The third group, called the copper carbonates, consists of malachite and azurite.

32. What is the characteristic property of the carbonates?   All the carbonate minerals dissolve in acid with the release of carbon dioxide gas, which produces the fizzing and hissing effect known as *effervescence*. Not all do so with equal vigor, however, and with some it is necessary to powder the mineral or heat the acid. Any acid will do, and calcite reacts readily with even so weak an acid as vinegar contains. Cerussite, the lead carbonate, is best dissolved in nitric acid.

33. What is Iceland spar? Water-clear calcite is known as Iceland spar, from its original occurrence in a large cavity in basalt near Helgustadir, on the Eskefjord, in Iceland. Numerous other localities are known in Mexico, New Mexico, Montana, and elsewhere. Iceland spar is especially noted for its strong double refraction (see Question 676), whereby a dot or line seen through it appears double. Because of this property it is useful in petrographic microscopes and other optical instruments.

34. What are sand crystals? Few minerals attract attention more quickly than the so-called sand crystals from the Bad Lands of South Dakota. Gray in color, rough in texture, but having a pearly luster, these are crudely formed crystals of calcite which enclose a large percentage of sand grains. Solutions of calcium carbonate percolated through loose sand until they deposited the calcite as a binding or cementing agent. The specimens occur singly and in clusters, some of large size.

35. What is Mexican onyx? This banded calcite, so frequently used for pen stands and small ornamental objects, is not true onyx, which properly is a variety of chalcedony quartz (see Question 727). Its decorative colors, however, have made it popular, and it is easily worked. A number of localities produce this variety of calcite, but the original is Tacali (officially Tecali de Herrara), in Puebla, central Mexico. A strikingly beautiful kind comes from the extinct crater of Zempoaltépetl, in Oaxaca, southern Mexico.

36. What is calcareous sinter? As deposited at Mammoth Hot Springs in Yellowstone National Park, and along the Anio River at Tivoli, near Rome, Italy, calcareous sinter is a precipitate of calcite from stream and spring waters. It is also known as calcareous (or calc) tufa, and is perhaps more often called *travertine*. The mineral is usually porous and often contains leaves and twigs enveloped within it, as the waters splashed and bubbled over them. Substantial blocks of travertine make good building stone.

37. What is mountain milk? Also called rock milk, this is a soft and spongy variety of calcite.

38. Which mineral resembles coral? Aragonite that looks like white coral, with its delicately branching arms, is known as flos ferri. The name means "flowers of iron" in Latin; this variety is common in beds of iron ore, especially at Hüttenberg in southern Austria, where the mines have been worked since ancient times.

39. What are Indian dollars? Six-sided disk-shaped twin crystals of aragonite, which have altered to calcite but retained their outer form, occur in large numbers in northern Colorado, where they are known as Indian dollars. In New Mexico they are referred to as "Aztec money." "Pioneer dollars" is another term, used in western Kansas.

40. Which mineral is natural baking soda? Nahcolite has the composition of sodium bicarbonate or baking soda. It was formerly known in small white crystals lining the walls of an old tunnel in the Phlegrean Fields, west of Naples, Italy. Since then it has been found to be rather common as concretions and in pockets in the sedimentary rocks of Colorado and Utah.

41. What is phosgenite? Related in composition to cerussite, the lead member of the aragonite group of minerals (see Question 31), phosgenite is a chlorocarbonate of lead, $Pb_2Cl_2CO_3$. It is a much rarer mineral than cerussite, but is found with it and has formed under similar conditions. A most interesting occurrence is at Laurium, Greece, where sea water has acted upon lead slag from the ancient mining operations, producing phosgenite.

42. Which is the most important nitrate mineral? Only one mineral in the chemical class of nitrates is of any importance. This is soda niter, $NaNO_3$, also known as nitratine or Chile saltpeter. Because it absorbs moisture and is easily soluble in water, as are the few other nitrate compounds that occur in nature, soda niter is found only in very arid regions. The largest deposits are situated in the deserts of northern Chile, such as Atacama. They are mixed with rock salt, gypsum, guano, clay, and sand in a material referred to as caliche (see Question 789). Soda niter has a cooling, saline taste.

43. What is saltpeter? This is the mineral known more technically as niter, which is potassium nitrate, KNO_3, in composition. It forms in certain soils, as well as in the loose soil of limestone caves. Delicate crusts of it appear on the surfaces of rocks, walls, and earth.

44. What are the borates?   Various kinds of mineral compounds contain boron. A familiar group of these are the colorless or white minerals known chemically as borates, which are compounds of boron and oxygen. Boracite, borax, kernite, ulexite, and colemanite are among the most important of the borates.

45. What is the unique history of kernite?   Probably no other mineral in centuries has when first found assumed importance as a first-rate source of a commercially valuable substance. Named after Kern County, California, kernite was discovered near Kramer in the Mohave Desert in 1927 and soon became the principal mineral from which boron was obtained. Kernite is soluble in water and after evaporation it yields borax. Borax, incidentally, occurs as a natural mineral as well.

46. Which mineral is known as cotton balls?   Owing to the loose rounded masses of silky fibers of which it is composed, the borate mineral ulexite is referred to as cotton balls or cotton-ball borax. This source of borax is abundant in the arid regions of California, Nevada, Chile, and Argentina.

47. Which is the most common sulfate mineral?   Gypsum is the most abundant sulfate mineral, although barite and anhydrite can hardly be considered scarce. A product mostly of the evaporation of inland seas, gypsum occurs in several distinctive forms. Ordinary scaly or granular gypsum, also called *rock gypsum,* is sometimes impure and earthy enough to be termed *gypsite*. The compact variety is *alabaster* (see Question 736), the fibrous variety is *satin spar,* and the transparent crystalline variety is known as *selenite*. The crystals of selenite from Wayne County, Utah, are of exceptional size.

48. What is glauberite?   So named because it contains Glauber's salt, which is sodium sulfate, glauberite is a sodium-calcium sulfate mineral occurring in thin tabular crystals in deposits formed by the evaporation of salt lakes. When exposed to the atmosphere it absorbs water and falls to pieces (see Question 987).

49. Which minerals belong to the barite group?   Four minerals of similar chemical composition—they are sulfates—and closely related crystallography are members of the barite group. These are barite, celestite, anglesite, and anhydrite.

50. What are barite roses?   Tabular crystals of barite often grow in such a form as to resemble flowers with open petals. These highly interesting clusters are termed barite roses or crested barite. Near Norman, Oklahoma, is one of the favored localities for brown barite roses.

51. How can barite be told from celestite?   These two minerals often occur in very similar appearing forms and colors. Celestite is somewhat lighter in weight, but it may be necessary to compare the colors that these minerals impart to a blowpipe flame (see Question 99). Barite gives the yellowish green flame of barium, while celestite shows a crimson flame.

52. Which mineral may have a core of galena?   Because it alters from galena, anglesite may contain a core of the former mineral in its unchanged state. Both are lead compounds, galena a sulfide and anglesite a sulfate.

53. What is the story of antlerite?   At the world's largest copper mine, that of Chuquicamata in Chile, a green mineral called brochantite was believed until 1925 to be the principal ore mineral and source of copper. In that year the similar-appearing mineral known as antlerite, which was well known but from fewer localities, was identified as the chief copper mineral, instead of brochantite. Thus the two minerals changed places in importance, as a result of a more careful examination of the material. Both minerals are hydrous copper sulfates, very close in composition.

54. What is hairsalt?   Silky fibers of epsomite, which is also epsom salt, are known as hairsalt. This is a hydrous magnesium sulfate, $MgSO_4 \cdot 7H_2O$, common in mineral waters, from which it deposits as delicate coatings on rock walls and mine timbers. Its astringent properties make it sting the skin and bite through flesh cuts, and so it is unpleasant to be around, though entirely harmless. Epsomite was named in 1824 after the locality of Epsom, in Surrey, England. Loose masses resembling snowballs adhere to the ceiling of Mammoth Cave in Kentucky.

55. Which mineral is blue vitriol?   The chemical known as blue vitriol has the same composition as the mineral chalcanthite. Both are hydrous copper sulfate, $CuSO_4 \cdot 5H_2O$, but the artificial substance is the one used industrially for such purposes as an insecticide and in calico printing.

56. What is alumstone?   Used in the production of alum, the mineral alunite has been called alumstone. It is a basic potassium aluminum sulfate, $KAl_3(OH)_6(SO_4)_2$. Because it so much looks like several common white or gray sedimentary rocks, a chemical test is required to identify alunite.

57. What is mountain butter?   A peculiar variety of alunogen, one of the hydrous aluminum sulfate minerals, has been spoken of as mountain butter.

58. Which are the chromates?   Although there are several minerals that are defined chemically as chromates, including vauquelinite and others, the brilliantly colorful mineral crocoite is much the most important. This hyacinth-red mineral is a lead chromate, $PbCrO_4$, and is of historic interest because in it the element chromium was first discovered.

59. Which is the most important phosphate mineral?   Apatite is by far the most abundant and significant of the many phosphate minerals. As *fluorapatite,* the calcium fluophosphate, $Ca_5F(PO_4)_3$, or as *chlorapatite,* $Ca_5Cl(PO_4)_3$, or *hydroxylapatite,* $Ca_5(OH)$-$(PO_4)_3$, a complete series exists in which fluorine, chlorine, or hydroxyl substitute for one another. Most fossil bone and phosphate rock, much of which has been derived from the accumulation of animal remains, consists of a massive, densely crystalline, impure variety of apatite known as *collophanite.* Apatite—rather appropriately, it seems—is the crystalline material of which our tooth enamel is made, although the origin of the name bears no relationship to this fact. When attractively colored in yellowish green, blue, or violet, apatite is cut into gems.

60. What is wavellite?   This is one of the most distinctive of minerals; almost always does it consist of radiating crystal aggregates. Green specimens from Arkansas are familiar, but this mineral may occur in white, yellow, or brown. Wavellite is a hydrous basic aluminum phosphate, $Al_3(OH)_3(PO_4)_2 \cdot 5H_2O$.

61. What is vivianite?   A hydrous ferrous phosphate, with the chemical formula $Fe_3(PO_4)_2 \cdot 8H_2O$, vivianite is a mineral that changes appearance readily. When it is fresh it is colorless and clear, but upon exposure it becomes translucent and turns blue or green.

62. Which are the arsenates?   Several oxidized arsenic compounds occur as minerals. Mimetite, scorodite (see Question 63), and erythrite are perhaps the most abundant minerals in this chemical class.

63. What is scorodite?   This mineral does not have a single typical property suitable for easy recognition. It is a hydrous ferric arsenate, $FeAsO_4 \cdot 2H_2O$. Its color ranges from pale green to "liver brown." Scorodite has been found amidst the hot springs of Yellowstone National Park.

64. Which are the vanadates?   Vanadinite and carnotite are among the best known vanadate minerals. Each has merits of its own. Vanadinite is one of the most attractively colored of the minerals (see Question 85). Carnotite is a major ore of uranium (see Question 629).

Scheelite crystal

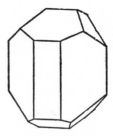

Wolframite crystal

65. Which are the tungstates?   Scheelite and a group of iron-manganese tungstates, of which wolframite is the principal one, constitute the tungstates. They are important sources of the metal tungsten (see Questions 552–556).

66. Which are the molybdates?   Of the few molybdate minerals known, wulfenite is outstanding for its beauty. It is a lead molybdate, $PbMoO_4$, and occurs in tabular crystals, often resembling butterscotch in color. It may also be red and orange, as well as less vivid hues.

67. Why is quartz classed with the silicates?   Chemically, quartz is an oxide of silicon, SiO_2, and used to be grouped with the other oxide minerals. The tendency now, however, is to place quartz at the beginning of the silicates, as is done in the current Dana system

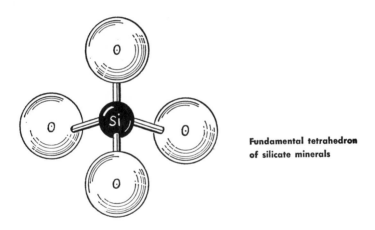

Fundamental tetrahedron
of silicate minerals

(see Question 14). This is because the structure of quartz—a tetrahedron consisting of four oxygen atoms surrounding one atom of silicon—is the fundamental structure of all the silicate minerals, which can be built up from it by the addition of aluminum, iron, calcium, and the other common metallic elements.

68. How are silicates classified?   The most satisfactory classification of the silicate minerals is based upon their atomic structure. There are six ways of arranging the fundamental tetrahedron (see Question 67), linking the oxygen atoms with those of the other elements. These are classified as (1) three-dimensional networks, (2) sheet structures, (3) chain structures, (4) ring structures, (5) double tetrahedral structures, and (6) independent tetrahedral groups. The properties of many minerals may be deduced from the type of structure, such as the fibrous nature of asbestos, the granular nature of olivine, and the easy cleavage of mica flakes.

69. How does quartz control radio frequency? Because quartz has a low degree of internal symmetry—in spite of the apparent external symmetry of a quartz crystal—it possesses the curious and useful property of *piezoelectricity*. When pressure is applied even slightly in the right directions, an electric current is set up, which can be magnified and measured. Reversing the effect, an alternating current will cause the quartz section or plate to expand and contract, thereby vibrating or oscillating at a fixed rate or frequency. In this way a carefully sized and oriented plate, referred to as a wafer, can control the frequency of radio and electronic devices. Its first large-scale use was in walkie-talkies during World War II.

70. What are Herkimer diamonds? So lustrous, transparent, and well formed are the quartz crystals that are found in large quantities at Middleville, Little Falls, and elsewhere in Herkimer County, New York, that they have become known as "Herkimer diamonds." They occur embedded in loose earth or lying loose in cavities in the rock. In size they range from individuals or clusters several inches long, down almost to the point of being invisible.

71. What is tridymite? Named from the Greek word meaning "threefold" because it occurs so often in trillings or crystal "triplets," tridymite is the equivalent of quartz, but forming at a higher temperature, above 870 degrees centigrade. (A still higher form is called *cristobalite,* and beyond that only *silica glass* develops.) The twins of tridymite may be united in fan-shaped groups. Tridymite is much more common than was once thought, for it is widely distributed in lava rocks of many countries. Mount Rainier National Park, Washington, is an important American locality.

72. What is flint? Flint, so valuable to primitive man for his artifacts, is a variety of chalcedony quartz (see Question 727). Its usefulness lies in the sharp cutting edge with which it breaks. Flint also gives sparks when struck, and has been used to set fires and ignite gunpowder. (The "flint" of cigar lighters is an artificial metal that serves the same purpose, see Question 584.) Flint usually occurs in gray, smoky brown, or black nodules having a white coating of chalk. The lumps of flint from the Cliffs of Dover and elsewhere along the English Channel are especially noteworthy. This material is a product of the silica-secreting power of diatoms, sponges, and other marine organisms.

73. What is touchstone?   Because they can be used to test the purity of gold and silver, pieces of flinty jasper, a variety of chalcedony quartz (see Question 727), are known as touchstone. The metal is rubbed upon the velvety-black surface of the mineral, a drop of nitric acid is applied, and the strength of color that remains on the streak indicates the percentage of the metal. This name goes back to 1530. Touchstone is also known as basanite or Lydian stone.

74. What is geyserite?   Rounded, concentric deposits of common (not gem) opal, white or gray in color, are called geyserite when they form around the geysers of Yellowstone National Park, Iceland, and New Zealand, and the few other places in the world where these intermittent thermal features exist. The material is more or less porous and arranges itself in shapes imitative of icicles, felt, and cauliflower, often attractive and certainly curious.

75. What is petrified lightning?   Sand or even solid rock fused by a bolt of lightning becomes silica glass. This material is known as *lechatelierite,* and the particular phenomenon seen especially in sand dunes is referred to as a *fulgurite,*—a narrow hollow tube of silica, often branching into twisted shapes. A beard of glass threads hangs from the outside of such tubes. When bare rock instead is struck by lightning, the result may be a thin crust resembling a film of varnish.

76. What are the zeolites?   Similar to one another in their ability to fuse at a low temperature, boiling and hissing—this is called *intumescence*—as the water in them escapes, the zeolites are nevertheless a most diverse group of minerals. Their composition covers a range of elements, although in their underlying composition, they are analogous to the feldspar group (see Question 161). They crystallize, moreover, in several different systems (see Question 107), and have unlike appearances. But, because they are fundamentally the same in their origin—usually being found as secondary minerals in cavities in dark rocks—they are more apt to occur together than separately.

The zeolites contain water, but they differ from other hydrous minerals in that the water is given off continuously as heat is applied, instead of in certain amounts at definite temperatures, as is true of the rest. Furthermore, they will again absorb steam, and other vapors as well, if exposed to them. The name zeolite comes appropriately from the Greek word meaning "to boil." Among the best known zeolites are stilbite, analcime, natrolite, chabazite, and heulandite. There are many others.

77. What is the appearance of stilbite?   This zeolite mineral typically occurs in sheaflike groups of crystals, resembling bundles of grain. It is usually white but may be yellow, brown, or red, and it has a pearly luster on the cleavage face (see Question 93).

78. How does analcime differ from leucite?   Apart from its laboratory tests for fusibility and water content, analcime (a zeolite) can be recognized by its growing in open cavities, especially in lava rocks. Leucite, which otherwise resembles it, is always imbedded in the surrounding rock matrix.

79. What is chabazite like?   Chabazite, a zeolite, occurs in rhombohedral crystals (see Question 122), which are nearly cubes in shape. Its color may be white, yellow, pink, or red.

80. What is distinctive about heulandite?   This mineral can be distinguished from the other zeolites by the diamond shape shown by the side of the crystal, which also has a pearly luster. Mostly colorless or white, heulandite can also be yellow or red.

81. What is meerschaum?   This unusual substance, used extensively for pipe bowls and cigar holders, is actually a mineral known as *sepiolite,* a hydrous magnesium silicate. Most of it is found on the plains of the province of Eskisehir, in west-central Turkey It is so porous that when it is dry it floats on water, hence its name, from the

German "sea foam." Meerschaum occurs only in irregular masses, which will adhere to the tongue. In spite of this porous nature, it takes a good polish and can be easily carved or worked on a lathe.

82. What is a mineral habit? The habit of a mineral is the crystal form or imitative shape that it customarily assumes. If it is a crystal form, the habit will be referred to as "cubic," "octahedral," "prismatic," etc. Otherwise, the terms are designed to describe the appearance of the mineral in its resemblance to some familiar object. Thus, a *granular* habit refers to a mineral consisting of an aggregate of individual grains. A *botryoidal* habit indicates rounded nodules like "a bunch of grapes," which is the meaning of this word. A *bladed* habit means flattened like a knife blade. A *reticulated* habit (from the Latin word for net) shows a network of slender crystals held together. A *stalactitic* habit looks like icicles. There are dozens more of these terms used for minerals; many of them can be recognized from the derivation of the words.

83. How are minerals identified? Recognizing the physical properties of minerals at sight or applying simple tests for streak, hardness, specific gravity, and magnetism (see Question 91) usually enables one to identify most of the common minerals. Tables have been published in a number of books that make it possible to track down their identity in a systematic fashion. Noting the geologic occurrences and mineral associates is enormously helpful to the trained student of minerals. Beyond that, the mineralogist may employ *blowpipe tests* (see Question 99), using more extensive tables of a similar sort, or he may go directly to the use of complex and expensive instruments. These include the *petrographic microscope,* which reveals the optical properties of minerals, the *spectroscope,* which analyzes by means of their spectra the chemical elements of which minerals consist, and various *X-ray* methods, particularly *powder photographs,* which present a series of curved lines on a film, indicating when decoded the exact identity of the mineral, much as do the fingerprints of a person. Among the newer instruments for the identification of minerals is the microprobe, which works on the smallest amount of material.

84. What makes the color in minerals? Mineral colors are due to a variety of causes. In many minerals the color is the result of small amounts of chemical impurities, such as the iron that makes feldspar pink or some related hue. Other minerals, such as smoky quartz and blue halite, owe their color to radioactivity, which distorts the crystal lattice (see Question 104) and permits the absorption of light that would otherwise be transmitted. Still others have a color that depends upon their natural crystal structure; thus malachite is green and azurite is as conspicuously blue, though they have nearly the same chemical composition. Interference of light (see Question 680) causes the rainbow colors of opal and labradorite.

85. Which are the most colorful minerals?   Perfection of form, richness of color, and an appealing luster combine to make a mineral attractive. Considering hue alone, apart from these other attributes, the most colorful minerals are probably those found in the upper levels of the earth's crust in the so-called *oxidized zone*. Here occur in wonderful profusion, brightly colored minerals containing copper, vanadium, uranium, and other metals, so deserving of front positions in any mineral cabinet. The blue and green copper minerals—among them azurite, malachite, chrysocolla, brochantite, chalcanthite—are difficult to surpass in their choicest shades and tints. The hyacinth red of crocoite, the butterscotch color of wulfenite, the fine red of vanadinite, and the range of green, yellow, and orange of numerous uranium compounds (see Question 627) are among the choicest treasures of the Mineral Kingdom. It is specimens such as these— and a hundred more like them—that, even more than the gems, make mineralogy a study of deeply satisfying aesthetic pleasure.

86. What is streak?   The color of the powder of a mineral is known as its streak because it is obtained by rubbing the specimen on a piece of unglazed porcelain, such as a tile. When used for this purpose the tile is called a *streak plate*. A mineral may be so hard that it scratches the plate instead of leaving a trail of its own powder, or it may leave only a white powder—in both instances it is said to have no streak. Many minerals produce a gray or black streak, and others have a streak of the same color as the solid mineral, but paler. For a few minerals, however, the distinctive color of their streak is a very useful means of identification. Foremost among such minerals is hematite, with its Indian-red streak—even the word hematite (from "blood-like") indicates its appearance, and this mineral was crushed to provide the war paint of the American Indian.

87. How is the hardness of a mineral measured? Although there are various ways of measuring hardness—by abrading, impact, and others—the mineralogist uses *Mohs' scale,* which is based solely upon the ability of a mineral to resist being scratched. This scale was developed by Friedrich Mohs, a German mineralogist, about a century ago. It reads as follows:

1	Talc	6	Orthoclase
2	Gypsum	7	Quartz
3	Calcite	8	Topaz
4	Fluorite	9	Corundum
5	Apatite	10	Diamond

This table is interpreted to mean that no mineral can be scratched by any that is lower in the scale, but in turn it will scratch all those beneath it. Diamond is the hardest of all minerals, and no known substance of any kind is harder. For this reason diamond dust is used to cut diamonds, and this mineral is the most effective industrial abrasive. Mohs' scale is usually supplemented by common objects, such as the fingernail ($2\frac{1}{2}$) and window glass ($5\frac{1}{2}$). It is important to remember that these are relative values only, and do not indicate that number 9, for example, is three times as hard as number 3, because it needn't be.

88. What is specific gravity? The relative weight of a mineral is its specific gravity. This is often referred to as *density.* Although the terms are not exactly synonymous, they are both expressed in the same numbers, which indicate how the weight of the mineral compares with the weight of an equal volume of water. At its heaviest. water weighs 1 gram per cubic centimeter at a temperature of 4° centigrade; therefore a mineral of the same weight would have a specific gravity of 1.00. If exactly twice as heavy as water, its specific gravity would be 2.00. The typical specific gravity of nonmetallic minerals is between 2.60 and 2.75 because the commonest of such minerals are quartz (2.65), feldspar (2.59–2.76) and calcite (2.72). The typical metallic mineral runs slightly over 5.00, which includes pyrite (5.02), magnetite (5.18), and hematite (5.26), which are among the most common minerals of this kind.

89. What is a Jolly balance? The most convenient way to determine the specific gravity of a mineral is by means of the Jolly balance, named after Philipp von Jolly (1809–1884), the German physicist who invented it. This is a spiral spring balance which measures the weight of the specimen by the amount that the spring is stretched. The weight is found both in air and in water. Any substance, like a swimmer, weighs less in water than in air, and the loss in weight is proportional to the specific gravity of the mineral, according to this simple formula:

$$\frac{\text{Weight in air}}{\text{Difference in weight}} = \text{Specific gravity}$$

90. Which are the lightest and heaviest minerals?   Ice—a true mineral—has a specific gravity of 0.9167 and so, of course, it floats on water, the next lightest mineral. Nitromagnesite, at 1.46, ranks third. At the other end of the scale is platiniridium, a natural alloy of two members of the platinum group, which has been recorded as high as 22.84 and as low as 22.65. Next heaviest is aurosmiridium at 20.0, and then pure gold at 19.3. Native silver (as much as 11.1) is only about half as heavy as gold. Native mercury, reading 13.596, is extraordinarily heavy, considering that in its familiar state it is a liquid mineral. The number of figures used after the decimal point to express specific gravity merely indicates the degree of accuracy with which the measurement or calculation has been made.

91. Which mineral is a natural magnet?   Magnetite is an iron oxide mineral (Fe_3O_4), so named because it is attracted to an ordinary bar or horseshoe magnet. Certain specimens, moreover, are naturally magnetic themselves and can pick up bits of metal—these are known as *lodestone*. Floating on water they were the first compasses, because they have the polarity, as well as the pulling power, of a magnet. A suspended fragment will point toward the north and south magnetic poles of the earth. Magnet Cove, Arkansas, is a noted locality for lodestone.

92. How does elasticity differ from flexibility?   Flexible minerals, of which chlorite is an excellent example, can be bent with the fingers and will stay bent. Elastic minerals, however, resume their original shape after the pressure is released, unless they have been bent beyond the "elastic limit." This property of elasticity is characteristic of muscovite, biotite, phlogopite, and all other true members of the mica group.

93. What is cleavage?   A mineral is said to exhibit cleavage when it breaks in definite directions to give flat surfaces. This results from the tendency of the atoms in its structure to hold together less firmly in some directions than in others. The easy way in which mica splits into sheets is a simple example of cleavage highly developed. The cleavage of diamond makes it possible for the diamond cutter to remove undesirable or flawed areas without the slow process of sawing them away. Galena breaks into smaller and smaller cubes, as does halite. Sphalerite has six directions of cleavage, giving it a peculiarly confusing appearance.

94. What is parting?   Some minerals show a false cleavage called parting. This resembles cleavage but takes place only on certain specimens of a mineral and its direction is usually determined by crystal twinning (see Question 123) or by external pressure to which it has been subjected.

95. What is fracture?   Minerals that do not possess cleavage or parting are said to fracture when they break. The most distinctive kind of fracture is *conchoidal,* which appears in an arc-like pattern resembling broken glass; quartz usually breaks in this way.

96. What is a hackly fracture?   The breaking of a mineral into jagged fragments, typical of the edges of metals, results in a hackly fracture. The native metals, such as copper and silver, break this way.

97. What is a sectile mineral?   Minerals that can be cut into thin shavings with a knife, instead of crumbling to powder, are said to be sectile. The shavings themselves will then powder, however, when struck with a hammer. The clear variety of gypsum, known as selenite, is a good example. Several silver minerals, including argentite and especially cerargyrite, are also sectile.

98. What are ductility and malleability?   These are physical properties of materials, including minerals, that pertain to the way in which they yield. A ductile mineral can be drawn into a wire; copper is a superior example. A malleable mineral can be hammered into thin sheets. Copper is also malleable, but some minerals are much more able to yield in one way than in the other, while still retaining their coherency.

99. How is a blowpipe used?   The blowpipe—a hollow metal tube through which can be blown a narrow stream of air against a small flame—is a cheap but very versatile piece of equipment for testing minerals. When held in forceps, or placed upon a small block of charcoal, many minerals fuse, yielding bright colors in the flame of a Bunsen burner, alcohol lamp, or even a candle. Coatings, also called *sublimates,* may deposit upon the charcoal. The mineral may be oxidized by heating it in the outer part of the blowpipe flame, or reduced (deprived of its oxygen) in the inner part of the flame. "Buttons" of certain metals—gold, silver, copper, cobalt, nickel, tin, iron, antimony, lead, and bismuth—can be obtained from minerals containing these metals. The addition of various chemicals makes possible still other tests on charcoal. *Bead tests* can also be made with the blowpipe, by melting a little of the powdered mineral in the loop of a platinum wire, in which a blob of borax or other flux has already been fused. Thus, chromium-bearing minerals give a green bead, cobalt minerals a blue bead. Distinctive reactions are also obtained by directing the blowpipe against powdered minerals enclosed in "open" or "closed" glass tubing.

100. What is the scale of fusibility?   Minerals fuse at various temperatures. To aid in an easy comparison between different minerals, the scale of fusibility has been devised, which reads as follows:

1   Stibnite
2   Chalcopyrite
3   Almandite garnet
4   Actinolite
5   Orthoclase
6   Bronzite
7   Quartz

Stibnite is readily fusible in a candle flame, whereas quartz is infusible even in the hot flame of a blowpipe, and the others represent in-between gradations.

101. How do minerals "grow"? Unlike animals and plants, which grow from within, minerals become larger by the addition of new material on the outside. As long as conditions are favorable and the proper chemical solutions are available, a mineral will continue to enlarge until its growth interferes with that of an adjacent mineral. Hence, large minerals differ from small ones only in size, though as they increase in weight they tend to become coarser and lose their transparency. The smaller specimens are the more nearly perfect in form and clarity, as shown by micromounts (see Question 970).

102. What causes a mineral to develop into crystals? Open space —room to grow—is the best advantage that a mineral can have in its tendency to develop well-formed crystals. This, together with a slow enough rate of cooling so that the separate centers of crystallization can enlarge to conspicuous size, makes the contrast between crystals and ordinary specimens of minerals that lack clearly defined plane surfaces. Thus, quartz crystals deposited slowly from groundwater solutions in a cave or rock cavity may be handsomely formed, but quartz grains in granite, where they must adapt themselves to what little irregular space has been left for them by the other minerals, occur always in rounded blobs without any crystal faces whatsoever. Some minerals, furthermore, tend naturally to form good crystals more readily than others. Garnet is an excellent example, often growing into geometric shapes while many of the associated minerals fail to do so under similar conditions.

103. What is a malformed crystal? The ideal crystal is as rare as the perfect female figure, and perhaps for analogous reasons. Crystals are subjected to so many stresses and strains during the course of their development that they become misshapen, distorted, or—most accurately—malformed. One face of the six terminations or endings on a quartz crystal frequently grows larger than all the rest combined, and cubes of cuprite may be stretched so long that they resemble velvety red needles. Nevertheless—and this is so important an observation that it is referred to as the "law of constancy of interfacial angles"—the angles between adjoining crystal faces of any given mineral are always the same, no matter where the crystal is found, how it was formed, or how large it may be. The angle between adjacent terminal faces of quartz is exactly 226°16′, whether

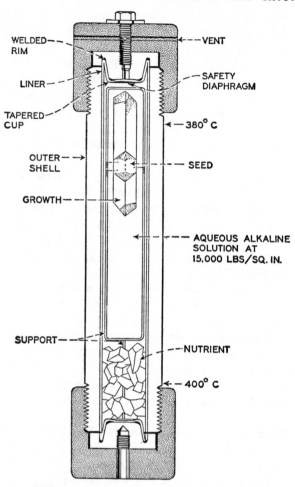

WELDED RIM

LINER

TAPERED CUP

OUTER SHELL

GROWTH

SUPPORT

VENT

SAFETY DIAPHRAGM

380° C

SEED

AQUEOUS ALKALINE SOLUTION AT 15,000 LBS/SQ. IN.

NUTRIENT

400° C

High-pressure bomb for growing quartz

the specimen comes from Argentina or Zanzibar, whether it grew in a cavern or in a vein, and whether it is of microscopic size or weighs ten tons. This law was first stated in 1669 by Nicolaus Steno (1638–1687), a Danish physician.

104. What is a crystal lattice? The three-dimensional pattern of atoms within a crystal constitutes the crystal lattice. This regular arrangement of the atoms, of which 14 fundamental types are possible, is revealed by X-ray photographs and is the real cause of the visible crystal form, the cleavage (see Question 93), and certain optical and electrical properties, which would be impossible if the atoms were situated at random.

105. How do crystals form? Crystals are formed in three ways: (1) From solution, whereby the substance precipitates out of a liquid as the fluid evaporates, the temperature cools, or the pressure is reduced. Halite or common salt is a familiar example. (2) From a state of fusion, as when water freezes to ice. (3) From a vapor, whereby a gas goes directly into the solid state. In this way chilled water vapor in the atmosphere turns to snow—snowflakes are a wonderful evidence of crystallization!—and sulfur deposits from sulfur gases around an active volcano.

106. What are the largest crystals? Geologists have reported seeing entire quarries being worked in single crystals of feldspar in the Ural Mountains. Such a crystal must have weighed several thousand tons. The largest known American crystals are the giants of spodumene in the Etta mine, near Keystone, in the Black Hills of South Dakota, near Mount Rushmore National Memorial. The largest was 42 feet long and weighed 90 tons; scores more are 20 to 25 feet in length. A crystal of phlogopite mica 33 by 14 feet in dimensions yielded 60 tons of useful mineral in Ontario. A 40-ton crystal of beryl, by no means a common mineral, was mined in Madagascar a few years ago, and many of 18 to 27 tons have come from New England and South Dakota. Siberian quartz crystals weighing 10 to 13 tons have been described as fairly numerous, and one was reported in 1959 as being as tall as a two-story building.

107. How are crystals classified? There are numerous ways to classify crystals according to their geometry. The *symmetry* of crystals—the manner in which the pattern of faces, edges, and corners can be repeated as the crystal is rotated—provides one way of grouping crystals of like nature. The internal symmetry of the atomic arrangement, revealed by X-rays, is another way. Still other classifications are used for special purposes, but the simplest and most generally satisfactory way to classify crystals is by the relationships of their *crystal axes*. A crystal axis is an imaginary straight line that is assumed to pass through the center of an ideal crystal. Using the axes as lines of reference, any crystal can be fitted into one of six *crystal systems*—isometric, tetragonal, orthorhombic, monoclinic, triclinic, and hexagonal. Each system has three axes except the hexagonal, which has four.

108. What are Miller indices? Devised by William H. Miller (1801–1880), an English mineralogist, these are numbers that represent the slope of a crystal face with respect to the crystal axes. They are derived mathematically from measurements taken on the crystal, and consist of three whole numbers (four in the hexagonal system). The simpler these indices, the more common is the face, usually. Indices such as (111)—read "one, one, one"—indicate that the particular face intersects all three axes at equal distances from the center of the crystal. Miller indices that have a zero in them, such as (110), represent a face that is parallel to a crystal axis.

109. What are crystal modifications? A modification or *truncation* exists when two or more kinds of faces occupy the same crystal, so that each member of the combination takes up room that would otherwise belong to one of the others. The slopes and hence the Miller indices (see Question 108) remain the same as though the faces were unmodified, but the size and shape of each face is different because of the truncation.

110. What is an isometric crystal? Crystals that belong to the isometric system are described by reference to three axes of the same length and perpendicular to one another. The axes are interchangeable. Typical faces are square or equilateral triangles. The smallest number of faces of a kind is six (the cube) and there may be as many as forty-eight (the hexoctahedron). Because isometric crystals are, when well formed, equidimensional in size, they tend readily to become nearly spherical when rolled in a stream bed, as is so often true of garnet.

111. Which are isometric minerals? Among the important minerals that crystallize in this system are garnet, diamond, fluorite, spinel, and halite; the metallic minerals galena, magnetite, pyrite, tetrahedrite, sphalerite, chromite, cobaltite, cuprite, bornite, argentite, and uraninite; and the native metals gold, silver, copper, platinum, and iron.

112. What is a tetragonal crystal? The three axes in a tetragonal crystal are mutually at right angles, as in the isometric system, but the vertical axis is either longer or shorter than the other two, which are interchangeable. In most minerals it is longer. Most tetragonal crystals have a square outline, the only important exception being chalcopyrite, with its wedge shape.

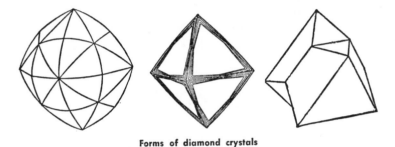

Forms of diamond crystals

113. Which are tetragonal minerals? Besides chalcopyrite, other familiar tetragonal minerals include zircon, rutile, cassiterite, idocrase, scapolite, scheelite, apophyllite, and pyrolusite.

114. What is an orthorhombic crystal? All three axes in an orthorhombic crystal are of unequal lengths, though they are still, as in tetragonal crystals, at right angles to one another. Such a crystal tends to be rectangular or boxlike in shape.

115. Which are orthorhombic minerals? Of the many orthorhombic minerals, among the most important are barite, celestite, staurolite, andalusite, topaz, chrysoberyl, stibnite, aragonite, olivine, anglesite, anhydrite, prehnite, anthophyllite, enstatite, columbite, chalcocite, carnotite, and witherite.

116. What is monoclinic crystal? The three axes in a monoclinic crystal are of unequal lengths, as in the orthorhombic system, but they are no longer all perpendicular to one another. The forward axis is inclined downward, while the side axis is at right angles to the plane of the other two. This arrangement gives a typical monoclinic crystal a forward-sloping look.

117. Which are monoclinic minerals?   Among the common ones are various members of the amphibole and pyroxene groups, arsenopyrite, the micas, gypsum, orthoclase, borax, spodumene, azurite, wolframite, colemanite, serpentine, ferberite, kernite, monazite, stilbite, and talc. Although not a mineral, sugar crystals are clearly monoclinic.

118. What is a triclinic crystal?   When all three axes are of different lengths and are inclined to one another, the crystal is triclinic. The resulting absence of all obvious symmetry is characteristic.

119. Which are triclinic minerals?   The triclinic minerals include microcline, the plagioclase feldspars, rhodonite, amblygonite, axinite, kyanite, ulexite, turquois, chalcanthite, and wollastonite.

120. What is a hexagonal crystal?   Belonging to the only crystal system that is marked by four axes, hexagonal crystals have a vertical axis either longer or shorter than the three horizontal axes, which are interchangeable and make 60 or 120 degree angles with one another. Hexagonal crystals are either three-sided or six-sided in outline and are generally long and often tapered.

121. Which are hexagonal minerals?   These include such important minerals as tourmaline, beryl, corundum, apatite, quartz, calcite, dolomite, cinnabar, hematite, magnesite, vanadinite, and pyromorphite. Ice is also a hexagonal mineral.

122. What are rhombohedral crystals?   One of the two main divisions of the hexagonal crystal system includes those crystals that have a three-fold symmetry, so that the pattern repeats itself three times with each complete rotation of the crystal upon an axis. This is the so-called rhombohedral division, in contrast to the hexagonal division, in which a six-fold symmetry is prominent. In Great Britain it is regarded as a seventh crystal system, separate from the rest of the hexagonal crystals. Calcite, quartz, and tourmaline, for example, would be called rhombohedral.

123. What is a twin crystal? Two or more crystals may grow together in any number of random orientations, but when they are intergrown according to a definite law they are twin crystals. A "twin" may actually consist of three or more individual parts, such apparent triplets (trillings), quadruplets, etc., being still thought of as twins. Some twin crystals occur in contact along an obvious surface known

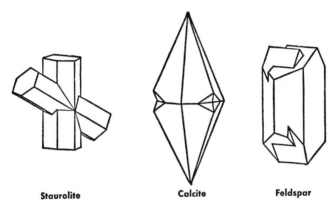

| Staurolite | Calcite | Feldspar |

TYPICAL TWIN CRYSTALS

as a *composition plane,* whereas others consist of interpenetrating individuals that look as though a jigsaw would be required to separate them. Some twins develop disk-shaped forms, perhaps with an opening in the center, like an angular doughnut. Common twin crystals may be given names to identify them, such as Dauphiné twin, a variety of quartz named after a locality in France.

124. What are enantiomorphous crystals? Crystal forms are said to be enantiomorphous when they occur in two positions that are mirror-images of each other. They cannot be converted into each other by any rotation, but instead are related as are one's right and left hands. Therefore they are designated as right-handed or left-handed. Quartz crystals are a common example of this phenomenon.

125. What is a hemimorphic crystal? Such a crystal has different faces at the opposite ends of a crystal axis. The word means "half-form" and suggests this unequal development. The zinc mineral hemimorphite (see Question 452) gets its name from this property.

126. What are vicinal forms?　These are complex crystal forms that take the place of the simple fundamental forms that usually develop in about the same position on the crystal. Because of their complexity they are rare, inasmuch as it is a rule in crystallography that the simpler forms—in their relation to the crystal axes—are the most common.

127. What are etch figures?　A fascinating array of peculiar patterns are produced on the faces of crystals that have been treated with solvents. These etch figures indicate the internal symmetry of crystalline substances and may tell much about the growth history of a mineral. Used for this purpose are acids, caustic alkalies, and steam at high pressure. Most of the figures are angular depressions, such as low inverted pyramids. Faces of different kinds on a crystal will show unlike patterns—the six terminal faces of quartz, for example, which may look alike, are proved to consist of two sets of three faces each.

Natural etch figures also occur on many minerals. Especially interesting ones have been noted on diamond, suggesting clues to the mystery of the origin of this most remarkable of all minerals.

128. What is a mineraloid?　Certain mineral substances do not have a regular atomic structure, hence never grow into crystals, and they do not have definite chemical formulas. Yet they resemble the more orthodox minerals in other ways. Dr. Austin Flint Rogers termed these mineraloids. They are believed to originate from a gel state. Opal is the best known example of a mineraloid, but now seems to be a mixture of a crystalline and a noncrystalline substance. Others, such as limonite and bauxite, are apparently mixtures of various oxides of respectively, iron and aluminum.

129. What is peculiar about whewellite?　This is a mineral—the only one, incidentally, that must be whistled instead of spoken!— that is the salt of an organic acid (oxalic acid). According to the rigid definition of mineralogists, it should not be considered a mineral because it is a crystallized organic substance. Whewellite, however, resembles the true minerals of inorganic origin closely enough to be accepted. It occurs in plant tissues and also in coal beds.

130. Which is the stalactite and which the stalagmite?　The stone icicle that hangs from the roof of a cavern is called a stalactite—it holds "tight" to the ceiling—and the deposit built up from the floor is a stalagmite—it has enough "might" to stand by itself without support. Some twisting stalactites rise up against the force of gravity, like coiling snakes—these are known as *helictites*. The National Speleological Society—devoted to the study and exploration of caves —a few years ago recorded a list of 67 minerals found in caves as stalactites and stalagmites, and probably a few more have been noted since then.

131. What is a geode? The word geode—meaning earthlike, because geodes resemble miniature stony planets—is used for rounded nodules of rock which have an outer mineral shell, inside of which is a lining of mineral matter in bands or projecting crystals. Some geodes are large, many are beautiful within, and all are interesting. Around Keokuk, Iowa, in Geode State Park in the same state, and elsewhere in the Mississippi Valley, geodes reach an outstanding development, both in number and in variety. Some contain petroleum stains from an unknown source. The geodes of Uruguay are noted for their magnificent crystals of purple amethyst quartz. Some geodes contain loose sand ("rattle stones") and others hold water which splashes around inside.

132. What are thundereggs? Geologists call them spherulitic geodes, because they are more or less round and contain mineral matter, often brightly colored, attractively banded, and showing mossy inclusions and other plantlike features. Although they are found in many parts of the world, the name thunderegg comes from Oregon, where they occur in the weathered outcrops of late Oligocene or early Miocene lava flows (see the geologic time chart, Question 258). According to Indian legend, the angry gods on Mount Hood and Mount Jefferson in the Cascade Range once fought a violent battle during a storm, using as weapons the eggs taken from the nests of thunderbirds. These have since been recovered over a wide area in this section of the country. A typical thunderegg reveals, when sliced open, a star-shaped pattern of chalcedony (see Question 727) with parallel bands of colored agate, which originated in a gel state within rock cavities.

133. Which mineral is shaped like an envelope? The crystals of sphene show acute angles and are rather surprisingly shaped like envelopes. The name comes from the Greek for "wedge," in allusion to this form. The mineral has also been called titanite, because of its chemical composition—a calcium titano-silicate—but the older name, given it in 1801 by René Haüy (1743–1822), has been restored to favor as the preferred one. Sphene is a common mineral in many rocks, though in small amounts.

134. What is spar? This is a term, used by itself or added to various other names, that refers to minerals that are cleavable and lustrous. Thus, we have feldspar, satin spar, fluorspar, and a host of others. When a miner uses the word spar, he may have in mind a particular kind of mineral with which he is rather familiar, but no one else can guess which it is without further information.

135. What is fool's gold? Three minerals may on occasion so much resemble gold that they have long been known as fool's gold. The most familiar of these is pyrite. Another, chalcopyrite, has an even deeper golden color. Weathered biotite mica looks astonishingly like flake gold and is' the kind washed up in stream gravels. Mark Twain tells of his sad experience with biotite when he thought for certain that he had made his fortune. "So vanished my dream. So melted my wealth. So toppled my airy castle to the earth and left me stricken and forlorn."

136. What is a desert rose? Not a flower at all but a mineral having a rosette form like that of a flower with its petals opened—this is a desert rose. It is usually composed of quartz or gypsum, though it may be some other mineral. Barite roses (see Question 50) may be found on the desert but these are well enough known to have their own name.

137. What is meant by asbestos?* Any fibrous mineral in which the fibers can be separated may be called asbestos. The most important commercial asbestos is a variety of serpentine known as chrysotile. This yields delicate fibers that are flexible and yet strong enough to be used for spinning. With its ability to resist flames, heat, acid, and vermin, asbestos is a material having hundreds of in-

*IMPORTANT: See new Publisher's Note on page v.

dustrial uses. For brake linings it has no substitute, and it is widely employed in roofing and fire-proof curtains. Other minerals that include asbestiform varieties are anthophyllite, tremolite, actinolite, and crocidolite (blue asbestos), all of which are kinds of amphibole (see Question 170).

138. What is mountain leather? Thin flexible sheets of interlaced fibers, like asbestos in nature and belonging to the amphibole group, constitute the material known as mountain leather. It can float on water.

139. What is mountain paper? An especially thin variety of mountain leather (see Question 138) is called mountain paper. It is white, gray, or yellowish in color.

140. What is mountain cork? Thicker pieces of mountain leather (see Question 138) are referred to as mountain cork. Buckingham, Quebec, is a locality for this odd mineral substance.

141. What is mountain wood? Resembling mountain leather (see Question 138) in structure but more compact, mountain wood looks like brown or gray wood. It too is an asbestoslike material.

142. What are the brittle micas? These are a group of minerals that occur in flakes, scales, or plates, and resemble the true micas (see Question 165) except that they cannot be bent without breaking. Chloritoid, a green mineral, is a so-called brittle mica, and so also is margarite, a pink mineral. Margarite is interesting because, although itself a soft mineral, it alters from crystals of corundum, the second hardest of known minerals.

143. What is a pseudomorph? When a mineral is altered in such a way as to change the internal structure while preserving the same external form, it is referred to as a pseudomorph. The word means "false form," implying that the outward appearance is deceptive because the mineral does not actually have the atomic structure (and hence the real nature) that it seems to have from surface indications.

There are several kinds of pseudomorphs, classified according to the process that has taken place. The most familiar, though not necessarily the most simple, is petrified wood, which has the look of wood but the atomic structure and chemical composition of chalcedony quartz (see Question 727). Another common pseudomorph is "limonite after pyrite"—originally pyrite, now chemically altered to limonite (more accurately, goethite); the cubic crystals are false, representing only the shape of the previous mineral, for nothing else remains of the earlier pyrite.

144. How is wood petrified?　A large number of chemical substances can replace the wood of trees by penetrating it in chemical solution, at the same time that some or all of the organic matter is taken away by the same fluids. This step-by-step or cell-by-cell substitution produces petrified wood, as it turns the wood to stone. Of the many minerals that are found in petrified wood, by far the most common is chalcedony quartz, and so the term petrified wood is almost synonymous with *silicified wood*. Because of its frequent bright agatelike colors and swirling patterns, petrified wood is often referred to as *agatized wood*. Opal likewise is abundant as a replacement of wood, giving us *opalized wood*. Of particular interest, surely, are the remarkable substitutions of uranium-bearing minerals (see Question 660).

145. Where are the largest petrified trees?　The standing stumps of petrified trees in the Pike Petrified Forest, on the west side of Pikes Peak, in Colorado, are the largest known anywhere in the world. The giant of these trees has a circumference of 55 feet and a weight estimated at 140 tons. More remarkable, really, is the group called the Trio, which consists of three stumps of similar height, girth, and appearance, said to have a unique single root system. These huge trees were sequoia, growing in the moisture climate of earlier times.

146. How long does wood take to petrify?　Time alone seems not to be a significant factor. Wood posts in mines where they have been saturated by mineralizing solutions for a few decades have been partly petrified, whereas logs that have been buried under natural conditions for much longer periods may be little changed. Some wood is undoubtedly more susceptible to petrification than others, and some chemical solutions are more active in producing this change —silica is perhaps the most effective.

147. What is a thin section? If carefully handled, rocks can be sliced so thin that most minerals in them become transparent to light. The standard thickness is 0.029 millimeters, scarcely more than that of a piece of paper. Viewed under a petrographic microscope, with light penetrating them from beneath, such thin sections reveal the identity of minerals by means of their optical properties. The space relationships and sequence of formation can also be learned in this way.

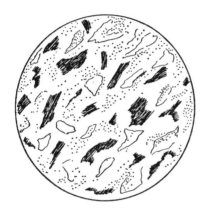

Thin section of igneous rock

148. Which localities have the largest number of minerals? Three mineral localities in the world seem to share the honor of being the most prolific. Each has yielded more than one hundred kinds of minerals, many of which have been found nowhere else. These three deposits are Crestmore, California; Franklin, New Jersey, and Långban, Sweden.

Crestmore is a cluster of quarries near Riverside, California. The most recent list included 137 names of minerals, from actinolite to zoisite, most of them satisfactorily authenticated; in addition are some minerals not included because not yet adequately described. The Franklin and Sterling Hill locality in New Jersey has yielded the most spectacular suite of fluorescent minerals ever discovered (see Questions 978–980). Långban, Sweden, is noted, among other minerals, for its native lead. Each of these localities has had a mineral named for it—crestmorite, franklinite, and langbanite.

149. Which state has the most minerals? The longest list of individual minerals in the United States has been recorded from the state of California. In 1892 Colorado was the leader, as enumerated in the sixth edition of Dana's *System of Mineralogy,* but this is no longer true. The comprehensive 1956 catalog, *Minerals of California,* by Joseph Murdoch and Robert W. Webb, names 523 species, perhaps one-quarter of all that have been described from the entire world. More are being noted each year, and doubtless many others still remain for future studies. California is indeed the Mineral State.

150. What are the Tri-State minerals? Although there are a number of points in the United States where three states come together, and hence a number of "tri-state" areas familiar to geographers and local residents, this term means just one particular place to the mineral collector. It means the broad district, centering at Joplin, Missouri, where the vast zinc deposits of Missouri, Oklahoma, and Kansas furnish some of the finest mineral specimens known. Superb sphalerite, excellent though lesser amounts of galena, fine marcasite, and shiny sprinklings of golden chalcopyrite and pink dolomite in a matrix of broken and recemented chert—these are among the most easily recognized of mineral associations and their presence fairly shouts "Tri-State" to anyone who has ever seen them.

151. Are minerals forming in the earth today? There is no reason to doubt that minerals like those we know in the earth's crust are being formed at the present time under conditions similar to those of past ages. A basic principle in geology, known as uniformitarianism, recognizes that the processes now working within the earth are the same as those that have always been in operation. This was stated as "the present is the key to the past" by James Hutton, the Scottish physician who was the father of modern geology. Oil is still being created from marine organisms in offshore sediments, as it has been since life began. Ore minerals are crystallizing from molten rock that cools beneath the surface in the same fashion as ever before. Because, however, Earth's processes are slow, these mineral resources are forming much slower than they are being consumed.

II. IGNEOUS ROCKS

Introduction. The original source of all the rocks of the earth's crust is presumed to lie in pockets of molten rock-matter, known as *magma,* which form at depth and cool to become the igneous, or fire-made, rocks. When this magma solidifies below the surface, surrounded by older rocks which it has invaded, the igneous rock is called *intrusive;* when the magma reaches the surface, it becomes *lava,* and the resulting product is an *extrusive* igneous rock. These igneous rocks may later be broken down by physical and chemical means, becoming sediment, which forms the sedimentary rocks described in Chapter IV; these in turn may be altered to the metamorphic rocks discussed in Chapter V. Or the igneous rocks themselves may be sufficiently changed to take on the character of the metamorphic rocks without an intervening sedimentary stage. Thus the igneous rocks are the primary rocks, and they include many of the most interesting of nature's products—granite, basalt, pumice, obsidian, and a host of others familiar in history and literature, essential to the sciences and arts.

152. What is magma like? Magma, the mother-liquid of the igneous rocks, has never been seen by man. Consequently, all that we know about its nature is what can be deduced from the rocks that apparently have been formed by its cooling and hardening. Lava, on the other hand, is commonplace in many parts of the world and can be seen to solidify daily somewhere. So, if lava were to be regarded merely as extruded magma, the problem would be rather easily solved. Yet the extrusive igneous rocks and the intrusive igneous rocks are so different in certain essential respects that lava cannot be considered simply as magma that has approached closer to the surface. They may come from the same early source, or they may have gone through a very different and entirely separate cooling history. Certainly, at least, magma has lost a large part of its fluid (gaseous and liquid) content while confined within the crust of the earth. Its original content of water and other volatile substances is estimated at 1 to 8 per cent; 11 per cent is the maximum amount that a silicate melt, as magma is, can hold in solution under any conditions.

The average water content of a fresh igneous rock, however, is only 1.15 per cent.

153. How does magma form?   The ultimate origin of magma is not known at all, but local pockets of molten material develop by the accumulation of heat, perhaps as a by-product of radioactivity. Any relief of pressure—such as by compression to form mountains, accompanied by the development of large fissures in the upper part of the earth's crust—may enable the semi-solid or plastic body of rock to liquefy to magma. Its own buoyancy and the pressure of the surrounding rock, as well as any chemical activity of the heated gases it contains, will cause this magma to rise within the crust until it begins once more to cool and solidify.

154. How does magma solidify?   The liquid magma solidifies as it cools, chiefly by transfer of its heat through conduction, partly by loss of heat through radiation into the cooler adjacent rocks. The outside of a body of magma cools first and most quickly, while the inner portions take a much longer time. A large magma may require more than a million years to cool to the temperature of its surroundings. The rapidly cooling areas of a magma may fail even to crystallize and the result will be glass, whereas the more slowly cooling areas may grow into coarse crystals of considerable dimensions. Eventually the whole magma becomes solid, whether crystalline or glass, and the volatile constituents escape toward the surface, perhaps making pegmatites or ore deposits before they end as mineral waters.

155. What is meant by the texture of a rock?   The pattern or size and arrangement of the mineral particles (and glass) in a rock is spoken of as its texture. It is chiefly of value as an indication of the cooling history of the rock, which depends upon the mode of occurrence as well as the properties of the molten matter. Numerous technical names are given to the various textures, but simple ones such as coarse-grained, fine-grained, and glassy serve most purposes. The usual equivalent of coarse grained is *phaneritic,* which means that the individual grains can be seen and determined with the eye or by use of a hand lens, though the range in size may be substantial. When the components are too small to be recognized by sight, the texture is *aphanitic*. More distinctive, probably, is the *porphyritic* texture, which contains one set of minerals conspicuously larger than the rest. The rock itself is called a *porphyry,* though there are many kinds of porphyry, depending upon the minerals that are present.

156. How are igneous rocks named and classified? The literature is cluttered up with hundreds of names of igneous rocks which have accumulated over the centuries. Any little difference was enough to encourage the coining of a new name; the only talent required was a knowledge of Greek and Latin prefixes. Some of these names are linguistic atrocities; katzenbuckelite is more euphonious than some. The trend now is to cull out the useless names, and an eminently workable system really needs only a few.

Igneous rocks are nearly always classified according to their texture (which suggests their origin) and their mineral or glass composition (which reflects their chemical composition and cooling history). Classifications are always arbitrary, because sharp lines cannot be drawn between things that are always transitional. "The trouble," says the distinguished petrographer Albert Johannsen, "is not with the classification but with nature which did not make things right." Even intrusive and extrusive rocks (see page 43) grade into each other.

157. What is a silicic rock? A high content of silica and a compensatingly low content of iron and magnesium make a rock silicic. *Acidic* is a synonym less favored than it used to be. Granite, rhyolite, and obsidian are common examples of silicic rocks. These are relatively low in specific gravity (see Question 88) and generally light in color, except obsidian which owes its darkness to structural peculiarities rather than to the presence of large amounts of dark-colored minerals.

158. What is a basic rock? The opposite of acidic is basic, but this term, too, meets with disapproval. Petrologists and petrographers, who are the scientists specializing in rocks, use the term (and various synonyms) to indicate rocks that are relatively low in silica and high in iron and magnesium. These elements make them heavy and dark. Gabbro and basalt are examples of important basic rocks.

159. What is an essential mineral? The essential minerals in an igneous rock are those that are abundant enough to be involved in the classification of the rock. By their presence they help to determine the composition and properties of the rock, and by their percentages they help to determine its name. The bulk of the igneous rocks are composed of a bare handful of minerals, which therefore may be said to make up the principal portion of the crust of the earth. These include quartz, potassium and plagioclase feldspar, mica, amphibole, pyroxene, olivine, and feldspathoids. Only certain members of these groups of minerals are likely to occur to any appreciable extent, and they serve as the dominant igneous minerals.

160. What is an accessory mineral? The minor constituents of an igneous rock, which may be present without influencing the classification or naming of it, are referred to as accessory minerals. Practically all are too small to be seen without a microscopic examination of a thin section (see Question 147). Of the accessory minerals, zircon, apatite, sphene, magnetite, ilmenite, hematite, and pyrite are perhaps the ones almost always to be found in granite, the most accessible of the igneous rocks.

161. What are the feldspars? The most significant constituents of the igneous rocks, the feldspars belong to a group of minerals that are all silicates of aluminum but have potassium, sodium, and calcium substituting for one another. They are alike in numerous respects, though they are divided into two main kinds—one, the potassium feldspars (see Question 162); the other, the plagioclase feldspars (see Questions 163–164). The classification and naming of the igneous rocks depends upon the kind and amount of feldspar present, and so the petrologist and petrographer are more concerned with feldspar than with any other mineral.

162. Which are the potassium feldspars? Orthoclase and microcline are the principal potassium or potash feldspars. They both have the same chemical composition, given as $KAlSi_3O_8$, though sodium replaces some or much of the potassium. Orthoclase is monoclinic in crystallization (see Question 116), while microcline is triclinic, but they look alike except under the petrographic microscope and are often confused with each other. If the potassium feldspar is transparent, it is probably orthoclase—*adularia,* including the moonstone variety, or *sanidine,* typical of rhyolite (see Question 199). If, on the other hand, it is green, it is certain to be the gemmy variety of microcline known as amazonstone (see Question 733). The usual color of both orthoclase and microcline is white to pale yellow, or pink to red. The largest known crystals are potassium feldspar (see Question 106).

163. Which are the plagioclase feldspars? A series of triclinic minerals, divided entirely arbitrarily, comprises the plagioclase feldspars. These are often referred to as the soda-lime feldspars because sodium and calcium ("lime") replace each other in all proportions. One hypothetical "end member" is albite, $NaAlSi_3O_8$; the other is anorthite, $CaAl_2Si_2O_8$. Based upon the relative amounts of these imaginary components, the division is as follows:

Albite	100 to 90	per cent "albite,"	0 to 10	per cent "anorthite"		
Oligoclase	90 to 70	" " "	10 to 30	" " "		
Andesine	70 to 50	" " "	30 to 50	" " "		
Labradorite	50 to 30	" " "	50 to 70	" " "		
Bytownite	30 to 10	" " "	70 to 90	" " "		
Anorthite	10 to 0	" " "	90 to 100	" " "		

164. How are the plagioclase feldspars distinguished? Measurements with a petrographic microscope are necessary to differentiate between the species. Labradorite, however, is likely to be dark—perhaps with a fine play of colors (see Question 680)—whereas the others are white or gray. Of the other members of the series, several include interesting varieties, such as *cleavelandite,* the platy albite, and *sunstone,* a shimmering golden variety of oligoclase. Any plagioclase may be told from the potash feldspars by the presence on certain cleavage surfaces of fine, straight lines or striations, which orthoclase and microcline do not show.

165. What are the micas? A group of aluminum silicate minerals characterized by elastic sheets, the micas crystallize in the monoclinic system (see Question 116), but occur in six-sided "books." They are named according to their chemical composition which is usually indicated by their color, and so we have white mica, brown mica, and black mica as major constituents of igneous rocks. Some of the largest crystals in pegmatite deposits are mica.

166. What is white mica? *Muscovite* is known as common mica or as white mica, even when it is green! But the green color results from the action of light within the thin layers, which actually are quite colorless in thin enough pieces. Fine flakes of muscovite are referred to as *sericite*.

167. What is brown mica? The addition of magnesium to the composition of muscovite gives *phlogopite* or brown mica. This, however, is typical of the metamorphic rather than the igneous rocks, but it sometimes occurs in large crystals, as in Ontario, and resembles the other micas in its properties.

168. What is black mica? Black mica is *biotite,* named after a French physicist, J. B. Biot. In thinner sheets biotite has a smoky brown color. To the magnesium of phlogopite is added iron to make biotite. This is the most abundant of the micas, occurring in many kinds of rocks. Whereas muscovite and phlogopite are employed industrially as an electrical insulator, the iron content of biotite interferes with such usage.

169. What is lithia mica? Different in its distribution from the other micas, *lepidolite* or lithia mica also has a different appearance. It is typically pink or lilac colored, and is found only in small flakes. Beautiful specimens occur in Maine, California, South Dakota, and Colorado—the Brown Derby mine near Gunnison, Colorado, yields the largest known crystals of lepidolite, yet they are only about half an inch across. Lithium-bearing tourmaline and beryl (both pink) are apt to be found with this lithium-bearing mica.

170. Which are the amphiboles? A strategic group of igneous-rock minerals, the amphiboles crystallize in the orthorhombic, monoclinic, and triclinic systems. They are complex silicates, some with unbelievably long chemical formulas. *Hornblende* is the common amphibole, widely distributed in many kinds of rocks; it is dark green to black, and has a cleavage angle of 56° and 124°, which distinguishes it—and the other amphiboles—from the related group of pyroxenes. Other important amphibole minerals are anthophyllite, the tremolite-actinolite series, arfvedsonite, and glaucophane. Several of them occur in asbestos forms (see Question 137).

171. Which are the pyroxenes? A group of related minerals are the pyroxenes, which resemble the amphiboles except that their cleavage is 87° and 93°, nearly right angled. They too are silicates in the orthorhombic and monoclinic systems. Augite is the common pyroxene, dark green to black. Enstatite, diopside, aegirite, jadeite (see Question 734), and spodumene—noted for its enormous crystals (see Question 106)—are other important pyroxene minerals. Each has its own kinds of rock in which it can be expected to occur; thus, spodumene is a typical pegmatite mineral (see Questions 181–184).

172. What is olivine? The mineral olivine is actually a series of silicate minerals important in igneous rocks. It grades from forsterite, Mg_2SiO_4 to fayalite, Fe_2SiO_4. Forsterite is the more common member of the olivine series, but they look alike and are both characterized by the green color that gives them the name olivine and by the granular nature of their growth. Olivine often occurs in sugary grains.

173. What is the feldspathoid group? When certain magmas are low in silica content and rich in alkalis, a group of minerals known as the feldspathoids form instead of the usual feldspars. Of this group leucite, nepheline, sodalite, and lazurite are the most important.

174. Which mineral is known as white garnet? True garnet can indeed be white but this color is not typical. A feldspathoid mineral, leucite, is often referred to as white garnet, because it has the same shape and forms in isolated crystals, as does garnet.

175. What is granite? The wide distribution of granite, which forms the framework of the continents, makes it to us the most important of the igneous rocks.

Stone used for monument or building purposes may be called granite but not correspond to the proper use of this name, which correctly applies to grained igneous rock consisting mainly of potassium feldspar and quartz. Other minerals may be present, of course, and a "thin section" of almost any granite will reveal the presence of perhaps a dozen different minerals.

The name granite is an ancient one. It has been used for several different rocks, as indicated above, and true granite has in turn been called by various names. The Welsh name is *givenith faen,* which means wheat stone, and this may be the word taken by the Romans who built roads and dug mines in Wales in the 1st Century A.D.

The color of granite may range from white to black; some is white and black; commonly it is mottled pink, white, and black. A porphyritic texture (see Question 155) is not unusual—crystals of feldspar 6 inches long occur in the Pyrenees at Port d'Oo.

176. How old is granite?   Books formerly taught that granite is the oldest of all rocks because it underlies the veneer of sedimentary rocks on the continents and seems to have changed in many places to the metamorphic rocks. Granite, however, may be of any geologic age (see Question 258 on the geologic time chart). Young granite (of Tertiary age) is present in Great Britain, Yellowstone National Park, and Jamaica, among other places. Granite is forming today, without any doubt. Nevertheless most granite is Pre-Cambrian—more than 90 per cent of it and perhaps 99 per cent.

177. What is meant by granitization?   It is only fair, when talking about granite, to bring out the views of those geologists who believe that a large portion of the world's granite, perhaps most of it, has originated by the reworking of deeply buried sedimentary and metamorphic rocks through the attack of very mobile solutions which penetrate them from below. Other mechanisms are also assumed, including the upward migration of electrified atoms called ions, and the local melting and recrystallization of sediments. This general process is known as granitization and the product would not be truly an igneous rock. There is no doubt that such is the case with a good deal of granite, but the conservative view is that it is greatly subordinate in amount to the granite of typically igneous origin.

178. What is two-mica granite?   Not related in any way to Two-Gun Harry from Tucumcari, this is a rock of the granite family containing both light and dark mica. The light mica is muscovite, the dark is usually biotite. Although not a particularly common rock, it occurs near Aberdeen, Scotland; at Saint-Nabord, France; in the Black Forest of Germany, and elsewhere.

179. What is orbicular granite? Rounded masses naturally cemented in a matrix of granite constitute the curious rock called orbicular granite. The "eyes" are known variously as orbs or varioles, and by other names. Some are as large as a foot across. Sometimes they are packed so closely together that their edges are modified by the contact. Although of world-wide occurrence, the largest number have been seen in Finland.

180. What is the Syene granite? One of the most famous of monumental rocks is the granite that is found near the old town known to the Greeks as Syene, lying on the east bank of the Nile, at the bottom of the first cataract, next to the modern town of Aswan, Egypt. From the Fourth Dynasty, about 5,000 years ago, to the beginning of the Christian Era, the granite quarries at this locality furnished rock for the face of the Pyramid of Chephren (adjacent to the Sphinx) and Cleopatra's Needle (now in New York City), for the obelisk of Karnak, the lining of the king's chamber in the Pyramid of Cheops, and other notable structures. In the present century the Aswan dam was completed with this same granite, which has a mottled look and a pinkish tint.

181. Which is the coarsest rock? A coarse grain size in granite, or any other igneous rock, reaches its maximum in the prodigious growths typical of *pegmatite*. Here occur crystals measured in feet and yards rather than inches—the giants indeed of the Mineral Kingdom. Pegmatites also contain minerals seldom found in other rocks, and a wide array of handsome crystals and gems. As characteristic of pegmatite as the large crystals, is the extreme variability in grain size, so that they grade readily from coarse to fine within a short distance. In addition, perhaps the most distinctive single feature of pegmatite is the presence of *graphic granite,* an intergrowth of quartz in (usually) microcline feldspar, so arranged as to resemble ancient Runic characters or hieroglyphics. This was, in fact, the original rock to which the word pegmatite (meaning "something fastened together") was applied by Abbé Haüy. No other rock is more intriguingly patterned.

182. Which minerals occur in pegmatite?   Well over one hundred different minerals have been reported from pegmatites all over the world. The common ones are quartz, several kinds of feldspar, and muscovite and biotite mica. Among the familiar gem minerals are garnet, beryl, apatite, corundum, tourmaline, spodumene, topaz, and chrysoberyl. The radioactive minerals include uraninite and allanite. The likeliest metallic minerals include cassiterite, molybdenite, wolframite, and arsenopyrite. There are so many more that a book could be (and should be) written about pegmatite minerals, in addition to the numerous geologic bulletins that have appeared over the years. The huge crystals described in Question 106 are all of pegmatitic origin.

183. What are the kinds of pegmatites?   Unless otherwise specified, the term pegmatite means granite pegmatite because most bodies of this rock are end phases of the crystallization of granite. There are, however, syenite pegmatite, diorite pegmatite, gabbro pegmatite, and other types of intrusive igneous rocks, but they are far from abundant. These bodies, as is true of granite pegmatite, contain principally the same minerals as those in the parent rock to which they are related.

184. What is the origin of pegmatite?   Although much is not yet agreed upon as to the details of their origin, pegmatites seem in general to be a late-stage solidification of exceptionally fluid portions of a magma, which fill openings in the main intrusive (which is usually granite) or in the adjacent "country rock." These residual liquids and gases are by then rich in water, other volatile substances, and silica. The solidification often takes place in separate zones, so that one area has a concentration of quartz and another of feldspar; and other minerals or associations of minerals are likewise segregated in a place of their own. Most of the pegmatites of unusual composition probably represent a replacement of an earlier deposit of ordinary pegmatitic quartz and feldspar, producing the rare and exceptional minerals for which pegmatites are noted.

185. Which rock is the opposite of pegmatite?   Complementary to pegmatite in grain size, *aplite* has a similar occurrence and is likewise an offshoot of granite and related rocks. Its tiny crystals and light color give it a sugary appearance. The difference between coarse pegmatite and fine-grained aplite is attributed to the stickiness of the liquid from which aplite has cooled, after the volatile fluids have escaped. Nevertheless, it remains a puzzle why pegmatite and aplite should be so intimately intermingled as they are.

186. What is syenite?   Given its name from the locality at Syene, Egypt, where it is found together with Syene granite (see Question 180), syenite may be thought of as granite without quartz. Hence its essential mineral is potassium feldspar. Its color depends upon the color of the feldspar, either pink or gray, modified by any additional minerals that may be present.

187. What is nepheline syenite?   When a magma has the composition of syenite but is even more deficient in silica, the mineral nepheline may be present along with the potassium feldspar. This relatively uncommon rock is termed nepheline syenite. It has a greasy gray appearance, sometimes tending toward green. The origin of nepheline syenite, with its rather peculiar chemical composition, is an unsolved problem in geology, because it requires an abnormally high concentration of the alkalies sodium and potassium; it is also high in aluminum, offsetting the low silica content. The Crazy Mountains in Montana are a well-known locality for this rock.

188. What are the intermediate igneous rocks?   This description pertains to chemical and mineral composition, not grain size. Such rocks are neither "acidic" or "basic" but lie in between, combining almost any proportion of the light and dark minerals. The classification is entirely arbitrary; the fundamental names are diorite, quartz diorite, and granodiorite. These, and other members of this large group, are divided mainly upon the basis of the kind and amount of feldspar present. Quartz may be common, moderate in amount, or entirely absent. Hornblende, biotite, and pyroxene are other major minerals in the intermediate rocks.

189. What is diorite?   The characteristic minerals of the granular rock called diorite are plagioclase feldspar (toward the sodic end), one or more dark minerals, particularly hornblende, but sometimes biotite or augite; absent are potassium feldspar and quartz. The color is usually medium gray, mottled black and white, or occasionally pinkish. Diorite does not usually occur in bodies as large as those of granite or syenite, but often forms a border around them. The presence of quartz (more than 5 per cent) in such a rock makes it *quartz diorite* or *tonalite,* named for Monte Tonale, in the Tyrol.

190. What is granodiorite?   The Sierra Nevadas are dominated by about 20,000 square miles of a white intrusive igneous mass of granodiorite. It is exposed in the gigantic domes and bold pinnacles of Yosemite National Park and Mount Whitney. At the Cassia City of Rocks in Idaho it has weathered into fantastic sculptured features. In appearance and composition this kind of rock resembles granite, but more than half of the feldspar is plagioclase, which is the feldspar in diorite, the rest being potassium feldspar. An orbicular variety (see Question 179) is the so-called pudding-granite of Craftsbury, Vermont.

191. What is gabbro?   The principal coarse-grained dark and heavy granular rock is gabbro. Plagioclase feldspar (usually labra-dorite in rectangular grains) and pyroxene are the chief minerals, but olivine is a common one. A mottling effect is pronounced, caused by islands of either the lighter or darker minerals set in a framework of contrasting color. Gabbro with a finer grained texture goes under the name *dolerite* or (in the United States) *diabase* (see Question 798). A special variety of gabbro, associated with the nickel deposits at Sudbury, Ontario (see Question 541), is named *norite.*

192. What are monomineralic rocks?   These are rocks composed preponderatingly of a single mineral. They occur in igneous, sedi-mentary, and metamorphic types. Among the important intrusive igneous rocks of such relatively simple mineralogic composition are anorthosite, pyroxenite, and dunite—these are all related to and associated with gabbro. Even though easy to recognize and describe, each of them has features of particular interest.

Anorthosite, consisting almost solely of plagioclase feldspar, is white or gray, though any play of colors that the labradorite present may show (see Question 680) adds an attractive bluish cast. This rock makes up large areas in Labrador, Quebec, Minnesota, Nor-way, and the Adirondack Mountains of New York.

Pyroxenite is dark and noticeably heavy. Its one essential mineral is pyroxene of any kind; when impure, it tends to have metallic minerals such as iron oxides and sulfides.

Dunite is composed exclusively of olivine and so is glassy, granular, and yellowish green. It was named in 1859 after Dun Mountain in New Zealand.

193. What is peridotite? Because olivine so rarely occurs by itself, dunite (see Question 192) is a scarce rock. But in combination with pyroxene it is widely distributed and represents the important igneous rock known as peridotite. This gets its name from the French word for olivine, which is, of course, a major, though not the sole, constituent. Another common mineral is phlogopite, the brown mica. Undoubtedly the most interesting kind of peridotite is kimberlite, the original home of diamond in South Africa (see Question 715), as well as in isolated occurrences in Arkansas, India, and elsewhere.

194. What is Bowen's reaction series? The normal order of crystallization of the mineral components in an intrusive igneous rock is indicated by the "reaction series" worked out by Norman L. Bowen. The high temperature minerals crystallize first in two distinct groups, beginning with olivine and plagioclase feldspar. (Preceding these are only the minor accessory minerals, see Question 160.) Further cooling causes olivine to change into pyroxene by reacting with the residual magma, then into hornblende, and finally biotite. The feldspar follows a continuous reaction, becoming richer in sodium and poorer in calcium. These two branches of the series then merge, and potassium feldspar is formed, changing into muscovite mica, and eventually into quartz, the last mineral to crystallize from a magma.

195. What is a phenocryst? The visible grains of the dominant mineral in a porphyry (see Question 155) are called phenocrysts. They stand against a background of another pattern, which is known as the *groundmass*. Feldspar is by far the most abundant mineral that serves as a phenocryst. In some coarse porphyries the phenocrysts of feldspar are several inches long, and they may weather out to yield loose crystals of interest to the specimen collector.

196. What are the felsites? Owing to the difficulty of identifying the individual minerals in most extrusive igneous rocks, the word felsite has come into use as a general field term for light or medium-colored ones. It includes the lava rocks equivalent to granite, syenite, diorite, quartz diorite, and granodiorite, already described. When these rocks contain phenocrysts in a dense groundmass, they become felsite porphyry.

197. What is a vesicle?   The gas cavities in an extrusive igneous rock are known as vesicles. They originate as bubbles while the gas is escaping from the congealing lava, and are flattened and elongated by the movement of the molten rock. When filled with later deposits of minerals they are known as *amygdales,* which may contain attractive deposits of quartz, calcite, and zeolites. These structures are common in the lavas of Paterson, New Jersey, and elsewhere.

198. What are lithophysae?   Translated from the Greek words for "stone bubble," these are concentric shells of rock with hollow spaces between them. They result from the expansion of gas bubbles as the pressure is relieved in erupted lava. Many are lined with dainty crystals of topaz, quartz, tridymite, cristobalite, feldspar, fayalite, and garnet. Lithophysae are prominently developed at such places as Obsidian Cliff in Yellowstone National Park and Rocky Mountain National Park, Colorado.

199. What is rhyolite?   The extrusive (lava) equivalent of granite goes under the name of rhyolite, which comes from the Greek meaning "lava stream." Its composition is like that of granite, but rhyolite has cooled upon or close to the surface of the earth, so that the minerals are somewhat different and the grain size distinctly so. Sanidine, a clear glassy kind of feldspar, is the common mineral in visible grains, and quartz is the other frequent phenocryst. A flow structure, produced by the solidification of a viscous mass of molten rock—which makes bands of contrasting color, parallel streaks of minerals, rows of air cells—is a typical feature. Porous and glassy varieties of rhyolite have their own names—pumice, obsidian, etc. Rhyolite may be found in numerous colors but most are light.

200. Which rock rings when struck?   No doubt many specimens of compact rock will give a ringing sound when hit with a metallic object—certainly slate will—but this musical property is especially pronounced among the igneous rocks in the one called phonolite. This name, from the Greek "sound" and "rock," was coined by Martin Heinrich Klaproth (1743–1817) from its common German name Klingstein, which meant the same thing but did not seem dignified enough. Phonolite is the extrusive or lava equivalent of nepheline syenite (see Question 187). It has a platy appearance. Occurrences of particular importance are at Cripple Creek, Colorado, where it is the host rock for the rich gold telluride ores (see Question 390), and along the Rhine, where it has been used to build some of the scenic castles.

201. What are the lava equivalents of the intermediate igneous rocks? The extrusive rock of granitic composition is called rhyolite (see Question 199), while that corresponding to syenite (see Question 186) is called *trachyte*. Among the intermediate igneous rocks, the equivalent of diorite (see Question 189) is *andesite,* named in 1835 for the Andes Mountains. Many of the volcanic peaks of the Western Cordillera of both continents consist largely of andesite. *Dacite* is the equivalent of quartz diorite and granodiorite (see Questions 189–190). When otherwise indistinguishable, these rocks (including rhyolite and trachyte) are all grouped together as felsite (see Question 196).

202. Which is the chief lava rock? The most widely distributed rock of extrusive (lava) origin, and the most easily recognized, is basalt. Dark green, gray, or black, in color, high in specific gravity (heavy), dense in texture—often with glassy, ropy, or vesicular phases—basalt is the foundation rock of the ocean basins, constituting the islands of the Pacific and representing vast areas of the continents where lava flows have spread out over the landscape and piled up to great heights in the geologically rather recent past. The rough cindery variety of basalt is known as *scoria* and is the basic equivalent of pumice (see Question 209). Balsaltic glass is called *tachylyte.*

The principal minerals of basalt are pyroxene (usually augite), a calcic or intermediate plagioclase feldspar, and, although not essential to this rock, olivine. The modern name basalt was introduced in 1546 by Agricola (see Question 12), but the word is an old one and has been ascribed to half a dozen ancient languages.

203. What are aa and pahoehoe?   These are Hawaiian words used by geologists to indicate the porous, rough surface form of basalt (*aa*) and the smooth, ropy or billowy form (*pahoehoe*). These are almost identical in composition, but differ only in the circumstances of flowage of the lava—the former quite viscous, the latter still fluid.

204. What are basaltic columns?   The most striking aspect of basalt is a columnar or prismatic "jointing" which this rock tends to develop upon cooling and contracting. More than half the columns have six sides, while others have four, five, seven, or eight sides; many are remarkably symmetric, and they occur in long, slender prisms as well as short, stubby ones.

The Giant's Causeway, on the north coast of Ireland, is the most famous group of basaltic columns. Projecting above the level of the Atlantic, they resemble stepping stones. Fingal's Cave, one of seven on the Isle of Staffa, on the west coast of Scotland, is constructed of columnar basalt which forms the roof, walls, and floor of the cave. Basalt columns likewise make the structure of Devils Tower National Monument, Wyoming, and Devils Postpile National Monument, in California.

205. What is pillow lava?   When basalt flows under submarine conditions or into a standing body of water, it seems to favor the development of a rounded or oval pattern known as pillow or ellipsoidal lava. Frequently this looks like a pile of huge pillows or half-filled grain sacks.

206. What is Pélé's hair?   Liquid lava of basaltic composition, blown out into reddish or brown threads by the emerging gas in the Hawaiian crater of Kilauea, was named after the goddess Pélé. Her "hair" is not too clean, for it contains numerous tiny droplets of black glass known as Pélé's tears.

207. Which is the common natural glass?   Most natural glass is obsidian. This is surely one of the most interesting of all natural substances Its name goes back to classic times, when a Greek phrase that described its ability to reflect images like a mirror was changed into a Latin name for the supposed finder of it, one Obsidius who is alleged to have discovered it in Ethiopia. Perhaps he did, at that.

Molten rock that cools too rapidly to crystallize into granite, or even into rhyolite, will chill to a glassy state and become obsidian. Thus it is the equivalent of granite and rhyolite, differing from these principally in origin. Nevertheless, virtually every piece of obsidian contains a myriad of embryonic crystals or crystallites (see Question 211) that make it dark. The color of obsidian is usually black, but some is red, some mottled black and red, and some dark brown or gray.

Obsidian Cliff in Yellowstone National Park is a flow 75 to 100 feet in thickness. No one has yet found the vent from which the glass came, but it evidently moved down from a high plateau into a stream valley, where it is preserved 200 feet thick. Material from here, made into Indian arrowheads, has been distributed throughout North America.

208. What is pitchstone? Obsidian with a water content between 4 and 10 per cent acquires a pitchy luster and so is called pitchstone. This rock is apt to be green, brown, or gray. Pitchstone from the Isle of Arran, off the coast of Scotland, is noted for its internal beauty of structure.

209. Which igneous rock floats? Dr. Albert Johannsen tells how, after the eruption of Krakatao, sailors could leave their ships and walk to shore over two miles of floating pumice. Puffed up with air bubbles until the pore space may be much greater than the glass, pumice is rock froth, a kind of obsidian expanded by escaping gas. It was described as early as about 325 B.C. and was well known to the ancients, for one of the chief regions for pumice is the Mediterranean. Fragments may float for years and tour the globe before they become waterlogged enough to sink. The glass in pumice is spun out into fibers. Pumice is used as a dentifrice, depilatory, and insulator.

210. What are spherulites? Rounded bodies in natural glass are known as spherulites. They are produced by rapid growth in a quickly cooling lava, and have been made artificially. Although described from a number of places the best known man-made spherulites came from Pennsylvania. At Kane a broken glass furnace spilled 6,000 cubic feet of molten glass into a pit; when cooled, the fibrous pellets of synthetic wollastonite were distributed through the entire mass. Green glass with this type of mothball has often been passed off as a natural substance.

211. What is a crystallite?   Embryonic crystals, just beginning to form and so small that they can be discerned only under high magnification, are known as crystallites. Nearly every glass contains great numbers of them, often strung out in wavy bands by the final movement of the lava. Crystallites grow in a wealth of forms—there are tiny rounded or beadlike ones and rodlike or hairlike ones. The basalt in Hawaii contains many of them.

212. What is perlite?   When natural glass cools and contracts, stresses are set up that may cause it to fracture into many small curved surfaces arranged like the layers of an onion or a pearl. Hence the rock is called perlite. These shells may separate, leaving cores of glassy pellets, irregularly rounded. These are *merekanite,* though mineral collectors know them as Apache tears and by other local names. Perlite is common in the Western states and is used as an insulating material.

213. Can a glass crystallize?   Solid and hard though it may appear, glass is unstable, and the natural tendency of its atoms is to rearrange themselves in the more stable structure of a crystalline substance. This process is *devitrification.* Because of its eventual effectiveness, no natural glass of any considerable geologic age is known anywhere in the world.

214. What are pyroclastic rocks?   "Fire-broken" is the meaning of the word pyroclastic, and so these rocks are associated with volcanic explosions, which shatter them and erupt them from the crater. Gas pressure is the cause. Some pyroclastic rocks are derived from the destruction of cooling lava, others from solid material. Thus the interior of a volcano, either deep or shallow, or the surrounding rocks may constitute the source. The products are named according to their size and shape. *Volcanic dust* or *ash* is extremely fine, rich in shards of glass; when deposited in layers it turns to the rock known as *tuff.* *Cinders* or *lapilli* are coarser, and *volcanic bombs* and *blocks* may reach a considerable size. The bombs are especially interesting because they are spirally twisted blobs of viscous lava, hurled into the air and streamlined in shape as they descended to earth.

215. Which is the most abundant rock of the earth's crust? This is a loaded question, with more than one barrel to the shotgun. First, since water is a rock, the bodies of the oceans contain the most abundant rock visible on the surface of our planet. In the polar regions, however, ice may be considered the most abundant rock (see Question 967). Ignoring the masses of water and ice that lie upon the surface of the earth and fill in its largest hollows, we come upon two other kinds of rock, one constituting most of the continents, the other making up the floor of the oceans. These are diametrically opposite in appearance, physical properties, and origin. Granite of the land, basalt of the ocean basins—these are then the most abundant rocks and both are igneous. At depth, however, other types of rock may extend down to the bottom of the crust—a boundary known as the M- or Mohorovičić discontinuity—and so they may possibly be present in a larger amount than granite or basalt, but this is unknown.

216. What are secondary igneous minerals? Not all the hot fluids are expelled readily from a crystallizing magma. A small amount is trapped in openings, where it remains to react with the already-solid minerals, altering them to typical secondary minerals, though they are still igneous. Serpentine, chlorite, and epidote, various clay minerals, certain carbonate minerals, and a shredded mica called sericite are among the most characteristic of these.

217. What is country rock? This is a term that refers to the older rock surrounding an igneous intrusion, through which it forced its way or was allowed to enter. The country rock may be of any kind, and usually is not related in any way to the intrusive rock itself. Thus, the country rock of African diamond pipes includes shale and other rocks very different from the kimberlite intrusive.

218. What is a xenolith? Meaning "foreign rock," a xenolith is a piece of "country rock" (see Question 184) that has been torn loose or otherwise surrounded by an igneous intrusion. The magma then rises with it. If chemical conditions are effective enough, the xenolith may be dissolved and absorbed by the magma.

III. METEORITES

Introduction. Meteorites are the only tangible evidence we have yet had of outer space—the only solid things we can actually handle and analyze that have had their origin beyond our own planet. Though recorded in ancient chronicles and the subject of much literature and speculation through the ages, they were long discredited by scientists anxious not to perpetuate mysteries and fables of any sort. Finally their existence was grudgingly admitted, and then used as a basis for the most generally accepted theory of the origin of the earth itself. No longer required for this purpose, these samples of infinity nevertheless tell us much about the probable nature of the earth's interior. In this Age of Space, moreover, they have now assumed an importance out of all proportion to the few precious specimens available to us. Meteorites are fascinating and often beautiful objects in themselves. Experience has shown that the best way to increase the small number of known meteorites is to acquaint people with their appearance and properties, for every observant person has the opportunity of finding them. Doubtless they have fallen equally on every area of the earth.

219. What are meteorites and meteors? Meteorites are the parts of the solar system that eventually reach the surface of the earth. They may be regarded as metallic and stony rocks of igneous type resulting from the break-up of a lost planet very much like our own. As they streak through the protecting atmosphere that envelopes the earth they are heated by friction to incandescence, leaving behind them a cloud of gas at a temperature of several thousand degrees— this is the visible part or the *meteor*. Meteors or "shooting stars" differ greatly in brightness and assume various aspects. Glowing streaks or trains are typical—appearing as a fine line, then brightening, fading again, and bursting in a final flash. Some make spinning flares; others split into several parts; a few trains consist of dust and smoke illuminated by sunlight. The larger the meteorite and the faster its speed, the brighter will be the meteor. Only the largest bodies survive the trip and land on the earth. Before they do so, they are called *meteoroids*.

220. What is a fireball? An unusually bright meteor is called a fireball or—especially if it explodes—a *bolide*. There is no real distinction between a fireball and any other bright meteor, though Dr. Fletcher G. Watson quotes the astronomer who said, "A fireball is a meteor sufficiently bright to make people report it." It should then be bright enough to cast a shadow. A few thousand meteors answering to this description appear in the sky daily. Most meteors can first be seen at a height of about 100 kilometers (60 miles), but the bright ones penetrate deepest into the atmosphere; fireballs rivaling the full moon may be visible down to 40 kilometers, while those that actually drop meteorites may flame to within 20 kilometers of the ground.

Answers to further questions about meteors and the other interesting inhabitants of the solar system, including comets and asteroids, are given by James S. Pickering in his book "1001 Questions Answered About Astronomy." The earth's atmosphere is examined more closely by Frank Forrester in "1001 Questions Answered About the Weather," another volume in this series.

221. How fast do meteorites travel? Radar and radio observations of meteorites show that upon entering the atmosphere they range in velocity between 12 and 80 kilometers per second. The majority fit into two prominent groups, from 30 to 45 kilometers per second and from 55 to 65 kilometers per second. Only 0.3 per cent seem to exceed the so-called parabolic limit which marks the dividing line between permanent members of the solar system and stray wanderers from intersteller space. Even if a meteorite were standing still when it began to be pulled by the earth's gravitational attraction, it would strike the atmosphere at 11 kilometers per second. Beyond this figure its actual speed depends upon the time of day. In the morning (A.M.) hours we are on the forward side of the earth, which is coursing around the sun at the rate of 29.8 kilometers per second, and so we encounter meteorites head-on, but in the evening (P.M.) hours we are on the back hemisphere of the globe and meet only those that are barely able to overtake us from the rear. Hence the difference in speed is substantial, ranging from a minimum of 7 miles per second to a maximum of 44 miles per second.

222. How many meteorites come to earth? An observer with a fixed field of view may see perhaps 10 meteors per hour on an average clear moonless night. Extended to the entire area of the atmosphere this comes to 24,000,000 meteorites that could enter the earth's blanket of air each period of 24 hours. Through binoculars, up to the eighth visual magnitude, this number increases to 500,000,000 per day; and through a low-power telescope, reaching out to the tenth magnitude, the light of 8,000,000,000 meteorites might be seen

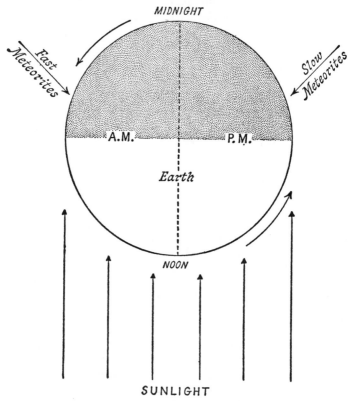

Day and night speeds of meteorites

daily. Additional smaller particles, entering as *micrometeorites* and interplanetary dust, do not encounter enough resistance to be vaporized and so escape being seen or photographed. The earth thus grows larger each day by the addition of an amount of material estimated at 5 million tons per year. Of this amount only about ½ ton represents the weight of the bodies that crash through the atmosphere and land as recognizable meteorites. The meteorites preserved in museum collections throughout the world total about 550 tons, according to Dr. Frederick C. Leonard. Some 10,000 tons of interplanetary dust, as measured from the noise it makes when striking space vehicles, falls to earth daily.

223. What is the size of meteorites? The countless number of particles that pass in orbits around the sun range in size from those that may be measured in miles—the *asteroids,* indistinguishable from large meteorites—down to the finest dust which sifts continually onto the earth's surface. The average weight of specimens collected from more than 400 falls is 20 kilograms, but about four-fifths of the material is estimated to be lost as the meteorite burns away or is scattered coming down. The average extraterrestrial particle weighs perhaps one twenty-millionth of an ounce.

224. What is the largest meteorite in the world? The largest of all meteorites is called Hoba and is a roughly tabular block, 9 by 9 feet across and 3¼ feet thick, having a metal content estimated at 60 tons; with the surrounding layer of iron shale, the original mass must have weighed about 100 tons. This genuine "space monster" lies where it fell and was found in 1920, in a bed of limestone near Grootfontein, South-West Africa. The size of a meteorite body lost in the desert near Chinguetti, French West Africa, though reported as 300 feet long and 60 feet high, has never been verified.

225. Which is the largest meteorite on exhibit? Ahnighito, which means The Tent, is the largest meteorite "in captivity." Brought back with much effort from Cape York, Greenland, in 1897 by the polar explorer, Admiral Robert E. Peary, it weighs 34 tons, 85 pounds, and is on display at the Hayden Planetarium in New York. It is owned by the American Museum of Natural History, together with two others of the same fall—The Woman, weighing nearly 3 tons, and The Dog, about ½ ton. A fourth large meteorite from the same area is called Savik and was taken to Copenhagen, Denmark, in 1913. These Cape York meteorites furnished valuable metal to the primitive Eskimos, from whom Captain John Ross first learned of their existence in 1818. A fifth specimen was found in 1963. The largest piece, representing the man, has not been located in modern times.

The world's third largest meteorite, unnamed, was reported in 1965 from the Gobi Desert. Said to weigh 30 tons, it is on display in Urumchi, Sinkiang, China.

226. How many meteorites are known?   The number of independent meteorites has now passed the 1,700 mark. Of these, somewhat less than half, referred to as "falls," were seen to land and were promptly recovered; the rest, designated as "finds," were picked up by accident and later identified as meteorites. There is a big difference between the two groups, however, in the kind of meteorite each represents. The metallic ones, on the one hand, are likely to attract attention because of their unusual nature, and so do not need to be seen to fall. Those that landed in past centuries in densely settled areas, such as India, were highly prized and are apt to have been fashioned into useful implements, and hence remain unrecognized today. The proportion of metallic meteorites in India is 5 per cent, contrasted with 56 per cent in Australia—where, furthermore, the arid climate helps to preserve them from rusting and the barren terrain serves to make them conspicuous. The stony meteorites, on the other hand, so much resemble ordinary rocks that they are likely to pass unnoticed unless their descent is witnessed, and so most of these have been seen to fall.

227. Where have meteorites fallen?   More than 70 per cent of the total infall of meteorites would be expected to end in the oceans, which cover nearly three-quarters of the globe. There is no reason to believe that the distribution is affected by any physical features of the earth itself, such as mountains. About 2,000 meteorites of recoverable size are believed to fall in a year; of these, perhaps 25 drop onto the United States. The number that have been recovered, however, corresponds closely to the familiarity that local residents have with the appearance of meteorites and to the opportunity they have for finding them. The Great Plains of the United States owes its fruitfulness as the leading source of meteorites to the fortunate combination of a stoneless, intensively cultivated soil—in which an unusual rock is readily noticed by farmers and ranchers—and a thorough educational campaign conducted in that region for three decades by Dr. Harvey H. Nininger. For several years this pioneer in locating meteorites accounted for half of all discoveries in the world.

228. What are meteorites composed of? There are three main types of meteorites—metallic, stony, and stony-iron. In some ways there are sharp distinctions among them, yet taken together they represent a sequence of material, so connected that they all must have had a single origin. In addition, there are the tektites which, if meteoritic, are the equivalent of glassy meteorites; also, certain very puzzling sedimentary bodies having a fused glassy crust, about which little else is known for sure; and possible combustible and organic matter remaining almost entirely in the realm of speculation.

229. What is the appearance of metallic meteorites? The metallic meteorites, known as *siderites* or simply as *irons,* are frequently grooved and pitted as a result of their flaming passage through the atmosphere. The grooves often radiate away from a single point, indicating the direction in which the specimen was consistently pointed while it fell, a feature known as orientation. The peculiar pits that are often present are referred to as "thumb marks." The fresh surface usually bears a thin crust of bluish black or gun-metal color, produced by the melting of the metal during flight. Upon exposure it rusts brown and weathers to an oxide scale.

230. What is the composition of metallic meteorites? The siderites consist largely or entirely of metal, through which may be scattered minor rounded grains of accessory nonmetallic minerals. The metal, referred to as nickel-iron, is essentially an iron-nickel-cobalt-copper alloy of three different kinds. One kind is called *kamacite,* occurring as cubic crystals and containing 5 to 6 per cent nickel. A second kind is called *taenite* and occurs as octahedral crystals containing more than 6 per cent nickel, and perhaps as much as 48 per cent in some specimens. The third kind is called *plessite* and has been proved to be merely an intimate intergrowth of kamacite and taenite. The principal accompanying minerals are troilite (iron sulfide), schreibersite (iron-nickel-cobalt phosphide), cohenite (iron-nickel-cobalt carbide), and graphite (native carbon).

231. What is the structure of metallic meteorites? When sawed open and the inside polished and etched with acid, the internal structure of the siderites is revealed. On this basis they are classified into three groups—hexahedrites, octahedrites, and ataxites. The *hexa-*

hedrites (containing 6 per cent nickel or less) show a rectangular pattern of fine lines called *Neumann lines,* which are planes parallel to the sides of a cube or hexahedron. The *octahedrites* (containing 6 to 15 per cent nickel) show triangular bands parallel to the sides of an octahedron—this so-called *Widmanstaetten figure* can be very handsome, whether coarse or fine. The *ataxites* show neither of these crystal patterns until they are subjected to sudden mechanical shock or heat at about 1,000° C., when they can be converted into one of the other kinds if they contain the right amount of nickel.

232. Are diamonds actually found in meteorites?   Yes. Diamonds were first found in a meteorite, the Novo-Urei aerolite, by Russian scientists in 1888. They were next discovered in the Canyon Diablo siderite in 1891, and they have continued to turn up in this same meteorite ever since. Generally their presence is made known by the rapid destruction of the grinding wheel. The American Meteorite Laboratory reports about 6 diamonds per pound of metal, but innumerable smaller ones are doubtless pulled out of the meteorite undetected. Meteoritic diamonds occur mostly as the carborado variety but also in small clear crystals or clusters. They are never of any useful size, however.

233. What is the appearance of stony meteorites?   The stony meteorites, known as *aerolites* or simply as *stones,* are generally not pitted or grooved like the siderites, because the minerals in them are not so readily melted or vaporized. Their corners are rounded, however, and they have a thin fusion crust of black glass, sometimes smooth and shiny like varnish, more often slightly crackled. Beneath the crust the color is variable, but usually is light gray; no indications of heat are shown, but tiny projecting parts of gray malleable metal can nearly always be detected. Upon weathering, the surface in spots —and eventually the whole body—rusts to a deep brown, and finally oxidation destroys the crust entirely.

234. What is the composition of stony meteorites?   The aerolites are composed of various nonmetallic minerals, mostly silicates. All except about half a dozen, however, show at least some trace of metal, which identifies them as of meteoritic origin. Many of them resemble closely the important basic rock of the earth's crust known as peridotite (see Question 193).

235. What is the structure of stony meteorites? The aerolites are subdivided into two groups on the basis of their internal structure. The *chondrites,* being more than 90 per cent of all stony meteorites, consist of small rounded grains, known as *chondrules,* embedded in a shattered matrix. The chondrules are chiefly olivine or pyroxene (mainly hypersthene or diopside), and the matrix consists of similar material, together with plagioclase feldspar, other minerals, dispersed bits of metal, and glass. Black veins of the same composition are a prominent characteristic of many chondrites. The other kind of aerolite, the *achondrites,* lacks both the rounded crystals and the shattered texture, but is composed of the same minerals though in different amounts.

236. What is the nature of stony-iron meteorites? These intermediate members of the meteorite family, known as *siderolites* or *stony irons,* are combinations in various proportions (often about equally divided) of the metallic and nonmetallic constituents of the other two types. In the *pallasites*—named for Peter Simon Pallas (1741–1811), a German naturalist and explorer—olivine occurs as large rounded crystal grains in a sponge-like continuous network of metal, and these specimens are probably the most beautiful of all the varieties of meteorites. The metal in the *mesosiderites* is probably discontinuous and the minerals are olivine, pyroxene (bronzite), and feldspar (anorthite).

237. What are tektites? First found along the Moldau River in Bohemia, small pieces of natural glass called tektites are now known in considerable quantity from a number of places, especially around the South China Sea and Australia. They go under various names according to their location, and the outward appearance is more or less distinctive for each area. Internally and in composition, however, they are all much alike, having a high content of silica and many bubbles and flow marks, whether *australites* from Australia or *billitonites* from the island of Billiton. Many of them have a button or dumbbell shape, suggesting that they solidified from a plastic state while whirling through the air. They are quite unlike any volcanic glass or other terrestrial material, but their origin is entirely unknown because nobody has ever seen one fall. Yet they seem to have come from outer space, although, on account of their erratic distribution, not necessarily as true meteorites. An origin from the moon, as a result of being thrown off when meteorites bombard the lunar surface and scatter bits of fused rock beyond the gravitational attraction of our satellite, as long propounded by Dr. Nininger, seems as reasonable an explanation as any. However, they well may have resulted from the skipping motion of an asteroid along the earth's surface.

238. How are meteorites named?   Meteorites are given the name of the nearest town, such as Tilden (Illinois) and Weston (Connecticut), or prominent landmark, such as Cabin Creek (Arkansas) and Lucky Hill (Jamaica). To avoid confusion the latitude and longitude are often added, and a code has been devised by Dr. Frederick C. Leonard, to provide this information in a kind of shorthand notation.

239. What is the largest North American meteorite?   Bacubirito, with an estimated weight of 27 tons, is the largest meteorite ever discovered on the mainland of North America. It was unearthed in Sinaloa, northern Mexico, and still lies in the same spot. Three other very large siderites of Mexican origin—the handsome 12-ton Morito, known to the Conquistadores, and the two pieces of Chupaderos, 15½ and 7½ tons, which remarkably fit together, are on exhibit in Mexico City.

240. Which is the largest United States meteorite?   The Willamette, Oregon, siderite is the largest meteorite ever found in the United States and ranks seventh in the world. Discovered in a forest in 1902, it was secretly moved by the finder to his own property nearby, but after he began to exhibit it, the owners of the land from which it had come sued him and were awarded custody of the huge specimen. This 15⅗-ton meteorite is especially interesting because of the curious cavities large enough for children to huddle in. Like the Cape York specimens (see Question 225), the Willamette can be seen at the Hayden Planetarium in New York.

241. Which is the largest stony meteorite?   The enormous meteorites described above are all metallic; this type survives the hazardous trip to earth most satisfactorily. The largest specimen of stony composition ever recovered is the Norton, Kansas, aerolite, which was seen to fall February 18, 1948. It burst twice, at altitudes of 40 and 18 kilometers, and left behind a dust cloud visible for 2 hours. The main piece, recovered from a hole in August of the same year, after a deliberate search, weighs close to 1 ton.

242. Which was the first meteorite preserved? The oldest meteorite on display anywhere in the world, the exact date of which is known, is the Ensisheim aerolite, which fell in Alsace on November 16, 1492. This 280-pound specimen, which buried itself in the earth to a depth of five feet, is still exhibited in the town hall. Prior to that, of course, many meteorites and other rocks now suspected to have been meteorites were kept for religious or sentimental reasons, but their history is obscure. Thirty-five different falls that took place before the year 1800 were represented in collections that were in existence in 1904.

The sacred Black Stone worshipped by Mohammedans at Mecca is claimed to have fallen from heaven and is almost certainly a meteorite. In China, India, and Japan, as well as most of the rest of the inhabited world, stones from the sky were regarded as portents from heaven. The American Indian also gave them his share of veneration. The Casas Grandes siderite, for example, was found in 1867 in an old tomb in ruins of the Montezuma Indians, in Chihuahua, Mexico, wrapped like a mummy.

243. Which is the smallest known meteorite? The smallest meteorite that constitutes an entire fall, as far as is known, is the Mühlau, Austria, aerolite in the Vienna Museum. It weighs 5 grains and is about the size of the end of one's finger. Much smaller complete individuals have been collected at Holbrook and Canyon Diablo, Arizona—as tiny as 0.0183 grains at the former locality—but these belong to a group of many specimens representing the same fall (see Question 226).

244. What is a meteorite shower? The breakup of an aerolite during its passage through the atmosphere, as it moves against a resistant front of highly compressed air, may result in a shower of meteorites, from which a dozen or more individuals are eventually recovered. The greatest of such showers was that of Pultusk, Poland, which dropped an estimated 100,000 stones on January 30, 1868. The Holbrook, Arizona shower of July 19, 1912 produced about 16,000 stones. Most famous of all is the shower of April 26, 1803, at L'Aigle, France, because it brought to an end the era of skepticism about the actual existence of meteorites as objects worthy of scientific study.

245. What is a meteorite crater?   Large circular or elliptical depressions, usually surrounded by a raised rim of upturned and shattered rock and filled with finely crushed rock, have been formed by the explosion of unusually large and sufficiently coherent meteorites. The shock of compressed air immediately preceding the actual impact of the meteorite itself seems to be responsible for most of the devastation. The outer part of the meteorite and the surface of the earth partly vaporize, the water in the ground turns to steam, and a terrific explosion both creates the crater and destroys the meteorite. A widely spreading blast of heated air and earth waves like those of an earthquake are accompanying effects. The battle-scarred surface of the moon reveals dramatically what a bombardment of meteorites having the size of asteroids can doubtless do.

246. Where are meteorite craters situated?   Eleven localities are universally accepted as having craters of meteoritic origin because meteorites are associated with them. The Barringer Crater on the plateau of northern Arizona, between Winslow and Flagstaff, was the first to be identified and is the best known and most accessible. Considering the story it has to tell, it can rightly be considered one of the wonders of the world. Other meteorite craters in the United States are near Odessa, Texas, and Brenham, Kansas; the latter was previously thought to be a "buffalo wallow." On June 30, 1908 the possible impact of a comet, as Russian scientists believe, produced 10 or more pits in central Siberia, and the general destruction in this isolated Tunguska region was tremendous. A second swarm of Siberian meteorites, on February 12, 1947, resulted in a cluster of 122 craters in the Sikhote-Alin Mountains. Saudi Arabia, Argentina, Australia, and Estonia contain the rest of the authenticated craters of the world. The crater in Chile announced in 1966 has furnished meteoritic material but no solid specimens.

247. How often are people hit by meteorites? The star that fell on Alabama and punched a hole in the roof of a house in Sylacauga in November 1954 is the only authenticated instance of a meteorite having struck a human being. Mrs. Hodges of that town awoke from an afternoon nap to find herself badly bruised, and an aerolite lay on the floor near her. Weighing 8½ pounds, it is now in the Alabama Museum of Natural History, in Tuscaloosa.

248. Where do meteorites originate? The modern opinion on meteorites, backed by the astronomical (photographic and radio) evidence as to their orbits and velocity, is that they have always been members of the solar system. The evidence of their mineralogy, with its continuous series of composition, indicates that they all must have had a common origin. The nature of their structure—large crystals in the metals, broken fragments in the stones, and cracks in both types—points toward their development by slow cooling from a liquid state and their later disruption. The chemical evidence (as to isotopes, radioactive and trace elements) suggests the original body to have been one or more planets intermediate in size between the earth and Mars, formed at a temperature of about 3,000° C. and a pressure of about 1 million atmospheres. Inasmuch as meteorites in motion swing around the sun, some probably go close enough to become intensely heated; about 3 per cent of the stony meteorites have turned black in a fashion that can be duplicated in the laboratory by heating them for a few minutes to 800° C. This effect, as well as the occurrence of the glassy meteorites and the Neumann lines, may instead be due to an ancient collision between two planetary bodies, which shattered to become the asteroid-meteorite family. The breakup of a planet once situated between Mars and Jupiter (where the asteroids now swarm), due to the tidal influence of Jupiter or a collision with a satellite of Jupiter, is a likely possibility.

IV. SEDIMENTARY ROCKS

Introduction. Sedimentary rocks are secondary rocks, made by the destruction and re-constitution of igneous, metamorphic, and previous sedimentary rocks. Although they are more in evidence than either of the other major types of rock, they are present only as a relatively thin veneer over the crust of the earth, except in restricted places such as the long troughs of sedimentation known as geosynclines and confined basins of deposition. In the Mississippi Delta, for instance, sedimentary materials have been penetrated to a depth of 22,000 feet without giving way to anything else, and in the Ganges River basin they are 45,000 to 60,000 feet thick. Altogether, however, they account for only about 5 per cent of the volume of the outer 10 miles of our globe.

249. What causes weathering? Weathering is the action of the atmosphere upon rock matter. The moisture, oxygen, carbon dioxide, and other constituents of the atmosphere react with the minerals of the rocks, serving to alter and decompose them, generally producing simpler chemical compounds. Soil is the major result of weathering, but various mineral deposits also originate in this way.

250. How do sedimentary rocks form? Three main processes are involved in the formation of sedimentary rocks. One is weathering in place, so that the altered rock covers like a cloak the fresher bedrock beneath, from which it has been derived. Clay is a good example. A second process is the accumulation of broken fragments of rock, either set free by weathering or else eroded bodily from the original source—sandstone illustrates this mechanism. These broken rocks are known as *fragmental, clastic,* or *detrital* rocks.

251. By what agents are sedimentary rocks deposited? The sediment that will eventually become part of a sedimentary rock is deposited mainly by streams, but also largely by the still waters of lakes, the waves and currents of the ocean, the moving air we call wind, and by glaciers and floating ice. Each of these geologic agents of erosion, transportation, and deposition has its own modes of action, and each leaves highly individual clues as to the extent of its participation in the sedimentary processes. Running water is by far the dominant agent in sedimentation, for it is the principal function of streams to wear away land and carry waste ultimately to the sea.

252. How is sediment changed into solid rock?   Converting loose sediment into firm sedimentary rock is called *lithification.* Circulating ground waters carrying dissolved mineral matter deposit it between the loose grains as a binding agent or *cement.* The most common cementing materials are calcium and magnesium carbonates, silica, and iron oxide—the last one (with or without water) adds much of the color to sedimentary rocks, the reds, yellows, and browns, as well as the greens. Gypsum and barite are other important cementing agents. *Compaction* of the loose rock squeezes out excess water and reduces the volume of the pore spaces. In addition, a new crystallization of minerals between the grains helps in the overall process of consolidation.

253. What is diagenesis?   The physical and chemical modifications that take place in a body of sediment, during deposition and also afterward, are classed under the heading of *diagenesis,* which is to that extent broader than lithification.

254. What are the distinctive features of sedimentary rocks?   Inasmuch as most sedimentary rocks are deposited in separate beds or strata, one on top of another, their most characteristic aspect is this layering or *stratification.* Lava flows are also layered, and some other igneous as well as certain metamorphic rocks likewise show parallelism of structure. But this significant feature is dominant in the sedimentary rocks and serves usually to identify them. The surface between the individual layers is the *bedding plane.*

The presence of fossils, which are the remains or impressions of animals and plants of the geologic past, is indicative of sedimentary rocks. Although fossils may on occasion be seen in igneous or metamorphic rocks, these are not their natural home.

Other structural features typical of sedimentary rocks include *mud cracks* due to the drying of muddy sediment; *ripple marks* made by wind, wave, and current; and lumps called *nodules* and *concretions.* Geodes (see Question 131) are a special kind of concretion.

255. What is the value of fossils in the study of rocks?　Fossils serve two distinct and principal uses in the study of rocks, apart from the fact that their presence is an indication that the rock is sedimentary. Fossils tell the age of sedimentary rocks according to the principles of organic evolution, whereby changing forms correspond to intervals of time. Thus, trilobites correspond only to the Paleozoic era and dinosaur bones to the Mesozoic era (see Question 258). Secondly, fossils indicate the environment in which the organisms lived or the rock accumulated. They often give the most reliable proof as to whether a rock is of marine or nonmarine origin, and often they suggest much more closely the exact conditions of deposition.

256. Can a leaf imprint be a fossil?　Yes, any evidence within the rock of former life on earth is properly regarded as a fossil. Fossils may range from an impression such as that, or the footprint of an ancient animal, even the cast or mold of one, all the way to the complete body of a mammoth deep-frozen in the Arctic tundra and well enough preserved for the dogs to eat of the flesh.

257. Are fossils often mineralized?　Many of the fossils that consist of the original hard or resistant parts of animals and plants have been replaced by mineral matter, so that little or none of the organic substance is left. This accounts for the great weight of dinosaur bones and the heaviness even of petrified shells and wood. Some have clearly been replaced so that the fossils appear to have been made out of stone; silicified wood (see Question 144) is the best example, but there are clam shells of pyrite and numerous other such kinds of preservation. The replacement of woody matter by radioactive minerals, such as carnotite, is of extraordinary economic significance (see Question 660).

258. What is the geologic time chart?　Most applicable to sedimentary rocks, although igneous and metamorphic rocks are also dated according to it, and especially appropriate when considering fossils, which give us most of our rock dates, the geologic time chart reads as follows. Note that the *eras* are divided into *periods* and these into *epochs*. The time chart is always printed with the oldest divisions at the bottom—as though it were a slice through the earth itself—and should be learned from the bottom up.

Era	Period	Epoch
Cenozoic	Quaternary	Recent Pleistocene
	Tertiary	Pliocene Miocene Oligocene Eocene Paleocene
Mesozoic	Cretaceous Jurassic Triassic	

Paleozoic	Permian
	Carboniferous:
	   Pennsylvanian
	   and
	   Mississippian
	Devonian
	Silurian
	Ordovician
	Cambrian	

Pre-Cambrian:
  Proterozoic
  and
  Archeozoic		

259. When did trilobites live? These three-lobed creatures, perhaps the most distinctive fossils in the rocks, lived in the seas of the Paleozoic era. Their presence indicates the age of the rock in which they are found, as well as giving proof of a marine environment.

260. When did dinosaurs live? All the reptiles known as dinosaurs thrived during the Mesozoic era of geologic time, and their bones are found in rocks of that age only.

261. What were dinosaurs like?   Dinosaurs were of all sizes, some no larger than a chicken, others ponderous animals that shook the earth as they plodded along. Some were vegetarians, others ferocious meat-eaters. Their habits were doubtless as diverse as their appearance, but we tend to think of them mainly as huge swamp-dwelling

| Stegosaurus | Brontosaurus | Triceratops |

THREE TYPES OF DINOSAURS

monsters with long necks and tails, being chased by others having heads full of sharp teeth. Some familiar types had horns, others were armor plated. Altogether, they were the most amazing creatures that ever dominated the earth—weird looking, long lived, stupid, like all reptiles cold blooded.

262. What is a formation?   The term formation is a technical one, having a special meaning in geology different from its popular use for any odd-shaped rock. A formation is the fundamental unit in rock subdivision and includes layers of sedimentary rock deposited under rather similar conditions during a fairly restricted interval of geologic time, yet large enough to be shown on a geologic map. In North America (and Australia) formations are named after some geographic feature in a place where they are well exposed and can be thoroughly studied. This then becomes the *type locality*. An example is the Pierre shale, named from its occurrence at old Fort Pierre, at a spot in South Dakota whose exact site is now unknown, but the same rock extends from eastern Minnesota to eastern Montana. Thousands of formations have been recognized in the United States; the Committee on Geologic Names of the U. S. Geological Survey keeps a card file of formation names and descriptions, to which reference can be made to avoid duplication.

263. What is correlation?   Correlation is the process whereby stratigraphers—who are the students of layered rocks—attempt to match formations from place to place in order to determine their mutual time relations. This may be done from outcrop to outcrop or, underground, from well to well. It is important in working out geologic history because in no single area is there a complete record of geologic time, and so the record must be pieced together from one region to another.

264. What is an unconformity?   A substantial break in the sequence of deposition of the sedimentary rocks, corresponding to a missing interval of time, is known as an unconformity. Several types are recognized, depending upon the kinds of rock involved and the bodily relationships. In 1859 Charles Darwin stated his belief that less of the total amount of geologic time is recorded by sedimentary beds than by the gaps between them. The evolutionary changes in fossils indicate the small proportion of time actually represented by the rocks of any given region.

265. What is a concretion?   Local concentrations of cementing material in nodular form are known as concretions. Often they begin with a nucleus of some foreign object, such as a fossil or grain of sand, and grow concentrically around it. Concretions may assume any size or shape as they develop, but in composition they resemble the cement of the rock and are almost always unlike the main body of the sedimentary rock in which they occur. Thus, a concretion of silica is apt to be found in a rock composed principally of calcium carbonate rather than of silica.

266. What are the textures of sedimentary rocks?   A clastic texture in a sedimentary rock is the result of the accumulation of broken fragments or particles later cemented together. A nonclastic texture is one in which the grains have grown in an interlocking fashion, resembling those of igneous origin, and this is typical of the chemically precipitated rocks, in which the individual crystals enlarge under the pressure and influence of the mineral-rich mud which settles down upon them.

267. What is the Wentworth scale? Revised by Chester K. Wentworth from an earlier system proposed by Johan A. Udden, this is a scale widely used to screen sediments and to measure the size of grains in sedimentary rocks. Each size is multiplied by a power of two to give the next larger size, and the samples are named accordingly. Thus, sand is coarser than silt, and granules are larger than sand. Other terms used include (in decreasing order) boulders, cobbles, and pebbles; and clay-size particles are even finer than silt.

268. Which are the quartzose rocks? This term applies to sandstone and conglomerate when they consist mainly of quartz fragments. *Silicious* also refers to these rocks, and both terms likewise indicate the presence of a cement predominantly silica.

269. Which are the calcareous rocks? The rocks that contain a substantial proportion of calcium carbonate are led by limestone, one of the most important of all rocks. When enough magnesium is present as a replacement of calcium, the term *dolomitic* limestone is used; pure dolomite would be composed solely of the mineral dolomite, the calcium-magnesium carbonate, $CaMg(CO_3)_2$. This was named after the French geologist with the mouth-filling name Déodat Guy Silvain Tanerède Gratet de Dolomieu. Named in turn after the mineral and rock are the Dolomites, a noted mountaineers' rendezvous in northern Italy, which contain much of this same rock standing in bold relief.

270. What is a carbonaceous rock? An abundance of organic matter (carbon), turning them black or dark gray, marks the carbonaceous rocks. This carbon is a strong reducing agent and should not be confused with the carbon in calcium carbonate (see Question 32), which acts very differently and is colorless or white when pure. Carbonaceous limestone, shale, etc., are typically dark.

271. How are sedimentary rocks folded? Although brittle at the surface of the earth, rocks assume a remarkable plasticity when buried deeply under enough confining pressure. They then can warp, bend, or fold. Upfolds of sedimentary rocks are called *anticlines;* downfolds are *synclines.* These may succeed each other across wide distances when a sedimentary trough is compressed to make folded mountains which have been uplifted and exposed by erosion.

272. Which is the coarsest sedimentary rock? The largest particle size of rounded sediment builds up the rock called *conglomerate.* Small and large fragments may occur together, but an appreciable proportion of them are granules (2 to 4 millimeters in diameter) or bigger, often referred to collectively as gravel. When the fragments are more or less angular, rather than rounded, the equivalent rock is called a *breccia*—this is the true sedimentary breccia, because this term is used for other kinds of shattered, angular rocks.

273. What is tillite? *Till* or tillite is a conglomerate deposited by glaciers and hence consists of rough pieces of rock irregularly heaped up by the ice, which lacks the ability possessed by a stream of selecting, sorting, and smoothing the sediment it carries.

274. What is the Nebraska till? The oldest of the glacial deposits of Pleistocene date in North America is called the Nebraska till, from its occurrence in that state—till being the general name for coarse unsorted glacial debris as it is dropped by the ice. The successive advances of the glaciers during the Ice Age have left 4,800,000 square miles of till, most of it north of the Missouri and Ohio Rivers.

275. What is a basal conglomerate? Gravel and coarse sand spread widely across the landscape in thin layers by the sea, as it encroaches upon a broadly eroded land surface at the close of a prolonged interval of erosion, become lithified to conglomerate. This particular type is referred to as a basal conglomerate because it will become the bottom layer of the next deposit of rock to be laid down in that region. Its presence assists the geologist in deciding the sequence of events and in finding which side of a series of strata is the bottom.

276. What is sandstone? Correctly speaking, sandstone is a sedimentary rock composed of sand-sized fragments, which are defined as more than $\frac{1}{16}$ millimeter in diameter and less than 2 millimeters. These fragments may consist of any kind of mineral or rock material. If hastily used, however, the term sandstone seems to imply sand composed of quartz, which is the most resistant of the common minerals and therefore accumulates in almost every sedimentary deposit, and which is certainly the most abundant constituent of sandstone.

There are, nevertheless, numerous minerals in some sandstones. Feldspar is a common one, and a sedimentary rock containing a fair percentage of it goes under the name *arkose*. The presence in the matrix of dark green and dark gray silt and clay produces *graywacke,* a name unfortunately misused for other rock types. On beaches of South Pacific islands, coral makes up the sand; in the Bay of Naples and elsewhere in volcanic areas, olivine is the sand mineral; White Sands National Monument in New Mexico contains acres of pure gypsum sand, derived from underlying beds of gypsum and, in places, being lithified again into solid gypsum.

277. Which is the flexible rock? Bearing the name *itacolumite* is a flexible sandstone which can be bent easily and will sag under its own weight. This strange rock is best known as a source of diamond, which is found in it in Brazil, India, the Ural Mountains, and Georgia and North Carolina. In Brazil, particularly, itacolumite is a host rock for crystals of diamond, though not the original source, inasmuch as any sandstone is secondary. The curious flexibility of itacolumite is due to a combination of some porosity, the presence of mica, chlorite, and talc—all three are flexible minerals—and an interlocking arrangement of quartz grains which provide an ability to rotate as do joints in bones.

278. What is the Potsdam sandstone? Named in 1838 from its occurrence at Potsdam, New York, this well known Cambrian formation (see Question 258) is especially prominent in scenic Ausable Chasm in northeastern New York. Almost two miles long, the gorge reaches a depth of 175 feet, and is a favorite tourist spot. The Potsdam formation originated from rock debris worn from the ancient Adirondack dome, from which is spread around the north and east flanks of the mountains of that name. It extends into southern Canada.

279. What is the Medina sandstone? Through the Medina sandstone has been carved the historic Delaware water gap, an important pioneer route in frontier time. This formation, of Silurian age, also outlines numerous prominent ridges in the Appalachian Mountains. It was produced by the erosion of an ancient mountain range known as the Taconic, which swung from Newfoundland through New England and at least as far south as New Jersey. This sandstone was named after Medina, New York, and is part of a thick group of related rocks, which seem to be favored today with the name Tuscarora.

280. What is the St. Peter sandstone? Remarkable for its pure quartz composition, consisting of rounded and chipped bits of quartz shaped by the wind and reworked by a clear, shallow sea, the St. Peter sandstone is one of the finest of its kind. Of Ordovician age, it occurs from Minnesota to Oklahoma. It was named in 1852 from outcrops on the St. Peter River, now called the Minnesota River, in southern Minnesota. The St. Peter formation furnishes glass and foundry sand for industry.

281. What is the Dakota sandstone? A vital source of water in the Great Plains states, the Dakota sandstone was deposited by streams flowing between two great arms of the sea that advanced to meet in one of the most extensive marine inundations in all of North American geologic history. This happened in the Cretaceous period. The Dakota sandstone now outcrops as sharply defined "hogbacks" along the Rocky Mountains and encircling the Black Hills of South Dakota. It was named in 1862, however, from the town of Dakota in Dakota County, Nebraska. Its steeply dipping structure and its porous nature make the Dakota an excellent carrier of water, which is obtained from thousands of artesian wells (see Question 936).

282. What is the Mesaverde sandstone? Capping certain of the large flat-topped lands in the Colorado Plateau region (see Question 659) is the Mesaverde sandstone of Cretaceous age. It was named in 1877 before the full revelation of the fascinating cliff dwellings that justified the later establishment of Mesa Verde National Park. In Mesa Verde itself the harder layers of this formation protect the caves in the softer layers. Here thrived a substantial culture which ended rather abruptly at the close of the 13th Century.

283. What is the Navajo sandstone?   Gray, buff, and red in color, the Navajo sandstone comprises the wonderfully scenic features of Rainbow Natural Bridge, a stone arch and national monument in southeastern Utah, and the towering Great White Throne and Angels' Landing in Zion National Park, in the same state. The most typical aspect of the Navajo sandstone is its cross-bedding, which reveals huge shifting dune sands of Jurassic times, when the deposit was laid down. This formation was appropriately named in 1915 from its many outcrops in the enchanting land of the Navajo.

284. What is the Tapeats sandstone?   The lowest sedimentary rock of the flat-lying beds that mark the cliffs of the Grand Canyon is the Tapeats sandstone. It is Cambrian in age. Like the other formations it is of significance in tracing the outlines of the structure of this region and interpreting the order of events that have taken place. This sandstone was named in 1914 for Tapeats Creek; below the mouth of this stream, the bed of the Colorado River itself lies within the formation.

285. Which is the thinnest rock?   The sedimentary rock consisting of particles smaller than $\frac{1}{16}$ millimeter in diameter is siltstone, mudstone, or shale—sometimes grouped together as *lutites*. A goodly share of such particles will prove to be one of the clay minerals (see Question 826), but there will also be tiny grains of quartz and feldspar, calcite and dolomite, and other minerals. The outstanding property of shale is its tendency to split readily parallel to the closely set bedding planes. Shale is the most common of the sedimentary rocks, constituting about 46 per cent of the total. It is also the softest, for physically it offers little resistance to erosion, but chemically it is quite stable because it contains so largely the final products of weathering. With the addition of foreign matter, shale becomes silty, sandy, or limy.

286. What is the significance of black shale?   Important as the probable source material of petroleum, black shale has been the subject of dispute among geologists for many years. The color is usually due to carbonaceous matter from animal or plant tissues, though sometimes iron sulfide is the pigmenting agent. Black mud, which will someday become shale, is being deposited today in such various places as Chesapeake Bay and the fjords of Norway. A particularly notable deposit of ancient black shale is the Chattanooga shale, which reaches from Oklahoma to eastern Kentucky; its origin seems to be different from that of other black shales but it is equally uncertain.

287. What is the Burgess shale? This fine-grained black shale, which outcrops along the mountains in British Columbia, is famous in the history of geology for its magnificently preserved fossils of Cambrian age, discovered by Charles D. Wolcott in 1910 when a pack horse walking along a trail on Mount Wapta, high above the town of Field, accidentally turned over a slab of rock in which they were preserved. These fossils represent carbon films of primitive soft-bodied animals previously unknown and unsuspected. The original environment was presumably that of the black shales discussed in Question 286. The Burgess shale is a member of the Stephen formation.

288. What are redbeds? Widespread throughout the world and of all geologic ages, the so-called redbeds are reddish colored fragmental sedimentary rocks, mostly land-derived and land-deposited—that is, of nonmarine origin. Most of them can be classified as sandstone, silt-stone, and shale, and their color is due to finely divided hematite. The source of the red color has been one of the persistent problems of petrologists, for these rocks are conspicuous and were among the first sedimentary rocks to be studied. The Old Red sandstone of Great Britain is an especially famous redbed in geologic history. So also is the Newark group of sediments in northeastern United States, noted for its great thickness and its dinosaur footprints. The most favorable environment for the creation of an initially red color in such sediments seems to be the deposition of hematite as a cementing pigment after the rock accumulated in hot and or semiarid climates. Perhaps Dr. Theodore R. Walker has finally solved this ancient problem.

289. What is lithographic limestone? The process of printing on stone with a greasy substance began in 1796 with the discovery by Aloys Senefelder (1771–1834) that the remarkably dense limestone at Solnhofen, Bavaria, was ideal for drawing and writing upon with a special ink, and that the image could be reproduced on paper by means of the mutual repulsion between grease and water. Thus lithography was born, though the process on a commercial scale now employs thin metal sheets and plastic "plates," with the intermediate step of a rubber blanket to transfer the image. Lithographic limestone is still used in Japan and elsewhere, however, and by individual artists. The original Solnhofen deposit is also noted for its astoundingly fine preservations of Jurassic fossils, including large flying reptiles allied to the dinosaurs, Archaeopteryx, the most primitive bird whose skeleton—with teeth!—shows many reptilian features.

290. What is the Trenton limestone? A widespread deposit of limestone, familiar to geologists both for its extraordinarily high content of fossils of Ordovician age and for its valuable petroleum resources, the Trenton formation is relatively thin but covers hundreds of thousands of square miles from Michigan to Virginia. It supports lovely Trenton Falls in Oneida County, New York, where it is more than 100 feet thick and from where it received its name in 1838.

291. What is the Onondaga limestone? This widely distributed formation, which belongs to the Devonian age, extends in an uninterrupted layer from the valley of the Hudson River to central Ohio. At Louisville, Kentucky, it forms the once-noted Falls of the Ohio—at this place the structure is that of an ancient coral reef. Among the other interesting fossils in this rock is the Methuselah brachiopod, *Leptaena rhomboidalis,* a long-lived marine invertebrate bearing a two-piece outer shell. The formation was named in 1839 from its outcrops in Onondaga County, New York.

292. What is the Ste. Genevieve limestone? Thousands of caverns, small and large, have been dissolved by underground water from the Ste. Genevieve limestone. These include Wyandotte Cave, in Indiana, and Mammoth Cave National Park, in Kentucky. This formation, named in 1859 for outcrops in the bluffs of the Mississippi River at Ste. Genevieve, in the Missouri county of the same name, is one of a number of limestone formations deposited during the Mississippian period of geologic history.

293. What is the St. Louis limestone? One of the most extensive bodies of limestone in the United States is the St. Louis limestone of Mississippian age. It lies directly beneath the Ste. Genevieve limestone (see Question 292). The bluffs of the Mississippi River near St. Louis are composed of it, and it is continuous from Iowa to Alabama. Except for its extent and homogeneity, this formation has little to remark upon, but those aspects of it are exceptional even in the central states where limestone is abundant.

294. What is the Fencepost limestone? In north-central Kansas one zone of the Greenhorn limestone is known locally as the fencepost bed because it breaks into pieces of a convenient size for making fence posts. The early settlers in this area also used it for constructing many of their buildings. The layers are of uniform thickness and the joints suitably spaced so that long slabs of the rock can be taken without any need for trimming them. The Greenhorn limestone is Cretaceous in age.

295. What is the Niobrara limestone? Named in 1862 from outcrops along the Missouri River near the mouth of the Niobrara River in Knox County, Nebraska, the Niobrara limestone is a Cretaceous formation extending from Minnesota to Montana and New Mexico. Within this large area it assumes diverse aspects. Part of it is known as the Niobrara chalk (see Question 299), which yields superb fossils of huge diving birds, marine reptiles, such as plesiosaurs and mosasaurs, and *Pteranodon,* the "winged dragon," climax of the flying reptiles. Elsewhere the Niobrara rocks become ordinary limestone and even shale.

296. What is the Capitan limestone? Of Permian age, the Capitan limestone is a massive white formation named in 1904 for El Capitan Peak in El Paso County, Texas. In addition to this sheer 1,300-foot cliff, most of spacious Carlsbad Caverns National Park, New Mexico, lies within the same formation, which is characterized as a reef-forming limestone.

297. What is the Kaibab limestone? This impressive formation, named in 1910 after the Kaibab Plateau on the north side of Grand Canyon National Park, frames the rim of the canyon in cliffs 500 to 600 feet high. It can be traced for miles on both sides of the Colorado River. Elsewhere in northern Arizona, such as in Walnut Canyon

National Monument, famed for its distinctive Indian cliff dwellings, the Kaibab limestone is also much in evidence.

298. What is the Redwall limestone?   Outstanding even among the other rocks of the Grand Canyon is the Redwall limestone, which delineates the 500-foot cliffs about halfway up the sides of this most magnificent of the world's canyons. The thickness remains about the same for more than 100 miles. The origin of this name, given it in 1875 by the noted geologist Grove K. Gilbert (1843–1918), is obvious from its splendid appearance, made red by the spread of shale from the rocks above. The Redwall is Mississippian in age.

299. What is chalk?   Chalk is a variety of limestone that is composed mostly of the remains of marine foraminifera, minute one-celled animals that create shells of calcium carbonate. Chalk is typically dead white, but it may be grayish or buff colored. It is soft because fine grained. Chalk is widespread in Europe and America, especially in rocks of the Cretaceous period (see Question 258), which was so called from the Latin name for chalk. The cliffs of the English Channel are the type locality for rocks of this age. Washed and purified chalk is known commercially as whiting, which is used for putty and silver polish.

300. What is the Selma chalk?   A soft clayey limestone known locally as the "rotten limestone" is the Selma chalk, a formation of considerable importance in eastern Mississippi and western Alabama and Tennessee. Where not stabilized by vegetation it erodes into badland topography because of its softness. Its age is Cretaceous, and it was named in 1894 from Selma in Dallas County, Alabama.

301. Which rock is made of shells?   Shells and shell fragments, partly cemented together in a porous mass, constitute the variety of limestone known as coquina. All coquina is of recent origin, and it is said to harden after exposure to the air. The best known deposits are in Florida, where coquina has been used as a building stone, especially in the old city of Saint Augustine, founded in September 1565. Here the Castillo de San Marcos and Fort Matanzas—both are national monuments—and the city gates erected in 1804 are all constructed of native coquina rock.

302. What is oölite? This is a variety of limestone composed of small rounded particles of calcium carbonate built up in a concentric and radial fashion. The term is less desirably used for the individual particles themselves. Chemical precipitation of aragonite or calcite takes place around a speck of foreign matter, say a grain of sand or bit of shell, when the water is agitated and a slight amount evaporates. The oölitic sands of Great Salt Lake are extraordinary in their abundance and symmetry; a handful of the dry grains slips through the fingers like a thousand tiny beads.

303. What is dolostone? To avoid confusion between the word dolomite as used for a mineral and at the same time for a rock composed of that mineral, the term dolostone was proposed in 1948 by Dr. Robert R. Shrock, though it has not yet been widely adopted.

304. What is the Lockport dolomite? Niagara Falls, the first of the world's great waterfalls to become known to Europeans and the very symbol of power, flows over the edge of the Lockport dolomite. Undercutting of the softer Clinton shale beneath it causes collapse of the brink from time to time and a steady decrease in the height and grandeur of the American Falls. Because the Lockport dolomite slopes toward Lake Erie, Niagara is gradually declining in elevation. This formation was named in 1839 from Lockport, New York, where it was excavated for the passage of the Erie Canal. Its age is Silurian.

305. What is the Bighorn dolomite? In the widespread seas of Ordovician time in North America was deposited a uniform bed of dolomite, which goes under the name Bighorn in the northern Rocky Mountains, after the Bighorn Mountains of Wyoming. Although it bears other names from Alaska to Greenland to northern Mexico, it is pretty much the same everywhere, as shown by its fossils of mollusks and coral.

306. Is a coral reef a sedimentary rock? Yes, because so-called coral reefs—they really owe less to coral than to other kinds of marine organisms—result from the chemical precipitation of calcium carbonate taken from sea water, and this is a major sedimentary process. The deposits, furthermore, are built up from the bottom and increase in height with the passage of time.

The entire reef complex consists of the remains of animals and plants which extract mineral matter from the clear tropical oceans and utilize it to form their structures along the island shores where the breaking waves can supply aerated water and nutriments to the growing organisms. More numerous than corals in the construction of a coral reef are calcareous algae and various marine invertebrates.

307. Where are coral reefs located? Modern coral reefs are developed in two main regions. One extends from the Tuamotu Archipelago and Hawaii in the Pacific Ocean to the east coast of Africa; the other is in the Caribbean–West Indies area, as far north as Bermuda. The Great Barrier Reef, fringing the northeastern coast of Australia, is the world's largest, attaining a length of 1,260 miles and a width from 10 to 90 miles.

308. What are evaporites? Chemical precipitation from solution, as a result of the evaporation of water, yields a large group of sedimentary rocks known as evaporites. Gypsum, rock salt, and anhydrite are the most familiar of these. The evaporation of sea water is the principal origin of the evaporites, though the locale may be an inland lake that is drying up, as is true of Great Salt Lake, the modern remnant of prehistoric Lake Bonneville, a much vaster body of water during the Ice Age. A fairly uniform sequence of precipitation takes place, with the less soluble minerals appearing on the bottom first, and the most soluble ones last. Some minerals are so soluble that a nearly complete disappearance of the water is necessary to bring them down; since this seldom happens, such minerals are rare.

309. Where is the Permian Basin? Situated in eastern New Mexico, western Texas, and northern Mexico is the thickest deposit of evaporites in the United States. The Castile formation, nearly 4,000 feet thick, consists more than 90 per cent of the three most common evaporites—gypsum, rock salt, and anhydrite. These were deposited in an enclosed basin, cut off from open circulation, during the Permian period of geologic time, when extensive aridity prevailed in this part of the world. The valuable potash beds associated with the name Carlsbad, which is the mining center, were also formed at this time (see Question 782).

310. What is the relationship between gypsum and anhydrite?
Both of these sedimentary rocks are composed of calcium sulfate, but gypsum contains water, and anhydrite, as its name suggests, does not. Anhydrite can change naturally to gypsum by the addition of water in the near-surface zones of the earth's crust. Conversely, but less readily, gypsum becomes anhydrite under pressure. Both rocks are white or gray when pure; anhydrite is both harder and heavier. Which of the two will form in the first place depends upon the temperature and salinity of the sea water from which they normally deposit.

311. Which rock is a food? The "mineral" content of every rock supplies food elements to the soil, from there to vegetation, and then directly or indirectly through animal sources to nourish our own bodies. But rock salt is a sedimentary rock indispensable to life because it is in itself a food substance. Thick beds of salt underlie certain parts of the earth's surface, and seepages bring salt to the top of the ground in "salt licks" and salt springs. The location of available salt has controlled caravan routes and sponsored the settlements of civilization in many countries. The extraction of salt from the ocean and from land-locked bodies of sea water was doubtless one of the earliest of human industries. Virtual underground cities have been excavated in the salt deposits of central Europe.

312. What is novaculite? A fine-grained but gritty, even-textured though sometimes porous siliceous rock, found in the Ouachita Mountains of Arkansas and Oklahoma, and a similar rock in the Marathon Mountains of Texas—in both places it helps to support a hilly topography—is novaculite. At first this word meant a certain whetstone used for honing razors, but now it has become a general petrographic term. The most active quarries of novaculite have been on the ridges northeast of Hot Springs, Arkansas, where two somewhat different kinds of material have furnished hard and soft stones, each adapted to sharpening particular kinds of tools.

313. What is greensand? When the green iron silicate mineral *glauconite* is concentrated in fairly pure deposits, a sedimentary material known as greensand is produced. Glauconite is forming slowly today on the bottom of the sea and presumably has done so throughout geologic history, for it is found in rocks of varying ages. There is, however, no general agreement as to the exact process involved. Especially good localities for glauconitic rocks are New Jersey; the Gulf Coast states of Texas, Mississippi, and Alabama; west of the Great Lakes in Wisconsin and Minnesota; and western Europe.

314. What are oozes?   Unconsolidated deep-sea sediments of the open ocean are referred to as oozes. They are derived from the ocean itself, and more than 30 per cent of their volume consists of the shells and other hard parts of very small marine organisms which extract mineral matter from the water to build their structures. Upon their death or when they shed their shells, these remains accumulate on the sea floor, usually at an inconceivably slow rate.

315. Which are the siliceous oozes?   The siliceous oozes include *radiolarian ooze* and *diatomaceous ooze*. The former comes from the protozoa (one-celled animals) called Radiolaria, and is most common in red clay in the Pacific Ocean directly north of the equator. The latter comes from the algae (simple plants) called diatoms and occurs in the North Pacific and Antarctic Oceans.

316. Which are the calcareous oozes?   The calcareous oozes include *globigerina ooze,* derived from foraminifera (one-celled animals) of that name; it is distributed throughout 50,000,000 square miles of the major oceans. Another is *pteropod ooze,* derived from certain gastropods (mollusks) and especially prominent between Africa and South America.

317. Which rock swells when wet?   Bentonite. There are several kinds of bentonite, but the usual definition applies to an altered volcanic ash—once of igneous origin, now sedimentary. As a result of the changes that it has undergone, bentonite has the remarkable property of absorbing several times its own weight of water. It is thus a kind of swelling clay, or *montmorillonite*. Thin beds of bentonite, derived from the volcanoes of the West, are widespread throughout the Great Plains and Rocky Mountains.

318. What is loess?   Silty wind-blown deposits intermixed with clay constitute the sedimentary rock known as loess. Its most usual color is grayish tan. Loess does not appear in layers, yet it was obviously deposited that way. Its most distinctive characteristic, in fact, is its ability to stand up in vertical walls, even though it is not cemented and it has not been compacted. The force of cohesion seems to be supplied by the remains of grass roots that once grew in it and now cause it to break into clifflike forms. Loess is very widely spread throughout central China, in the Missouri-Mississippi drainage system, and in northwestern Europe. The Chinese deposits are probably derived from the Gobi Desert, and the others have been reworked by streams and wind from the fine glacial "rock flour" released by melting glaciers of the Ice Age.

319. What is diatomaceous earth? The microscopic single-celled plants (algae) called diatoms extract silica from fresh, stagnant, and salt water. When their skeletal remains accumulate, a white powdery rock known as diatomaceous earth is formed. Although extremely

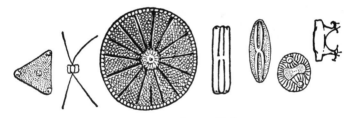

Diatoms, greatly magnified

fine, it has a harsh feel. It is used as a filter, as an insulation material, and in polishing powders. The thickest beds of diatomaceous earth are along the east and west coasts of the United States. The city of Richmond, Virginia, is built upon an 18-foot stratum of this chalky-looking rock.

320. What is the Cannonball marine member? This is part of the Fort Union formation, and is the only evidence still in existence—within 1,000 miles—of sedimentary rocks that had a marine origin during the Paleocene epoch of the Tertiary period. Elsewhere, marine deposits are found only along the shores of the continent. The Fort Union itself is widespread throughout the northern Great Plains of the United States and extends into Canada, but at the bottom of it lies this interesting relic of rock, containing oyster banks and other shallow oceanic features, the last remnant of an interior sea that had stretched from the Arctic Ocean to the Gulf of Mexico. The outcrops are confined mainly in the southwestern part of North Dakota. The formation gets its name from the Canonball River, which in turn was so called because of the countless round concretions in the rock.

321. What is the Morrison formation? Rich in remains of the gigantic dinosaurs that flourished in Western America, the Morrison formation has also come into prominence as one of the principal sources of uranium in this part of the world. These two aspects are intimately related (see Question 660). The formation is composed of shale in some places, siltstone in others, sandstone and conglomerate elsewhere—for it once covered more than 100,000 square miles from Montana to New Mexico and varied according to the local conditions of deposition that prevailed during the Jurassic period: streams, swamps, shallow lakes. The first discovery of the large dinosaurs occurred near Morrison, Colorado, in 1877 and the rocks in which they were exposed were named *"Atlantosaurus* beds" after the reptile found in them, being renamed Morrison in later years. The bizarre animals from Dinosaur National Monument likewise occur in the Morrison formation.

322. What is the Wasatch formation? The "dawn horse," Eohippus—with four toes in front and three in back—appears in the rocks of the Wasatch formation. He was about one foot high, had an arched back, a long tail, and a promising future, becoming the ancestor of all our modern horses. The Wasatch is composed largely of soft sandstone and consequently erodes readily into weirdly shaped scenery. The brightly colorful oddities of Bryce Canyon National Park was sculptured from lake deposits (they contain shells of aquatic snails) of the same rock, which received its name from outcrops in Echo and Weber Canyons in the Wasatch Mountains, Utah.

323. What is the Belt Sequence? This is an accumulation of sedimentary rocks of outstanding interest because, in spite of their great age, they are in many places little changed in position or nature from their original condition. They have certainly been elevated, however, no matter how flat they now rest—for they constitute the background of spectacular scenery in Glacier National Park, in Montana, and Jasper National Park, in Alberta. Originating in a shallow sea, the Belt rocks are Pre-Cambrian in age, yet mud cracks and ripple marks are still as well preserved as when they were formed more than half a billion years ago. The localities of the Big Belt and Little Belt Mountains in Montana gave their names to this sequence of formations, which has an aggregate thickness (including minor igneous additions) of as much as 35,000 feet.

324. What is the John Day formation?   Exceptionally fine skeletons of Tertiary mammals, identified as Oligocene or Miocene, have been taken from the John Day formation, in the John Day Basin of central Oregon. In few other areas have fossils shed so much light on the environment and life forms prevailing at a given time and place. Some of the strange beasts that called this part of Oregon home would have to be seen to be believed.

V. METAMORPHIC ROCKS

Introduction. By a change in mineral composition or texture, or both, igneous and sedimentary rocks can be transformed into the third major type of rock, the metamorphic rock. Rearrangement of the mineral grains into new patterns, called *recrystallization,* and reorganization of the chemical constituents into new compounds, called *recombination,* are the fundamental aspects of the process of metamorphism. The whole tendency is to adjust the stability of the rock to a new physical and chemical environment to which it is being exposed. The resulting products depend upon the nature of the original material, the particular processes involved, and the intensity with which they act. These products include some of the most interesting and distinctive appearing members of the Mineral Kingdom, though perhaps fewer in number and of less diversity than the igneous and sedimentary rocks. In its general principles metamorphism is easy to explain, but in detail the subject is enormously complex. Much of it is not easily understood because the conditions under which it takes place cannot be duplicated experimentally, and prolonged intervals of time seem to be necessary.

325. What causes metamorphism? Heat, pressure, and water—these three are the factors that turn igneous or sedimentary rocks into metamorphic rocks. High temperature increases the effectiveness of almost every chemical reaction and so speeds up the transformation. The pressure on rocks by simple burial at depth, or resulting from compression during folding, faulting, or mountain-building, causes changes to take place that will induce a greater stability in the material. Heat and pressure almost always accompany each other and act in conjunction. Fluids—gases and liquids—of any kind help metamorphism, serving to lubricate the slowly moving system, as well as to add themselves to the chemical composition in producing some of the new minerals. Steam and water are by far the most important fluids, but vapors and liquids of many common and rare kinds are involved. When a magma invades older rocks from beneath, in its molten, mobile state, it provides heat, pressure, and ample fluids—this *contact metamorphism* is one of the best recognized kinds.

326. Which are the minerals in metamorphic rocks?   Some of the most abundant minerals in the metamorphic rocks are identical with those of the igneous and sedimentary rocks from which they have been derived. Even when they are not the lineal descendants of these older rocks, many metamorphic rocks form under conditions of high temperature and strong pressure similar to that of igneous rocks, and so the minerals are much the same (see Chapter II). Quartz, feldspar, and mica are especially characteristic of both types of rock. Of the micas (see Questions 165–169) muscovite, biotite, and phlogopite are of both igneous and metamorphic origin but more frequently metamorphic—especially muscovite, which is rather rare in igneous rocks except pegmatite. Hornblende, olivine, and magnetite are other igneous minerals common enough in certain metamorphic rocks. Calcite and dolomite are familiar in both sedimentary and metamorphic rocks, as also is graphite, which comes from the carbonaceous matter in sedimentary substances. In addition to these, there are several minerals especially associated with metamorphic rocks—kyanite, andalusite, staurolite, wollastonite. More conspicuous in metamorphic than other rocks, though not confined to them, are garnet, actinolite, and tremolite. Of the minerals that originate in metamorphism, but also by hot-water alteration not so closely identified with this general process, chlorite, serpentine, talc, and epidote should be mentioned.

327. What is a relict mineral?   Minerals that survive the process of metamorphism without having lost their previous identity are spoken of as relict, for not all parts of the original rock are equally affected by the reorganization that it undergoes. A relict mineral may be recognized by some otherwise obscure feature that happens to have escaped destruction.

328. What is foliation?   This is the parallel alignment of minerals that have a flaky habit (see Question 82) so that they tend to orient themselves at right angles to the direction of pressure. Mica and the micalike minerals (such as chlorite and talc) are especially prone to this pattern. When the orientation is stretched out in one direction, as with elongated minerals (especially hornblende), it is termed *lineation.* These rocks split with a more or less ready "cleavage," but this term, though widely used, is too easily confused with the true cleavage of minerals (see Question 93).

329. What are the structures of metamorphic rocks?   Metamorphic rocks may be conveniently divided into those that show a parallel structure—such as foliation and lineation (see Question 328)—and those that do not and are said to be "massive." The emphasis is on at least a rough or wavy parallelism, even when faintly discerned, and this may be regarded as the dominant characteristic of metamorphic rocks, as much so as the layering of sedimentary strata and the interlocking texture of igneous rock bodies.

330. What is mylonite?   Taken from the Greek word for "mill," mylonite signifies a rock that has been drastically broken and crushed, even pulverized, by intense pressure which pulls out some of the material in the direction of movement. This takes place especially in areas of faulting in which one segment of the rock has been inexorably thrust over the other segment.

331. How do metamorphic rocks occur?   The home of most metamorphic rocks is in mountainous regions where intrusions of magmas, the heated solutions rising from them, and the horizontally directed forces that compress the rocks may be expected to act most effectively. These are the mobile or tectonic zones, where mountain structures and elevated landmasses are most apt to occur. Other areas contain metamorphic rocks only sporadically.

332. What is hornfels?   The baking effect of heat creates hornfels from clay or a clay-bearing rock such as shale. The original bedding is often well preserved. Conspicuous grains of biotite or andalusite may be visible, having formed at a late stage in the development of the rock. Small knots of graphite may also be present as a similar result. Hornfels is usually compact (sugary grained) and hard, as its name, meaning "horn rock" in German, suggests.

333. What is grade of metamorphism?   The degree to which the metamorphic agents have been effective in transforming a rock is referred to as its grade. Thus, a fairly small amount of heat and pressure produces low-grade metamorphism, recognized by a typical assemblage of minerals, which would be different from those expected to be found under high-grade metamorphism. When a geologic map is made of a metamorphic area, lines can be drawn to separate the zones where a given indicator-mineral is present, from those where it is absent, thereby producing a map of metamorphic intensity.

334. What is gneiss? In a limited sense, gneiss is the coarsest of the metamorphic rocks, having parallel streaks of feldspar or alternating light and dark minerals, of which feldspar, quartz, mica, and hornblende are the most representative. In a broader meaning, gneiss has come to signify a number of different kinds of rock, some of which have an unknown history not currently capable of being interpreted. Although gneiss is formed at higher temperature and pressure than schist (see Question 338), there is often a gradual transition between the two. Some petrographers require the presence of feldspar to make the rock a true gneiss; others consider only the spacing of the layers; still others expect gneiss to contain bands of varying mineral composition. Gneiss may be named according to its comparative composition, as a granitic gneiss; its origin, as a conglomerate gneiss; a mineral, such as garnet gneiss; or a peculiar structure, such as augen gneiss (see Question 335).

335. What is augen gneiss? Augen—the German word for "eyes" —is applied to gneiss that contains large rounded grains resembling giant eyes. These usually consist of feldspar or quartz or both minerals. The surrounding structure curves around them, accentuating the curious eyelike appearance as though shaded by thick eyebrows.

336. What is the Hinsdale gneiss? The oldest rock in the Berkshire Hills and Connecticut Valley of Massachusetts and Connecticut is the Hinsdale gneiss, named in 1892 for the place of that name in the state of Massachusetts. It is mainly a coarse, gray biotite gneiss.

337. What is the Idaho Springs gneiss? This ancient gneiss, well exposed in the mountains around the mining and resort town of Idaho Springs, Colorado, grades from gneiss to schist and contains lenses of silicate rocks. It is older than the Pikes Peak granite and other igneous rocks in contact with it, yet it seems to have come from an even older series of sedimentary rocks, as suggested by the mineral and chemical composition and the structure.

338. What is schist?   Derived from the Greek meaning "to divide," schist is a metamorphic rock usually so well foliated that it splits readily in the direction of the flat or elongated minerals of which it is principally composed and which are coarse enough to be identified at sight. These are chiefly mica, amphibole, chlorite, and talc. The presence of large percentages of any of these minerals gives it the convenient name mica-schist, chlorite schist, etc. Inasmuch as most schist consists of two or more minerals, compound names such as garnet-biotite schist are familiar. Schist grades in one way into gneiss (see Question 334), in another way into *phyllite* and then slate (see Question 344).

339. What is the Manhattan schist?   The principal rock of Manhattan Island is the Manhattan schist, several thousand feet in thickness, including other associated Pre-Cambrian rocks. The Manhattan schist extends into Westchester and Putnam counties and into western Connecticut. Its most constant characteristics are the presence of a white pearly mica, a coarse foliation, and a crumpled structure. It was once a sedimentary rock, prior to its profound metamorphism. It was described and named in 1890.

340. What is the Battleground schist?   This rock was so named in 1931 because of its occurrence on Kings Mountain Battleground in South Carolina, site of the American Revolutionary victory of October 7, 1780, though it occurs elsewhere in both North and South Carolina. It contains a large amount of fine-grained mica and is Pre-Cambrian in age.

341. What is the Kitchi schist?   A metamorphic rock marked by the presence of pebbles so rounded that they look like those of a sedimentary formation (conglomerate), the Kitchi schist was actually derived in Pre-Cambrian times from a volcanic material known as tuff (see Question 214). It was named in 1895 from the Kitchi Hills in northwestern Michigan.

342. What is the Visnu schist? This body of ancient (Pre-Cambrian) metamorphic rock consists of more than 1,000 feet of mica schist and quartzite at the bottom of the Grand Canyon, where it is exposed within the Inner or so-called Granite Gorge. It is a complex of mica, quartz, and hornblende schist, intruded by granite here and there and criss-crossed by a network of pegmatite dikes. Derived from still-older sedimentary rocks, the Visnu was given its Oriental name in 1889 from the splendid scenic feature known as the Temple of Vishnu, within the national park. The equivalent rock in the Bradshaw Mountains of central Arizona is called the Yavapai schist, so named in 1905 from Yavapai County.

343. What is the Abrams mica schist? Named in 1901 for Abrams post office in the upper Coffee Creek region of northern California, the Abrams mica schist is a metamorphic formation estimated at 5,000 feet in thickness. It is composed of dull-colored muscovite mica separated by irregular layers of white quartz which represent the original sedimentary beds of sandstone.

344. What is slate? A roofing and constructional stone of age-old acceptance, slate is a fine-grained metamorphic rock that splits easily because of closely spaced fractures or the parallel orientation of flaky minerals such as mica or chlorite, which impart a gloss to the surface. An original sedimentary bedding may often be seen in slate, but it appears at an angle to the newly formed planes along which the rock now separates. Slate comes in blue, gray, green, red, and brown colors; the material used for industry must be carefully selected to serve its purpose.

345. What is the Diamond Island slate? On Great Diamond Island and Little Diamond Island, in Casco Bay, Maine, occurs an interesting black slate studded with crystals and small masses of pyrite, which weather out and give iron stained surfaces. Equally distinctive are the numerous small crumpled quartz veins. The name Diamond Island slate was applied in 1917. This rock seems to be Pennsylvanian in age.

346. What is the Waxahatchee slate? Containing a good deal of fine-grained bluish slate, the Waxahatchee slate of central Alabama, named in 1940 after a creek in Selby County, has the substantial thickness of 5,000 feet. The rock also includes grayish and greenish colors. The age is yet uncertain as either Pre-Cambrian or Paleozoic.

347. What is the Mariposa slate?   Interbedded with volcanic rocks, the Mariposa slate of eastern California resulted from the intense metamorphism of earlier sedimentary rocks which were folded into mountains during the Jurassic period. The Mother Lode gold deposits (see Question 389), rising from hot solutions, penetrated this slate and produced some of the world's richest mineralization. The name comes from the old Mariposa estate in Mariposa County, California, where the rocks are about 10,000 feet thick.

348. What is quartzite?   Quartzite is the metamorphic equivalent of quartz sandstone which has undergone recrystallization. Unfortunately, and incorrectly, this name is often used also for a tightly cemented sandstone; this use should be discouraged, but it is difficult to discourage some people! The natural hardness and durability of quartz, to which has been added an interlocking texture of the individual grains, combine to make true quartzite without question the most resistant of all rocks. It stands as ridges and mountain peaks wherever erosion has exposed it.

349. What is the Baraboo quartzite?   One of the most attractive of metamorphic rocks is the famous Pre-Cambrian Baraboo quartzite, named after bluffs of that name in south-central Wisconsin. Much of it is deep red; other portions are gray and other colors, white being the least common. A feature of especial interest is the presence in several places in Baraboo and Pipestone Counties of a hardened and semi-metamorphosed red shale known as *catlinite,* which was used by the Indians for their peace pipes. The original locality was in Wisconsin, though quarries in Minnesota have been set aside as Pipestone National Monument.

350. What is the Sheridan quartzite?   The oldest rock in Yellowstone National Park is the Sheridan quartzite. Named in 1896 from its best exposure on the slopes of Mount Sheridan, it is found at only three places in the park. Its age is Pre-Cambrian.

351. What is the Gold Creek quartzite? A remarkably coarse-grained pure-white quartzite, containing many layers of large pebbles and preserving the original cross bedding, forms cliffs and ridges in northern Idaho and is known as the Gold Creek quartzite. It belongs to the Cambrian period.

352. What is marble? As quartzite is transformed sandstone, so marble is merely the metamorphic equivalent of limestone or dolomite. In pure material, the minerals remain the same—only the texture is altered to give the sugary or boldly crystalline appearance of the typical commercial stone. Pure marble, white enough for statuary, is not so abundant as impure marble, in which have developed the knots or streaks of other minerals that lend colored marble so much charm. No two marbles seem alike. Carbonaceous matter makes marble black or gray; iron minerals usually make it red or green. Swirls of serpentine and inclusions of other minerals yield a delightful array of patterns and hues.

353. What is eclogite? One of the heaviest of rocks is eclogite, a metamorphic rock consisting mainly of a mixed garnet and an aluminum-bearing augite called omphacite. Eclogite is usually interpreted as a metamorphosed basalt because its chemical composition is much the same as basalt, but some of it is thought to be of igneous origin because lacking evidence of parallel orientation.

354. What is serpentine? Serpentine is both a mineral and a rock. The mineral name includes at least two different but similar appearing minerals, *antigorite* (a platy variety) and *chrysotile* (a fibrous variety), both hydrous magnesium silicates, $Mg_3Si_2O_5(OH)_4$. The rock name refers to a mixture of chrysotile and talc, chlorite, and other green minerals.

The likeliest sources of serpentine are the igneous minerals olivine and pyroxene which have been acted upon by heated, late altering solutions from the same magma, or else those coming from nearby cooling igneous bodies. Pressure metamorphism is apparently responsible for some serpentine rock. This rock is greenish or gray, and it often contains veins of chrysotile in the form of asbestos (see Question 137).

355. What is talc?   The softest of all minerals, talc is most familiar for its use in cosmetics as talcum powder, though it has other and more important industrial applications. It is a hydrous magnesium silicate, $Mg_3Si_4O_{10}(OH)_2$, and is a product of metamorphism, as well as of certain hydrothermal (hot-water) alterations. Talc occurs in flexible leaves that can be cut with a knife without crumbling. In compact masses talc often goes under the name *steatite*.

356. What is soapstone?   Because of its slippery feel, the rock that is composed of an impure variety of talc has long been known as soapstone. This gray or grayish green rock is probably the result of hydrothermal (hot-water) alteration, as is most serpentine. Yet they are both usually considered metamorphic rocks, although the conditions under which they have formed is not clearly known.

Soapstone is quarried in the Appalachian Mountains, especially in Virginia, where it is sawed into blocks and slabs for use mainly as a heat-resistant material in the smelting furnaces of kraft-paper mills, and also for electrical switchboards, chemical sinks, partitions, and other structural uses. Inexpensive carved objects of soapstone have long been sold as jade but can be recognized by their slippery feel.

357. What are skarn minerals?   The intrusion of a good-sized body of magma into carbonate rocks such as limestone causes a large-scale outward transfer of mineral matter from the magma, which in turn absorbs or dissolves material from the surrounding rocks. A significant product of this action is the complex marble-silicate rock called *tactite;* especially when iron oxides are also present, the contact metamorphic rock is known as *skarn* and new minerals as skarn minerals. The existence of such a body, lying usually at the margin of an intrusive igneous rock of intermediate composition (see Question 188) indicates the fact and effectiveness of metamorphism.

358. Which mineral has a variable hardness?   The only mineral that shows a conspicuous difference in hardness in two directions is *kyanite*. It can be scratched by a knife blade along the length of its crystals, but not at all across the width. Its name derived from a Greek word meaning "blue," kyanite may also be green or gray, and almost always shows some variation or streakiness by which it may be recognized. This is a typical metamorphic mineral, often found with staurolite, garnet, and corundum. In composition it is an aluminum silicate, Al_2SiO_5 (see Question 16).

359. What is staurolite? Staurolite is a metamorphic mineral of more than ordinary interest. Its brown crystals frequently grow in twins that form Maltese, Roman, and other patterns of crosses, where the component parts penetrate each other. The popular "fairy crosses" of the southern Appalachians and from near Taos, New Mexico, are of this sort, and they are also picked up in numerous other parts of the world. Staurolite is an iron-aluminum silicate. $FeAl_4Si_2O_{10}(OH)_2$.

360. What is andalusite? Having the same chemical formula as kyanite, Al_2SiO_5 (see Question 358), andalusite is likewise of metamorphic origin. It is usually reddish or olive green and comes in square crystals. A most attractive variety is *chiastolite,* which has inclusions of carbon arranged to form a cross, which changes size and shape as successive slices are sawed across the crystal. In eastern California andalusite has been mined in quantity for the manufacture of spark plugs.

361. Which is the pistachio mineral? So frequently is its color pistachio green that epidote has been called pistacite, from its German name, *pistazit.* This mineral is a widespread product of the metamorphism of feldspar and various common dark constituents of previous rocks. It is an hydrous silicate of calcium, aluminum, and iron. Epidote is often found with chlorite. It often makes handsome specimen material. Several other familiar minerals, including zoisite, clinozoisite, and allanite are members of the epidote group.

362. What is wollastonite? A simple calcium silicate in composition, $CaSiO_3$, wollastonite is a metamorphic mineral that may occur in large enough bodies to be the principal constituent of certain rocks. It is important as a "geologic thermometer" because it can form only below 1,200° C.; above that temperature (allowing for the influence of pressure) the mineral that will occur is pseudowollastonite, a quite different substance. Hence any rock containing wollastonite must have originated at a lower temperature.

363. What are tremolite and actinolite? These are typically metamorphic members of the amphibole group of minerals (see Question

170). They grade into each other according to the amount of iron. When more than 2 per cent is present, white tremolite takes on a green color and becomes actinolite, and so the identification can be made by the color. Actinolite is often fibrous, one of the kinds of asbestos (see Question 137), and both minerals can be tough and compact, being then known as nephrite jade (see Question 734).

364. What is diopside? A member of the pyroxene group of minerals (see Question 171), diopside is associated with metamorphic rocks. It is a calcium-magnesium silicate, $CaMgSi_2O_6$. In the United States diopside is especially prominent in New York and New England; abroad, it is found in the Alpine countries, Ural Mountains, and Scandinavia.

VI. THE PRECIOUS METALS

Introduction. *Gold, silver, platinum*—these three are the "precious metals," named in the order that they would be described in any textbook and the order in which they became known to the human race. Other metals are much rarer, more costly, and more "precious," being priced also by the ounce or even by the milligram. But these three have a world-wide market, are abundant enough to serve many practical uses, and have been employed as media of exchange—gold and silver for many centuries, platinum only recently. All occur as native elements, all as natural alloys, and all in natural chemical compounds. Gold is doubtless the first metal familiar to man. In spite of its antiquity and the Biblical references to it, silver may rightfully be regarded as a Western Hemisphere metal, for it is only in North and South America that it attains a predominant position as a metal. Platinum, from the Latin for "silver," was so named because it was thought to be silver when discovered in the New World.

365. In what forms does gold occur? Gold, the noble metal, is found in the free state as native gold, in chemical compounds with tellurium, and as an "impurity" in base-metal minerals. In its native

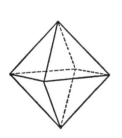 

Forms of gold crystals

state gold is nearly always alloyed with silver, though if much silver is present the mineral is known as *electrum* and is pale yellow to white. The natural alloy with mercury, called *gold-amalgam,* is known in a few deposits as small grains or lumps, metallic white to

yellow in color. Pure gold, when found, has a melting point of 1,063°
C., a boiling point of 2,600° C., and a specific gravity of 19.3, being
that many times as heavy as an equal volume of water (see Question
88). There are many kinds of gold ore, each having its own assemblage of associated minerals.

366. What is meant by gold ore?   The term ore is both a scientific
and a commercial one. It is properly applied to rocks and minerals
that upon treatment yield one or more metals, and do so profitably.
An ore deposit may revert to the status of a body of common rock if
the price of the metal should drop or the expense of mining become
too great. Conversely, ordinary rock may become ore simply by a
rise in price or the discovery of new metallurgical techniques that
make possible a cheaper recovery. Gold ore, therefore, is the entire
body of rock material that is mined for gold in reasonable expectation
of profit.

367. What is the gangue in gold ore?   Gangue refers to nonmetallic minerals associated with ore deposits and to the metallic
minerals that are regarded as waste. Quartz is the usual nonmetallic
gangue in gold ore, though calcite and other carbonate minerals,
fluorite, and tourmaline, as well as a few others, may also occur.
Pyrite and other sulfide minerals are the most common metallic
gangue, but frequently these minerals and their oxidation products
yield worthwhile amounts of gold that is present as a chemical impurity, and then they are truly ore minerals rather than gangue.

368. What is meant by the tenor of gold ore?   The tenor of gold
ore, as with any other metals, is the richness of the deposit and is
expressed in dollars per ton or, in the case of gold, as ounces per ton.
At the current price for gold, $35 per ounce, 1-ounce gold would be
worth that much, less an allowance for the silver content and the
cost of refining or coinage. When the price of gold was advanced in
the United States in 1934 from its previous value of $20.67 per
ounce, gold ore of a lower tenor than formerly could be worked at a
profit, and abandoned dumps were gone over a second time. With
rising labor and other costs, but with a fixed price set by the Government, the minimum tenor of gold ore that can be mined successfully
has gradually increased.

369. What is the fineness of gold? This is the proportion of pure gold in the native metal or in manufactured articles such as coins, bullion, or jewelry. It is expressed in parts per thousand. Thus, 900-fine, which was that of the now-suppressed gold coinage of the United States, means that there are 900 parts of gold to 100 parts of other metal used to harden it; this is equivalent to 13.714 grains of gold per dollar. The pale natural gold of the California veins has a relatively low degree of fineness (averaging 850), while the richer gold from the placer deposits (930- to 950-fine) has a deeper color.

370. What is gold leaf? This remarkable material is gold foil pounded so thin that as many as a quarter of a million sheets can be piled on top of one another in the space of one inch. As many as 300,000 sheets can be produced before the gold disintegrates. In this form, the metal, properly alloyed to overcome a certain stickiness, takes on a translucent greenish color not otherwise seen. Gold leaf for lettering glass, for inlaying glass and porcelain, for book binding, and for gilding various other objects is usually sold in small books of 25 leaves about 3¼ inches square, held between pieces of soft paper. This product is made possible only by the extraordinary capacity of gold for retaining its strength when spread extremely thin. One ounce of gold will cover about 100 square feet of surface.

Gold leaf has its substitutes in the form of a kind of brass called tombac, and silver leaf, which is colored after being applied.

371. What is the karat mark on gold? The fineness of jewelry gold is stated in karats, which is the number of parts in twenty-four that consist of gold. Twenty-four-karat gold is pure gold; 12 K stands for an alloy that is half gold and half copper or other metals. Further standards of quality in karats are given in the following table.

Karat	Fineness	
22	917	
21.6	900	United States coinage
20	833	
18	750	
14	583	
10	417	
8	333	

372. Why is gold alloyed? Pure gold is too soft (2.5–3 in Mohs' scale, see Question 87) to be used for most purposes without being alloyed with some other metal. Copper, silver, nickel, tin, or palladium are generally used, and a wide variety of colored gold is the result. The attractive "pink gold" and "green gold" in souvenir jewelry sold in the Black Hills in South Dakota are familiar examples. A reddish tinge is intensified by the use of copper as the alloy. "Green gold," mostly 14 to 18 karat, utilizes silver or silver plus cadmium or zinc as the alloying metal.

373. What is white gold? White gold, originally made to imitate platinum, is usually an alloy containing 25 per cent nickel and zinc; when stamped 18 karat it is thus three-quarters pure gold. Its whiteness makes it especially suitable for mounting diamonds; even in settings of normal "yellow gold," the top is usually white gold or platinum.

374. Which is the largest gold nugget? To date the largest nugget on record is the Welcome Stranger found at Ballarat in Victoria, Australia. It weighed 2,280 ounces and could not have traveled far from its source. A single mass of gold taken from the Hill End mine in New South Wales and weighing about 200 pounds was, however, even larger, and it is from unusual pieces such as this that the large and historic nuggets come.

375. Which are other large nuggets? Second to the Welcome Stranger, and also from Victoria, was the Blanche Barkley, weighing 1,752 ounces. A nugget of 1,050 ounces came from the Ural Mountains in 1936. The largest American nugget is the Carson Hill, a 1,296-ounce chunk of stream gold from California. The largest reported from the Yukon was 85 ounces. Thomas A. Rickard noted a nugget of 47 ounces from Arizona and one of 40 ounces from Montana.

376. Where were the great gold rushes? The 19th Century was the era of the great gold rushes, when men roamed the world in search of the glittering metal, exploring remote regions and pushing back frontiers. In many primitive lands gold, however, has long been the forerunner of civilization, of settlement, agriculture, and industry.

The legend of the Golden Fleece is a true story of the first known gold rush, when Jason and his Argonauts sailed in the ship *Argo* to the land of Colchis by the Euxine. There placer miners extracted stream gold by shoveling the gravel into sluice boxes made of hollowed trees and catching the gold in a lining of sheepskins, from which the coarse gold was shaken and the fine gold was beaten.

Payable gold was discovered in the United States in North Carolina in 1801 and then in Georgia in 1828; a Federal mint operated at Dahlonega, Georgia, from 1838 to 1861. The find of a flattened nugget of gold by James W. Marshall in the saw mill of John A. Sutter near Coloma, California, culminated in the gold rush of the forty-niners. In 1851 the excitement had moved to Australia, and then back again to the western United States. In 1859, for example, gold was discovered in Colorado, near Denver, and more spectacularly at Cripple Creek in 1891. Meanwhile the incomparable Rand was opened up in Africa in 1886 (see Question 384). The romantic era of the 19th Century gold rushes came to a close with the tragic Klondike rush of 1896.

377. What is a gold placer? When rocks that carry gold in its metallic state, rather than in chemical combination, are exposed by erosion, they crumble and partially decompose, thereby releasing the particles of free gold. Because it is physically and chemically resistant, the gold is little changed, although some of its silver content may be dissolved out. Hence it works its way downward to accumulate in grains and nuggets in stream beds, forming stream placers. Some finer pieces may be carried to the sea and concentrated in beach placers. The stream placers may be buried by later sediments or lava flows, or they may be uplifted above the stream channel as the water cuts downward within a narrower valley. The beach placers likewise may be drowned by a rise in sea level or may be uplifted above the strand line by a fall in sea level.

378. What is flour gold? Thin disc-shaped gold particles, so minute that 5,000 of them make one cent in value, are washed by the waters of the Snake River in Idaho, and elsewhere in the world. They are small enough to be carried in the air, and 17 million of them are estimated to weigh only one ounce. This size gold is not easy to recover!—but it is easy to see anyway.

379. What byproducts are recovered with gold? Besides the constant association of silver with gold, the over-all average ratio being 1 part silver to 4 parts gold, there are other metals that are frequently found with gold. Platinum is one of these; in certain places in Colombia platinum is a coproduct rather than merely a byproduct. Cassiterite, the principal tin mineral, occurs in gold placers in Alaska. Uranium is a valuable byproduct in the gold ores of the Union of South Africa. Rare-earth minerals, together with uranium and thorium minerals, come from some placer deposits of gold. And, of course, gold itself is a byproduct in many placer workings and vein mines primarily devoted to other minerals—especially the base-metal minerals discussed in Chapter 7, but it is the large tonnages handled, rather than the richness of the gold content, that accounts for the substantial production that is recorded in this manner, equaling 42 per cent of the United States output at the present time.

380. What are gold tellurides? Gold forms chemical compounds readily with only one element, tellurium, which is itself a heavy white semi-metal. These tellurides include a number of interesting minerals not easy to distinguish from one another by appearance. Among them are sylvanite, calaverite, krennerite, hessite, and petzite. The gold tellurides occur in three principal parts of the world—Rumania, Australia, and the United States, especially Colorado.

381. What is the nature of sylvanite? This is one of the most important gold-silver tellurides, its chemical formula being $(Au,Ag)Te_2$. Either metal can substitute for the other, but the proportions are about equal at Cripple Creek, Colorado. This silver-white or steel-gray mineral is soft and heavy, and it fuses easily, which drives off the tellurium and leaves a globule of gold and silver. The crystals occur in blades and branching aggregates of crystals. Offenbánya, Rumania, is a prominent locality for sylvanite.

382. What is the nature of calaverite? This mineral is a telluride of gold, $AuTe_2$, but it always contains a small amount of silver. Its normal color is pale brass yellow, but when fused by heat it turns to a ball of gold. Named after Calaveras County, California, where it was first found in the Stanislaus mine, it is doubtless best known at Cripple Creek, Colorado.

383. What is the production of gold? The world-wide production of gold since the beginning of man's tenure on the earth is estimated at 50,000 tons. The year 1940 was the best in history, accounting for 41 million ounces. During recent years South Africa, Canada, the Soviet Union, and United States have been the four leading producers of the yellow metal.

384. What is the Rand? More fully known as the Witwatersrand, this is by far the world's greatest gold district. Although the Rand is very real and not in the least dependent on mythology for its importance, the over-used word fabulous may be applied to it. Since 1886 it has yielded more than 16,000 tons of gold valued at more than 12 billion dollars. This district extends around Johannesburg, Republic of South Africa. Its mines go down 9,000 feet vertically and have 6,600 miles of underground workings, including air-conditioning necessary in the heat at that depth. The gold is recovered from thin beds of ancient (Pre-Cambrian) conglomerate, known as reefs, of which there are eight chief zones, the Main Reef Leader being the most persistent and prolific.

385. Which are the chief gold camps of North America? The Porcupine district in Ontario stands as the premier gold-producing area of North America. Of its 36 mines, the Hollinger is the largest, having been for some time the world's leading gold mine. The Hollinger-McIntyre zone, in the so-called North Break, yielded about 600 million dollars' worth of metal. Some of the mines are more than a mile deep.

Second in rank, and also situated in Ontario, is the Kirkland Lake district, with a production close to that of Porcupine. Its Lake Shore mine, going to a depth close to 7,500 feet, is the second largest single gold mine on the continent.

Lead, South Dakota; Cripple Creek, Colorado; and the Mother Lode, in California, would take third, fourth, and fifth places in a listing of this sort, although the California deposits are spread over a much larger area.

386. What is the importance to the United States of a gold-mining industry? A healthy gold-mining industry is a real source of strength in the national economy. In time of war, gold reserves are important to maintain solvency. The main use of gold in time of peace, also, is as a monetary reserve of governments and central banks to give stability to paper currencies, to stabilize credit, and to settle international trade balances, even when the "gold standard" has presumably been abandoned. A small amount of gold is used in industry and a considerable quantity in the arts, especially for jewelry. For some purposes, such as dentistry, gold is indispensable. Altogether the commercial uses of gold in the United States have greatly exceeded domestic production in recent years; for this reason alone imports must be maintained.

387. Which states produce the most gold?   The total known production of gold in the United States from 1492 to 1956 was 292,678,085 ounces. California led the nation with 105,079,394 ounces, Colorado was second with 40,256,738 ounces, Alaska third with 28,571,577 ounces, Nevada fourth with 26,591,106 ounces, and South Dakota fifth with 26,461,980 ounces. Montana, Utah, and Arizona also produced more than 10,000,000 ounces each. Although still behind such states as Idaho, Oregon, Washington, and New Mexico, the leading producer in the East was North Carolina, which reached its peak in 1887 and has accounted for 1,165,887 ounces of gold altogether. Peak production in California came in the year 1852, but Utah did not pass its prime until 1953.

388. Which is the largest gold mine in North America?   The Homestake mine at Lead, South Dakota, is the most productive gold property, not only in North America but in the Western Hemisphere. Since 1879 it has furnished about 470 million dollars in metal and its reserves are still the largest in the United States. There is exceptionally little silver in the gold, which is noted for its uniform character. The folding of the Pre-Cambrian rocks has closely controlled the distribution of the ore bodies so that they follow the crests of the uparched strata of the Homestake formation.

389. What is the Mother Lode?   A "mother lode" anywhere is the original zone of veins from which secondary or placer minerals have been derived. For this the prospector searches longingly, in order to come upon the original source of all riches, but true mother lodes in such a sense are usually as unreal as the crock of gold at the end of the rainbow.

In California, however, the Mother Lode exists. It is represented by a belt of mines 120 miles long and one mile wide, generally regarded as extending along the western foothills of the Sierra Nevada from Mariposa County on the south to El Dorado County on the north, or, in a broader sense, even farther from Mariposa to Downieville, within a width of 6½ miles. About half of its 300-million-dollar production has come from a 10-mile segment in Amador County. Mining has reached a depth of 5,912 feet. The numerous stone-built "ghost towns" of this part of California are one of the most distinctive features of the American countryside. The Mother Lode also furnished the gold for the Sierra Nevada placer deposits, which since 1848 have yielded about $1,300,000,000 in metal from a much broader area, about 150 by 50 miles in dimensions.

390. What is the Cripple Creek volcano? During the Tertiary period of geologic time, complex volcanic eruptions broke through the ancient Pikes Peak granite and adjacent Pre-Cambrian rocks, bringing with them the gold telluride ores that have made this locality famous. The volcano is about 3 miles in diameter and tapers downward into 9 roots or subcraters. A late explosion in the central part of the "volcano" formed the Cresson pipe—one pocket in this pipe gave $1,200,000 in metal. Cripple Creek lies at an altitude of 9,375 feet. It is one of a cluster of towns which were supported by 64 mines, among the best known of which were the Portland, Cresson, Vindicator, and Independence. Gold was found in 1891 on a cattle ranch, and the population of the district soon grew to 50,000, so that a new county, Teller, was established.

391. In what forms does silver occur? Silver, like gold, is found in the free state as native silver; in numerous compounds; and as a chemical impurity in base-metal minerals. Its important occurrence with native gold as an alloying agent has already been mentioned (see Questions 365, 379). There are about 60 well-known silver minerals, many of which are found rather widely distributed. Most lead, copper, and zinc ores contain some silver—particularly the sulfides and the secondary minerals derived from them. Silver is also a frequent associate of cobalt minerals. Antimony, arsenic, and bismuth are sometimes byproducts of silver mining; tin is a coproduct of silver in some Bolivian ores.

392. Which are the main silver minerals?   The principal minerals that are regarded as compounds of silver are argentite, cerargyrite, polybasite, pyrargyrite, and proustite. Native silver is another of the leading economic minerals of this metal. Other silver minerals, though of somewhat lesser value, are stephanite, stromeyerite, and pearceite. Silver-bearing galena, tetrahedrite, tennantite, chalcocite, bornite, and chalcopyrite are of major importance, the base-metal ores accounting for 68 per cent of the 1964 output of silver. The telluride minerals (especially sylvanite) have been referred to under gold (see Question 380).

393. How is massive silver found?   Native silver occurs as masses and slabs, sometimes of great size. Magnificent specimens have come from the centuries-old mines of Kongsberg, Norway. The "silver sidewalk" of the La Rose mine at Cobalt, Ontario, was almost solid silver for a length of 100 feet, and to a depth of 60 feet it yielded 658,000 ounces of the white metal. One outstanding specimen 5 feet long and 1,640 pounds in weight contained 9,715 ounces of silver. A chunk of nearly pure silver weighing 1,842 pounds was taken from Aspen, Colorado, and had to be hauled out of the Smuggler mine in chains because it was too heavy for an ore bucket.

394. What is wire silver?   Silver in intimately coiled wires is one of the most attractive of metals. These vary in size and degree of delicacy from very slender to rather thick. Guanajuato, capital of the state of the same name in Mexico, and Aspen, Colorado, are noted for their wire silver, as was Kongsberg, Norway, where specimens several feet long were formerly obtained.

395. What is the nature of argentite?   With a silver content, when pure, of 87.1 per cent, argentite is nearly as valuable as native silver. This heavy gray mineral is a silver sulfide, Ag_2S. It can be cut with a knife like lead. Because argentite is bright on a fresh surface and gives a shining streak when rubbed, it is also known as silver glance. Argentite is especially important in Nevada and Mexico, although it is widespread in many silver deposits.

396. What are the features of cerargyrite? From its waxy look and its sectility, so that it can be cut with a knife, like horn, cerargyrite is also known as horn silver. In chemical composition it is silver chloride, $AgCl$. Its pearl-gray color quickly darkens to violet-brown when it is exposed to light. Leadville, Colorado, was formerly a major source of cerargyrite, as were the Comstock Lode in Nevada and Poorman's Lode in Idaho.

397. What is polybasite? The word polybasite refers to the many metallic bases found in the mineral, although fundamentally it is a compound of silver, antimony, and sulfur, $Ag_{16}Sb_2S_{11}$. It is a gray or black mineral, not very distinctive in appearance unless it shows recognizable crystals with triangular markings on certain faces. But polybasite is a significant, though not too common, ore of silver. Ouray and Leadville, Colorado; Silver City and Delamar, Idaho; and the Comstock Lode and Tonopah, Nevada, are important localities in the United States.

398. What are the ruby silvers? *Pyrargyrite,* or dark ruby silver, and *proustite,* or light ruby silver, are two closely related minerals, both ores of silver. Their popular names indicate the difference in their color as seen in thin pieces or fine crystals. In ordinary masses both look somewhat gray, but they are the only gray minerals that become red when rubbed or broken. Pyrargyrite is a silver-antimony sulfide, Ag_3SbS_3. As the antimony is replaced by arsenic, it grades into proustite, Ag_3AsS_3, the lighter and more brilliant of the two, but the less common. These minerals occur together in various silver veins; Idaho is a leading source.

399. Is silver an ancient metal? Yes, though apparently it was known and used later than either gold or copper. As attested by slag dumps in Asia Minor and on islands in the Aegean Sea, man had learned how to separate silver from lead ores as early as the third millennium B.C. During the first millennium B.C. the silver mines at Laurium, Greece, the most famous in history, were worked for several centuries. The total production there is estimated at more than 250 million ounces of silver. Most of the silver deposits in what was then the Roman empire were known to the Romans, who mined the metal on a large scale. During the Middle Ages the silver output in Europe was maintained at a relatively low level.

400. Where is the greatest silver deposit of all time?   The conquistadores found the New World vastly richer than the Old in its prodigious yield of silver and gold. Unexcelled by any other single spot as a treasure house of silver was Cerro Potosí in Bolivia, discovered in 1544. This conical volcanic peak is said to have had 2 billion ounces of silver taken from its sharply defined veins, and some is there yet. Because of Potosí, Bolivia was the leading silver country up to 1700, giving place then to Mexico, with its many sources of metal. The Huanchaca and Chocaya districts in Bolivia still remain substantial silver producers, however, and there are a number of smaller mining camps, such as Oruro, Colquiri, Colquechaca, and Negrillos.

401. Where is silver mined in the United States?   Until the discovery of the Comstock Lode at Virginia City, Nevada, in 1859, the production of silver in the United States was slight, most of the metal being brought in from Mexico. Since that date, however, the United States has had a number of large deposits, so that it kept first place from 1871 to 1900, although its highest production of nearly 75 million ounces came as late as 1915. The high-grade silver ores are now largely depleted, most of the output being a byproduct of gold or base metals. Twenty-seven states have been listed as silver producers. Of these, the Western states have accounted for 99.5 per cent of the total. Montana, Utah, Colorado, Idaho, Nevada—in that order—have supplied 85 per cent of the silver of the United States. Outside of the West, Michigan and Missouri have been the chief silver states, but obviously of very minor significance.

402. Where are the most silver reserves in the United States? Idaho, which is currently by far the largest producer of silver among the states—more than double the output of second-ranking Utah— also has the largest reserves, which are classified as inferred, indicated, and measured, according to the methods used. The total of these three kinds is 225 million ounces.

403. Which is the largest silver mine in the United States?   The

Sunshine mine in the Coeur d'Alene district of northern Idaho is the largest producer of silver in the United States and the second largest in the world. It is also the only large straight-silver deposit in this country. The ore occurs in a broad zone of quartz veins in quartzite, which are richer below the 1,500-foot level, in contrast to the typical base-metal deposits which decline in value with depth.

The second-largest straight-silver mine in the United States has been the Tintic Standard mine in Utah.

404. What is the Comstock Lode? By far the most profitable scene of silver mining in the United States, the Comstock Lode is a zone of silver minerals occupying a fault in volcanic rocks. Although discovered in 1857 by two Grosh brothers, from Pennsylvania, its existence was not made public until 1859 by a man named Comstock, known locally as Old Pancake. Virginia City became the capital of the booming three-mile stretch of mines and dependent enterprises. At a depth of 3,000 feet the mines were flooded by hot waters, which helped to bring to a close the bonanza period of the 1870's. John W. Mackay and Adolph Sutro were among the best known of the "silver kings" who got rich on the Comstock.

405. What are the uses of silver? The photographic industry (including motion pictures), which is based upon the chemistry of silver compounds, would not be possible without silver. The outstanding use of silver, however, is for coinage and as a monetary reserve to support paper currency. The jewelry industry consumes a great deal, especially for tableware, the principal nonmonetary use. Dentistry and medicine are major users. Silver solder is vital to aviation, and other silver alloys are of growing importance to modern technology. Silver has, besides its brilliant luster and handsome color, strong antiseptic properties; it is the most highly reflective of all the metals. The future of silver seems most promising.

406. What is seigniorage on silver? This is the amount of money that the Government charged for the minting of silver coins. It is the difference between the circulating value of the coins and the cost of the bullion plus the charge for handling. All legal United States coins except the penny and nickel were made mostly of silver. Earlier prescribed by Presidential proclamation, and then by act of Congress, the seigniorage deduction was 30 per cent. The so-called "Treasury price" was thus fixed at $0.90505 per fine troy ounce, while the coinage value of silver in the silver dollar (which weighs 412½ troy grains) was $1.2929+ per fine troy ounce. The Treasury was authorized to sell silver on the open market to industrial users at the figure of $0.90505.

407. What is sterling silver? Perhaps originating in the word *steorling,* meaning "coin with a star," because some of the early Norman silver pennies had a small star on them, the term sterling is now the standard of quality for articles containing 92.5 per cent silver and 7.5 per cent copper. Since 1920 the lawful content of British coinage has been reduced to 50 per cent silver.

408. Which are the platinum metals? Six metallic elements make up the platinum group. Platinum itself is the most abundant and widely used; the others are palladium, iridium, osmium, rhodium, ruthenium. They always occur together and they are very much alike in most ways. All except palladium bring prices substantially higher than gold, and so they are the most precious of the precious metals. Besides their rarity, they have a splendid appearance, high resistance to corrosion, and unusual properties that make them valuable to commerce and industry.

409. How does platinum occur? Like gold and silver, platinum occurs as a native metal, always alloyed in varying proportions with one or more of the other members of the platinum group. The current production runs about 44 per cent platinum, 52 per cent palladium, and 4 per cent the rest altogether. Platinum may also be alloyed or mixed with gold and iron. Platinum also occurs in chemical compounds, though few in number. These include sperrylite (which is the chief source of platinum at Sudbury, Ontario—see Question 411), cooperite, and braggite; laurite and stibiopalladinite are compounds of ruthenium and palladium, respectively. Platinum also is found as a chemical impurity in base-metal minerals, associated especially with chromium, nickel, copper, gold, and silver. In each of these general respects platinum is analogous to silver and gold. All three metals, furthermore, have closely similar crystal structures.

410. Which is the heaviest of the platinum metals? Osmium, with a specific gravity of 22.48 (see Question 90), is the heaviest of the platinum metals, and has the highest melting point (about 2,700° C.) as well. Iridium is a very close second in both properties. The tensile strength and hardness of platinum or palladium, and also the resistance to tarnish and corrosion, are increased by the addition of any of the other four metals of the group.

411. Who discovered platinum? The natives of Colombia are credited with discovering the first platinum and using it for ornaments along with gold. In 1735 some of this metal was taken to Europe. In 1819 it was recognized in the gold placers of the Ural Mountains in Russia, which then became the world's main source of supply and remained so for almost a century. With a growing demand Colombia again became the chief producer for a few years after 1916. In the mid-1930's the placer field of Goodnews Bay in southwestern Alaska became an important producer, and by 1934 the recovery of platinum from the nickel-copper ores of Sudbury, Ontario, reached huge proportions. This has been since 1934 the leading producer of all the platinum metals. It faces intense competition, however, from South Africa, which is likely to surpass Canada in the near future, as it did from 1951 to 1957. Soviet production may be even larger but the amount is not revealed, although it is known to be remarkably high in palladium.

412. Has platinum been used in counterfeiting? Strange as it seems today, the principal use of platinum at one time was to make counterfeit coins which were plated with gold. The two metals are about of equal weight and such a coin would be hard to detect. Spanish doubloons were counterfeited in this manner. Considering that in 1788 crude platinum from Colombia was sold in Spain at 14 cents per ounce, compared to $17 per ounce for gold, the temptation was great. From 1828 to 1845 the price of platinum was supported in Russia by the issuance of legal coinage and such coins can be seen in numismatic collections today. This minting of platinum coins ceased when the value of the metal, then of growing importance to industry, exceeded the denomination of the coins.

413. What are the uses of platinum? Many uses for the platinum metals and their alloys were found as a result of the rise of industrialization during the second half of the 19th Century. Today the chemical and electrical industries consume approximately equal amounts of platinum, followed by the glass, jewelry, and petroleum industries. Platinum is an important catalyst, causing chemical reactions to take place that would not do so otherwise, or so rapidly. It is used, appropriately alloyed, for making rayon and fiber glass. Platinum utensils and equipment have long been used in chemical laboratories. Numerous are the electrical applications of platinum, palladium, and their alloys, such as for telephone relays and special sparkplugs. The appealing color and workability of platinum, hardened with iridium or ruthenium, have created a demand for it as a favored setting for diamonds; palladium alloyed with ruthenium is gaining in favor for the same purpose. An alloy of platinum and cobalt is the most powerful magnet material known.

VII. BASE METALS

Introduction. Those metals not classified as noble or precious have been referred to as base metals, thereby including all except gold, silver, and platinum. Yet there are other groups of metals that are best considered separately because of their general uses, such as iron and its alloys (Chapter 8), the radioactive metals (Chapter 10), and certain unusual metals not quite enough in demand to be called "precious" but still not thought of as base metals because of either their relative rarity or their only occasional use in industry and the arts (Chapter 9). With this consideration copper, lead, and zinc are the principal base metals—lead and zinc have always been so regarded. Tin should be added, for it serves many of the purposes of the base metals, with which, in fact, it is often alloyed. Modern practice would place aluminum and now magnesium in the same category, even though their chief employment is as structural metals akin to iron and steel, but they have within recent decades become enormously common and certainly cheap. These are all, except perhaps magnesium, termed the *nonferrous metals,* which may sound better than base metals.

414. What is the importance of copper? Standing next only to iron as the most important metal in modern living, copper is vital to national security and a high standard of industry. Both in quantity and value of world output, it is surpassed only by iron, and it is thus the most important of the nonferrous metals. Because of its superior conductivity, it has made possible the "electric age." Conductive of heat as well as electricity, resistant to corrosion, strong, malleable, and ductile, copper is indeed a remarkable metal as well as, next to gold, the most attractive one. Its use antedates the Bronze Age, for which it is responsible, by at least a thousand years, and it marks an exciting chapter in the long story of human development. Copper ornaments and simple utensils and tools were in everyday use by inhabitants of the Middle East and adjacent areas by 3500 B.C.

415. What is the importance of bronze? Bronze is the substance that advanced man from the Stone Age into the age of metals. Minor uses of gold, silver, copper, and meteoritic iron—though significant in themselves—were not sufficient to offset man's dependence upon raw rocks and minerals, but the introduction of bronze, doubtless come upon accidentally, opened up an entirely new dimension in human civilization. The effect on the hardness of copper by the addition of about 10 per cent tin was recognized by perhaps 2500 B.C. in the ancient countries of the Middle East and Egypt.

416. What is bronze? There are numerous kinds of bronze in daily use. Typical bronze is a brown-colored alloy of copper and tin, sometimes also containing zinc or zinc and lead, sometimes silver and aluminum. Historically, bronze was included under the term *brass,* and bronze is the Italian word for brass. We think today of brass as a yellow-colored alloy of copper and zinc, usually in proportions of two to one.

417. What is gun metal? This is one of the special varieties of bronze. The so-called "government bronze" consists of 88 per cent copper, 10 per cent tin, and 2 per cent zinc. Once used extensively for making guns, gun metal for this purpose has been supplanted by steel, but it is employed in the casting of machine parts. Imitation gun metal is often steel, treated to make it resemble the original alloy, though certain other alloys of copper, tin, and lead likewise make an effective substitute.

418. Where has copper been found in the United States? American copper was first produced at Simsbury, Connecticut, in 1705. Paul Revere was the outstanding figure in the early copper industry, establishing a copper-rolling and brass-casting foundry at Canton, Massachusetts. The great increase in copper output followed the opening of the rich deposits in Michigan; although known in 1771, they were first mined in 1830 and on a reputable scale in 1845— one of the most significant developments in the mining history of the United States. Copper mining started at Ducktown, Tennessee, in 1843. The next stage was set in the West, as gold placers were found in Montana in the 1870's and silver deposits a decade later, leading to the inevitable discovery of the copper at Butte. Shortly afterward the tremendous operations at Bisbee, Arizona, began, followed by the era of the "porphyry coppers," which slowly spread from Bingham Canyon, Utah, throughout the entire Southwest (see Question 419).

419. What are the porphyry coppers?   These are low-grade, large-tonnage deposits of copper minerals scattered "like pepper and salt" throughout rock of igneous origin and the surrounding rocks into which the molten magma intruded (see page 43). From the veins accompanying the igneous bodies, hot solutions were given off that also penetrated the adjacent area and replaced the rocks in a selective fashion whenever local conditions were favorable. The porphyry coppers are blanket in shape and have been more or less oxidized and enriched by descending secondary solutions after weathering took place. Because of their low grade these deposits must be mined by open-cut methods or underground caving.

420. Where is copper found?   About 90 per cent of the world's known copper reserves are in five regions, and 85 per cent of the total resources are in 12 districts or individual mines, each of which has enough ore to give more than 3 million tons of the red metal. Adding 16 more districts to the list raises the coverage to 94 per cent, leaving 6 per cent of the world reserves distributed among 34 countries.

The leading regions are south-central Africa, Chile, the western United States, eastern Ontario and Quebec in Canada, and Kazakhstan, a constituent republic of the Soviet Union in central Asia. Most of the copper produced in the United States comes from Western states—Arizona in the lead, with a production of 21 million tons from the earliest record to the end of 1966. Utah stands second in current production and third in total output, while Montana is third in current production and second in total output. Other major copper states in both categories are New Mexico, Nevada, and Michigan.

421. Where are the great deposits of native copper?   The once-vast but largely depleted copper deposits of the Keweenaw Peninsula of Michigan are truly unique, for there is nothing remotely resembling them anywhere else on our planet. Their origin is uncertain and probably complicated, but the native metal that they contain speaks for itself. Veins of massive copper, one weighing 500 tons; combinations of native copper and silver as "halfbreeds" (see Question 18); and copper minerals of uncommon occurrence elsewhere form a remarkable assemblage of mineralization. Prehistoric Indians mined here; the great glaciers of the Ice Age had strewn samples of the ore as far south as the Ohio River. Until surpassed by Butte, Montana, in 1887, this district, 100 miles long and 2 to 4 miles wide, was the premier copper producer in North America, and still ranks second in the world in its total yield. The incredible Calumet lode, an ore deposit shaped like an upright funnel, has been mined by 200 miles of workings down dip for 9,000 feet and for a length of 18,000 feet.

 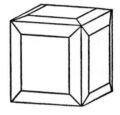

Forms of copper crystals

422. Which are the main copper minerals? About 165 copper minerals are known, for copper occurs in rocks of nearly all kinds and ages and in many different types of ore deposits. The principal copper minerals are native copper; chalcopyrite, chalcocite, bornite, enargite—these are sulfides; cuprite, an oxide; and malachite and azurite, which are carbonates. Other minerals of economic importance are covellite, tetrahedrite, tennantite, tenorite, chrysocolla, antlerite, brochantite, and atacamite. In addition to these copper minerals, copper also occurs as a chemical impurity in other minerals, especially pyrite, which may contain copper as it does gold—as an extraneous element of commercial value.

423. Where is Río Tinto? The largest pyritic copper deposits in the world are those of the Río Tinto or Huelva district in Spain and Portugal. Río Tinto is a town, Huelva a province, in the region of Andalusia. The mines were worked 3,000 years ago by the Phoenicians for their gold content, and then became a major source of copper and sulfur. About 50 ore bodies have been mined, mostly in large open cuts.

424. What are the properties of chalcopyrite? The most widely occurring copper mineral, chalcopyrite is a brass-yellow copper sulfide, $CuFeS_2$. It is one of the minerals known as fool's gold (see Question 135). It is softer than pyrite, another fool's gold, and can be scratched with a knife. Unlike true gold, it is brittle. Chalcopyrite may carry sufficient gold or silver to be valuable mainly for those metals. The crystals, though tiny, are often bright, wedge-shaped ones, as are those from the zinc mines of the Tri-State district (see Question 150). Masses of nearly pure chalcopyrite from the Rouyn district of Quebec are especially fine.

425. What is peacock ore? Peacock ore is a miners' name for bornite, which is also called purple copper ore, horseflesh ore, and other odd names, alluding to the distinctive variegated purple and blue tarnish that this mineral so readily assumes. Bornite is copper-iron sulfide, with the formula Cu_5FeS_4. So often does it contain microscopic impurities of other minerals that the formula took a long while to be derived correctly. Freshly broken bornite has a brownish-bronze look but the tarnish develops rapidly until the mineral turns nearly black.

426. What is the nature of chalcocite? Known also as copper glance, chalcocite is not quickly recognized by the novice because it appears as just another gray mineral. It does, however, usually have a shining lead-gray color which is somewhat distinctive. It also is sectile and can thus be cut with a knife. Chalcocite is copper sulfide, Cu_2S. Some "sooty chalcocite" is soft and dirty-feeling. The Kennecott copper mine in the Copper River district of Alaska is noted as a source of chalcocite in large amounts.

427. What are the features of enargite? Enargite would not be too abundant a mineral were it not found in large amounts in certain important copper deposits, such as those of Butte, Montana. At Bingham Canyon, Utah, and in the silver mines of the San Juan Mountains, Colorado, enargite is also a significant mineral. It is a copper sulfarsenide, Cu_3AsS_4, gray in color and showing a prominent cleavage. Although it resembles stibnite it can be distinguished by a test for copper.

428. What is cuprite like? Cuprite is a most interesting red mineral; in clear, brilliant crystals it is magnificent. This mineral is cuprous oxide, Cu_2O, containing 88.8 per cent by weight of the metal. Material from Bisbee, Arizona, is of unusually fine quality. Cuprite usually has for its associates some of the other colorful copper minerals, by which it can be identified.

429. What is chalcotrichite? Needlelike crystals of cuprite are known as "plush copper" or chalcotrichite. These actually are cubes enormously elongated in one direction so that they appear as delicate hairs or needles. The richness of the color and the intimate way they have intergrown with one another make such specimens among the loveliest of all minerals.

430. How are malachite and azurite related? Both are basic carbonates of copper, differing only slightly in chemical composition but as much as conceivable in color. Azurite was named for its azure-blue color, malachite from the Greek word for "mallow," referring to its leaf-green color. Together they make a striking contrast. Malachite is the more stable of the two, and crystals of azurite often alter to malachite, maintaining roughly the original shape. Like all carbonates these two minerals effervesce in acid (see Question 32). Bisbee in Arizona is doubtless the chief American locality, while Tsumeb in South West Africa is among the best foreign sources. Banded malachite from the Ural Mountains, the Belgian Congo, and Rhodesia is a splendid ornamental stone.

431. What were the ancient uses of lead? One of the oldest metals known to man—and the heaviest and softest of the base metals—lead was used in pipe, weights, sheet metal, coins, solder, ornaments, glass, and glaze for ceramics by the Egyptians, Phoenicians, Greeks, and Romans. Our word plumber comes from the Latin word for lead, *plumbum;* lead water pipes have been found in Pompeii. The Chinese used lead for money before 2000 B.C., and for debasing coins.

432. Where was lead mined in early times? The Phoenicians operated lead mines in Cyprus, Sardinia, and Spain. In 1200 B.C. the Laurium deposits of Greece supplied both lead and silver in amounts valuable enough to make this the treasury of Athens. The Romans mined lead within the borders of present-day Rumania, France, England, Spain, and Italy; the valuable byproduct of silver from Spain, Sardinia, and Britain enriched Rome for 6 centuries. Ancient deposits of lead were also worked in India, China, Persia, and Arabia.

433. Where has lead been produced in the United States? Mining and smelting of lead was carried on in Virginia as early as 1621. In the Upper Mississippi Valley lead was discovered in 1690 and was an important product during the 19th Century. The French discovered lead in the now-prolific area of southeastern Missouri in 1720, but production did not get well under way until 1763. A new spurt of activity began in 1867, and in 1957 this district celebrated its half century of world leadership. Western discoveries of lead followed the completion of the first transcontinental railway in 1869, and from the 1870's on there was a sharply increased output from localities such as the Coeur d'Alene in Idaho; Eureka, Nevada; Bingham Canyon, Park City, Big and Little Cottonwood Canyons in Utah; Leadville, Colorado; and Cerro Gordo, California.

434. What other countries produce lead today? Australia has moved into first place as a producer of lead—the Broken Hill lode in the desert of New South Wales has long been outstanding, and Mount Isa in Queensland is a flourishing newcomer. The Soviet Union ranks second. Following the United States come Mexico, Canada, and Peru. Together these six countries account for 60 per cent of the world total, an amount equal to about 2,800,000 tons of metal.

435. Where is the world's largest lead mine? The Sullivan mine at Kimberly, British Columbia yields 98 per cent of Canadian lead, as well as three-quarters of its zinc, and stands as the largest lead-zinc mine in the entire world. Its byproduct silver is likewise substantial. This mine is a huge lens of sulfide mineralization formed by the replacement of Pre-Cambrian sedimentary rocks.

436. Which are the ore minerals of lead? Galena is by far the principal ore of lead. Anglesite, cerussite, and pyromorphite are other major lead minerals, but there are few other minerals that can be regarded, even on occasion, as commercial sources. In this respect lead is much simpler than gold or silver. All these lead minerals are typically heavy and all have high percentages of the metal. Unlike the native metals previously described under gold, silver, and copper, lead as a native element is extremely rare, being found in Sweden but little elsewhere.

437. What are the properties of galena? A lead sulfide, galena (formula PbS) is a soft, heavy, bright-metallic gray mineral distinguished by its prominent cubic cleavage. Silver is almost always present, and other elements frequently are. When galena does not

Crystals of galena

contain silver it is known as "soft lead." Crystals such as cubes and octahedrons are sometimes of fairly large sizes. The localities for galena are pretty much the same as the localities of lead mining— the two are almost synonymous.

438. What is steel galena? Fine-grained galena, which shows the otherwise characteristic cleavage only when seen through a magnifying glass, is referred to as steel galena because of its compact appearance. This variety of galena is the kind that most typically contains silver as a chemical impurity and a valuable byproduct of lead mining.

439. What is the nature of anglesite? The oxidation of galena, lead sulfide, to lead sulfate produces anglesite, $PbSO_4$. Within it can usually be seen some of the unaltered galena, and the two minerals are frequently associated. In colorless or white crystals anglesite has a bright luster, but otherwise it is likely to be a dull gray mineral recognized by its heaviness and the bits of fresh galena still remaining (see Question 52).

440. What is cerussite like? The action of carbonated water on galena changes it to cerussite. This lead carbonate, $PbCO_3$ often occurs in a network of twinned crystals crossing one another at 60-degree angles. Other crystal forms are also common, but the usual masses of white or gray cerussite are not readily distinguishable aside from their bright luster and considerable weight. Cerussite is often found with galena and anglesite. Magnificent crystals come from Tsumeb, South West Africa.

441. What is the description of pyromorphite? Though of lesser importance than the previously described minerals as an ore of lead, pyromorphite is nevertheless a mineral of significance. Pyromorphite is a lead chlorophosphate, with the formula $Pb_5Cl(PO_4)_3$. Its six-sided crystals are remarkable for their rounded barrel shape, often hollow inside. They are usually some shade of green and have a high luster. Of course, they are heavy.

442. What are the main uses for lead? The largest single use of lead is for storage batteries, which use somewhere nearly equal parts of antimonial lead and lead oxides. The second largest use is in tetraethyl fluid, the anti-knock ingredient in gasoline. Third in importance is the use of lead as cable covering and for calking, and fourth is its use in pigments, especially as red lead and litharge.

443. What is red lead? Red lead and litharge, from which it is made, constitute the widest use of lead in the pigment industry. Litharge (or lead monoxide) is produced by roasting metallic lead in a reverberatory furnace in the presence of air. In turn, the powdered litharge is heated at 900 to 950 degrees Fahrenheit, converting it into the Pb_3O_4 compound for use in glass making and other applications.

444. What is white lead? This is the popular name for basic lead carbonate, which is produced from metallic or "pig" lead as it comes from the smelter. White lead is one of the oldest of the paint pigments. It is produced by a number of different methods, such as the Carter or "quick process," which takes only 12 to 14 days to transform metallic lead to the carbonate, in contrast to the more than three months required by the former Old Dutch process. The Sperry electrolytic and Thompson-Stewart processes are also employed.

445. How was zinc first utilized?   The earliest uses of zinc came more or less by coincidence. Brass, an alloy of copper and zinc, was first made in the time of Caesar Augustus by adding smithsonite, a zinc mineral (see Question 451), to copper to produce a metal that was harder than copper and yellower than bronze. Although bracelets filled with zinc were found in the ruins of Cameros, which was destroyed in 500 B.C., the metal itself was perhaps not purposely isolated until 1520; in the 16th Century zinc was imported into Europe from India and China, and in 1740 it was mined in Europe. Zinc is still the least known of the common metals and yet it is one of the five produced in the largest quantity, both in war and peace.

446. Where was zinc first used in the United States?   In 1835 at the Government Arsenal in Washington, D.C., John Hutz smelted the first zinc in the United States. He used ore from Franklin, New Jersey (see Question 449); the resulting metal was made into brass for the fabrication of standard weights and measures. The first commercial smelter was erected at Newark, New Jersey, in 1848 by the predecessor of the huge New Jersey Zinc Company.

447. What is galvanizing?   This large industrial use for zinc consists of coating steel to prevent rusting by dipping it into molten zinc. It is the most economical means of protecting steel products from atmospheric corrosion. This was first done in the United States in 1864 and the demand for the product expanded the use of zinc way beyond its previous and ancient employment in brass.

448. What else is zinc used for?   Exceeding galvanizing, the zinc-alloy industry is the largest consumer of the metal, most of it going into die castings. Brass products—first sheet, strip, and plate; next, rod and wires; third, tube—these constitute the third largest use for zinc.

449. Which are the zinc minerals?   Sphalerite is the principal ore of zinc. Smithsonite and hemimorphite are also important. At the unique deposits, now inactive, at Franklin and Sterling Hill, New Jersey, three other minerals—franklinite, zincite, and willemite—were mined on a large scale but they are of little significance anywhere else. Prior to the recent abandonment of this so-called Franklin deposit, these minerals would have deserved serious consideration as zinc ores, but their interest is now largely historical and as specimens for the collector intrigued by the phenomena of luminescence (see Questions 978, 980).

450. What are the characteristics of sphalerite?   This zinc sulfide (ZnS) has a distinctive resinous luster most of the time. Its good cleavage is usually apparent. In color, however, sphalerite ranges from white to black; yellow or brown is most common, green and red less so, but the variations are deceptive. Sphalerite consequently goes under several names given it by miners. Blende or zincblende is a familiar one. Black jack, resin jack, and ruby zinc are others, referring to the color or luster. Iron is nearly always present, manganese and cadmium to a small extent.

451. What are the features of smithsonite?   Even more variable in appearance than sphalerite (see Question 450) is the zinc carbonate, smithsonite, $ZnCo_3$. It was named for James Smithson (1754–1829), the Englishman who founded the Smithsonian Institution, yet British mineralogists formerly called this mineral calamine. How confusing in appearance smithsonite is can be told by its popular names turkey-fat ore for the yellow variety and dry-bone ore. It is substantially heavier, however, than either turkey fat or dry bones; it is fairly hard for an ore mineral, and it effervesces, like all carbonates, in acid. The color is usually a dirty brown, but fine ornamental material is translucent green or greenish blue, and it may be white or pink.

452. What are the properties of hemimorphite?   Previously called calamine in the United States, in conflict with the English name for our smithsonite, hemimorphite was agreed upon as the universal name for the hydrous silicate of zinc, $Zn_4Si_2O_7(OH)_2 \cdot H_2O$. Its most recognizable feature is its tendency to grow in groups of colorless or white crystals having one end pointed and the other stubby and flat. This difference in the opposite halves of the crystals has given it the name hemimorphite, meaning "half forms" (see Question 125).

453. Where is zinc mined? The United States is the chief producer of zinc ore as well as of zinc metal from the smelter. The Tri-State district of Missouri, Kansas, and Oklahoma (see Question 150) was for a long while the leading zinc-mining area in the country, but it has now been surpassed by the Butte and Coeur d'Alene districts in Montana and Idaho, respectively, and even more by deposits in Tennessee and Colorado. Canada ranks second among world producers of zinc. The Soviet Union, Australia, and Mexico are listed next among zinc-mining countries.

454. What is the importance of aluminum? Not only is aluminum the most abundant metallic element in the crust of the earth, but it ranks first among the primary nonferrous metals produced in the United States. Its importance is increasing as it becomes used for more and more purposes. It is light, relatively strong, resistant to atmospheric corrosion, and highly conductive of electricity. It is used in 30 industries and has more than 4,000 applications. Aluminum production in the United States is, nevertheless, concentrated in three giant companies, which operate 19 plants situated from New York to Louisiana to Washington.

455. What is the history of aluminum? Unlike all the metals discussed so far, aluminum is a modern phenomenon. Prior to the independent discovery in 1886 by Hall in the United States and Héroult in France of a continuous electrolytic reduction process, aluminum was regarded as a rare metal and a chemical curiosity. Since that time the aluminum industry has experienced a phenomenal growth.

456. What is the source of aluminum? If aluminum could be extracted profitably from back-yard soil, it would be the most abundant of metals, for it makes up an estimated 8.07 per cent of the earth's crust. However, only one rock furnishes commercial aluminum. That rock is bauxite, a mixture of various hydrous aluminum oxides. It was formerly referred to as a mineral, but has since been proved not to be homogeneous. The principal mineral in bauxite is *gibbsite,* $Al(OH)_3$, and some bauxite approaches that composition. *Boehmite* and *diaspore* are other minerals present in bauxite, and there is a fine-grained amorphous constituent known as *cliachite.* Named from a locality at Baux, France, bauxite used to be pronounced "beau-

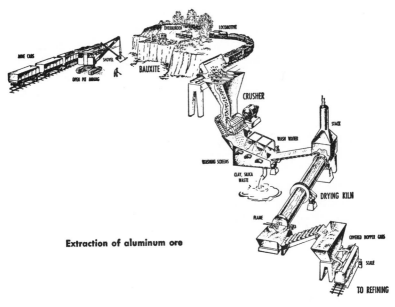

Extraction of aluminum ore

zite," but the usual American way is "box-ite," and this is the way the town that is the mining center in Arkansas is pronounced.

457. What is the appearance of bauxite? In its typical form one of the most distinctive of earth products, bauxite occurs in rounded concretionary grains resembling nodules stuck together with clay. The lumps are either darker or lighter than the surrounding material, and a red color is common, because of the presence of iron oxides. When earthy or claylike itself, bauxite is difficult to identify, but it most generally looks as described above.

458. What else is bauxite used for? The principal use of bauxite is, of course, as an ore of aluminum, which in the United States accounts for 94 per cent of the total output. In addition, however, bauxite is employed as an abrasive in the manufacture of synthetic corundum (2 per cent); in the chemical industry, mostly for aluminum sulfate (2 per cent); as a refractory or heat-resistant material (2 per cent); and in miscellaneous ways, such as a high-quality cement, these totaling less than 1 per cent.

459. Where is bauxite mined?   Surinam, often called Dutch Guiana, is the world's leading source of bauxite. Its neighbor, British Guiana, ranks second. The United States is third, with most of the production concentrated in Arkansas. Jamaica—which has the largest known reserves of ore—Hungary, France, and the Soviet Union, in that order, supply the next largest amounts, leaving only about 14 per cent for the various other countries of the world. Most of this bauxite travels long distances, as France is the only self-sufficient user of bauxite. The United States, it is true, does mine substantial amounts of bauxite, but it must import most of its needs.

460. Where is aluminum produced?   Aluminum plants require enormous amounts of dependable, low-cost power running to 17,000 kilowatt-hours per ton of virgin aluminum. Hence they are located near sources of such power instead of near the ore deposits. Even then, the competition for power has put aluminum plants at a disadvantage in comparison with other consumers; for this reason a plant even at Niagara Falls was obliged to cease operation in 1949, and four plants erected during World War II in metropolitan areas were also closed because of the uneconomic power situation.

The United States and Canada produce two-thirds of the world's metallic aluminum. The Soviet Union stands third, and a host of other countries combine to yield about one-quarter of the total. These nations include such as Japan, Switzerland, and Norway, where the obvious advantage is one of cheap hydroelectric power.

461. Where else in the United States does bauxite occur?   Besides the major deposits in central Arkansas, bauxite is known to occur on the continent of North America in only two places—the Coastal Plain in Georgia, Alabama, and Mississippi; and the Appalachian Valley in Georgia, Alabama, Tennessee, and Virginia. It has not yet been found feasible to extract aluminum from the high silica or iron *laterites* in Oregon and Washington. Laterite is a residual product of warm-climate weathering under conditions of good drainage.

462. Is tin a cheap metal?   In spite of disparaging references to the lowly "tin can" and, a generation ago, the "tin Lizzie," tin is anything but a cheap metal. The Model T, which had less than half a pound of the metal, would cost about $9,000 if made of tin. On a recent date picked at random, tin sold for more than 3 times the price of copper, 7 times the price of lead, and 8 times the price of zinc. The price of tin is quoted in many markets but the principal quotations are those in New York in cents per pound, in London in pounds sterling per long ton (2,240 pounds), and in Singapore in Straights dollars per picul (133⅓ pounds).

463. Which are the tin minerals? Because tin is a relatively scarce mineral, its ores are not numerous. Cassiterite is the only one of commercial importance, except that stannite is a source of tin in Bolivia, along with cassiterite. Teallite, cylindrite, franckeite, and a few other rare minerals yield tin when they occur with cassiterite, but they are never mined separately.

464. What is the nature of cassiterite? An oxide of tin, cassiterite (SnO_2) is a remarkably heavy and hard mineral. It is often difficult to identify otherwise because its color and texture are variable— witness stream tin, which looks like ordinary stream pebbles, and

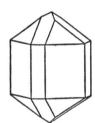 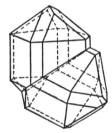

Single and twin crystals of cassiterite

such peculiarities as wood tin and toad's-eye tin. Cassiterite, nevertheless, is one of the few minerals for which a specific test is available. When treated with hydrochloric acid into which a piece of zinc has also been placed, cassiterite develops a coating of metallic tin, which shines brightly when rubbed.

465. How is tin traded? Tin, one of the few metals used by prehistoric man, has always been an object of international trade. The Phoenicians were drawn to Cornwall, England, in search of tin more than 2,000 years ago, and the name Cassiterides or Tin Islands referred to any of the North Atlantic tin lands, but especially to

Cornwall and the Scilly Isles, which may have served as depots for Cornish tin. This commerce in tin was ended by the fall of Carthage in 146 b.c., so that coins minted after this time contain increasing quantities of lead as a substitute. The traffic in tin has been transferred from one region to another with the passage of time, as new deposits were discovered. In modern times it is a characteristic of tin commerce that countries of substantial production have little use for it, while almost all of it must be imported by the highly industrialized nations in which it is almost entirely absent.

466. Where is tin chiefly mined? The one outstanding source of the world's tin supply is a strip of land in southeastern Asia about 1,000 miles long and 120 miles wide. It embraces the new countries and some of the older and more familiar names associated with Malaya and Indonesia. From Burma and the province of Yunnan in China on the north to the tip of the former Netherlands East Indies, this great zone of cassiterite furnishes tin for the entire world. It has been productive for more than 2,000 years.

467. Where else is tin mined? South America became a tin-producing continent with the opening up of the deposits in Bolivia about 1860. Since 1910 the Belgian Congo and Nigeria in Africa have become important tin exporters. Australian mines, now of diminishing value, began to produce tin about the middle of the 19th Century. Tin is one of the most crucial mineral deficiencies of North America, which consumes most of it. The efforts to recover tin in Canada, Mexico, and the United States have gone largely unrewarded, although the Aztecs worked on a small scale in Mexico, and tin has been known in the United States for 125 years. "Nothing," say Abbott Renick and John B. Umhau, "is more common in the United States than 'tin' cans nor more scarce than tin mines."

468. What is the tin yield of Alaska? About 90 per cent of the total output of tin in the United States has come from Alaska, where it was first discovered in 1910. These deposits are of placer type and are situated near York in the Seward Peninsula. From the intensive studies conducted from 1939 to 1945 by the U. S. Bureau of Mines and Geological Survey, it is believed that this district holds the greatest promise for domestic production, insignificant though it may be in terms of national needs.

469. How is tin brought to the United States? The utter dependence of the United States upon imported tin makes for a serious consideration of the ways in which this strategic metal is taken into the country. The possibility that shipments of tin will be interrupted by sinkings has a significant aspect in terms of national defense.

Most of the tin arrives at North Atlantic ports from the Far East by way of the Suez Canal and the Mediterranean—a trip of 55 to 60 days. Ore from Bolivia moves from the west coast of South America through the Panama Canal to the Gulf of Mexico in about 2 weeks. Some ships from Asia also traverse the Panama Canal, and some trips, especially of small lots, require much longer than two months.

470. What were the early uses of tin? A mummy wrapping of tin was used in Egypt in 600 B.C. Tinning of copper was done by the beginning of the Christian era. Tin-plated iron was first fabricated in the 16th Century. At the beginning of the 19th Century tin was employed mainly in bronze for cannons and bells, in pewterware (see Question 474), as a lining for copper cooking utensils, and as template for roofing. Most of the present-day uses for tin have been developed since 1800 but have enormously expanded within the past few decades.

471. What is block tin? This is solid tin, usually about 99.8 per cent pure. The term is used to distinguish articles actually made of tin from those in which template is really meant—this being thin sheet steel coated with tin, as in "tin cans." Tin foil is made of pure tin because it flows readily under pressure and may easily be rolled into foil—one pound can cover 14,000 square inches—or extruded into tubes for such familiar products as tooth paste and lotions.

472. What are the modern uses of tin? The most important single use of tin at the present time is in the making of tinplate. This is also a major product of the steel industry. Tinplate is black plate (thin, mild sheet steel) coated with tin by the hot-dip process and the electrolytic process. Although of some interest in antiquity, tinplate manufacture as now understood was begun in Germany between 1240 and 1575; it dates in the United States from 1872.

The second largest use of tin is in solder. Bronze and brass are in third place. Babbitt is the fourth largest user of tin.

473. What is babbit?   Babbit metal is a general term for soft, white, antifriction alloy metals used for bearings. In proportions of tin used babbitt contains either 24 per cent ("hardening babbitt") or 96 per cent ("lining babbitt"), the rest being lead, antimony, and copper. This alloy was named after an American inventor, Isaac Babbitt (1799–1862).

474. What is pewter?   Various white alloys consisting chiefly of tin go under the name pewter. Modern pewter consists of 93 per cent tin, 6 per cent antimony, and 1 per cent copper. The other metals that have been most used are lead, bismuth, and zinc. The higher the concentration of tin, the brighter the color. Pewter of Roman origin is known, and the metal was early used in the Far East. Until superseded by porcelain (china), pewter was the main tableware in England, which was a center of pewter making during the Middle Ages and later. Large amounts reached the American colonies, where it was also made in quantity, so that pewter was extremely common in Revolutionary days. Its popularity in collections has lately been renewed.

475. What is Britannia metal?   Essentially a tin alloy, Britannia metal contains antimony in variable proportions and smaller amounts of copper, zinc, lead, bismuth, or other metals. High-grade Britannia metal is quite similar to pewter (see Question 474), for which it is often substituted.

476. How is tin sold at Singapore?   The Singapore tin market operates in an unusual way, without open bidding yet at a fair price. Bids are submitted in writing by potential buyers. At the same time the two Malayan smelters notify the market manager of the supply that is available. Then the highest bid is accepted, and down through the list until all the tin is gone. The price is pegged for all of that day's purchasers at the lowest of the bids that was accepted. Any tin not requested must be carried over to the following day, so that there is a constant balance between supply and demand.

477. Which metal is being extracted from the ocean? Magnesium, one of the lightest of all the "wonder metals" of the 20th Century, is the only metal presently being taken from sea water. It is recovered as magnesium chloride. With cheaper sources of power, however, the future is certain to see the extraction from the sea of other metals on a large scale. The ocean is a virtually inexhaustible storehouse of mineral wealth, most of which it has acquired from the land by the processes of weathering and erosion during the vast extent of geologic time. Undetermined billions of tons of gold, for example, are dissolved in the seas, and the magnesium value is estimated at $3,000,000,000. Vast resources in manganese and phosphorus have been proved to exist on the floor of the ocean in the form of nodules.

478. How else is magnesium obtained? Apart from sea water, in which it amounts to 0.13 per cent, magnesium and its compounds have been obtained from large bodies of the minerals dolomite and magnesite (both carbonates, see Question 31) and brucite, as well as minor amounts of olivine and serpentine (see Questions 172, 354), and from well brines and sea-water "bitterns." The sea-water process itself also involves the use of high-grade dolomite and limestone for reaction purposes.

479. What are bitterns? Bitterns are the liquid residue from the extraction of sodium chloride (common salt). They contain 6.0 to 8.7 per cent magnesium chloride ($MgCl_2$) and 4.2 to 6.1 per cent magnesium sulfate ($MgSO_4$). These and other bittern compounds are so extremely soluble that sea water must be almost entirely evaporated before they will settle out.

480. What is brucite like? Brucite is an interesting pearly-white mineral that somewhat resembles mica except that the leaves are flexible but not elastic; they can be cut into slices with a knife. In composition brucite is magnesium hydroxide, $Mg(OH)_2$. A deposit at Gabbs, Nevada, produced a considerable amount for a number of years.

481. What are the uses of magnesium? As the lightest of all structural metals, magnesium is a critical factor in air transportation. Its recognized merits resulted in an expansion in its uses from 1918 to 1943 unparalleled by any major basic metals industry in the United States. In addition to lightness, magnesium alloys have good machining properties. They may be fabricated by various methods. Castings constitute the major use, aluminum alloys being next in importance. Wrought products produced by sheet and extrusion techniques also consume large amounts of magnesium. This metal is very satisfactorily alloyed with titanium, zirconium, zinc, thorium, rare-earth metals, beryllium, manganese, and lithium, as well as aluminum.

482. What is the history of magnesium? The first isolation of impure magnesium metal was in 1808 by Sir Humphry Davy (1778–1829), who obtained it by electrolysis. In 1833 Michael Faraday (1791–1867), another English chemist, devised a different technique that had better results, and in 1852 Robert Bunsen (1811–1899) developed in Germany an electrolytic cell for this purpose. Based upon Bunsen's method, the manufacture of magnesium was begun on a commercial scale in 1909, using magnesium chloride obtained as a byproduct from the potash deposits of Stassfurt, Germany. Production started in 1915 in the United States—by the General Electric Company—when imports were cut off by World War I. Today the Dow Chemical Company is the main source of primary magnesium in the United States.

483. What is titanium? Titanium may well be the metal of the future. Surely it belongs among the "growing-metals group" consisting also of aluminum and magnesium, for enormous quantities are potentially available. As described by F. J. Cservenyak and A. F. Tumin, "the whitest pigments, the 'middleweight champion' in the metals field, and glamorous gems are all derived from the 'wonder' element, titanium."

A low-density, silver-white metal between silver and stainless steel in color, titanium owes its importance to its lightness, strength, and resistance to corrosion, altogether an unusual combination of properties. Titanium alloys have, in addition to strength and hardness, a high resistance to fatigue and impact. Titanium cannot be used, however, for long periods at temperatures over 1,000 degrees Fahrenheit (even though its actual melting point is 3,038 degrees Fahrenheit), and it is difficult to fabricate, as well as presently expensive. A need for it may overcome the last two unfavorable factors. Compounds of titanium enter into numerous products of a non-metallic nature.

484. Which are the ores of titanium? Two minerals, ilmenite and rutile, are the ores of titanium. With them are associated anatase (octahedrite), brookite, and some other titanium-bearing minerals which usually constitute part of the ilmenite or rutile ore as it is marketed. Ilmenite and rutile are each used for fundamentally different purposes—ilmenite mainly in pigments, rutile mainly as a source of the metal and in welding-rod coatings, and in smaller amounts for alloys, ceramics, and fiberglass. These two minerals, moreover, come from unlike kinds of rocks and from generally different parts of the world.

485. Where are the sources of titanium minerals? The United States and Canada are the largest producers of ilmenite. Norway and Australia rank next. Canada is a large, and the only, producer of titanium slag, made from titanium-bearing iron ores by a smelting process because the ilmenite cannot be recovered by standard methods. Australia is by far the major producer of rutile, the United States being in second place.

In the United States the largest ilmenite mine is at Tahawus, New York, but the world's largest known deposit is at Allard Lake, Quebec. Titanium minerals, along with others of the so-called "heavy minerals," occur widely in the sands of Florida; these originated in the rocks of the Piedmont region of North Carolina, South Carolina, and Georgia. After weathering out, they were carried to Florida by streams and ocean currents and deposited along the ancient shore lines, which have now been uplifted as much as 180 feet above sea level.

486. What are the properties of ilmenite? Ilmenite is a metallic-black mineral which usually occurs in compact masses, in grains, or as sand. It is often intergrown with magnetite, though it seems at times to be somewhat magnetic in itself. A magnetic separation is made of these two related minerals. In composition ilmenite is a ferrous titanate, $FeTiO_3$.

487. What are the characteristics of rutile? A titanium dioxide, TiO_2, rutile has a peculiar bright luster and a red color, grading to reddish brown and black. Crystals of rutile show interesting elbow-shaped and network forms. Slender needles are often found in quartz, making *rutilated quartz*. Rutile is one of the most familiar minerals in "heavy sands," together with zircon, garnet, magnetite, staurolite, ilmenite, chromite, and monazite.

488. What is quicksilver? Quicksilver, meaning "living silver," is a name for mercury, the only native mineral that is a liquid at ordinary temperatures and the only liquid mineral besides water. Its unusual physical and chemical properties give mercury an importance out of all proportion to the size of its industry. Not only is it a liquid metal, but it is extremely heavy, is electrically conductive, and, together with its compounds, is toxic—a remarkable association of properties.

489. How is mercury marketed? Mercury has been one of the prime examples of an international cartel in action. From 1928 to 1950 the dominant world producers in Spain and Italy channeled their output through a cartel called Mercurio Europeo, thereby encouraging increased production elsewhere. This cartel was effectively broken by the United States when it purchased Italian mercury with "counterpart funds" in 1949, and in spite of rumors it has not yet been reorganized. Except in the United States and Mexico, not more than a few mines yield mercury in any country, and in some countries only one mine is operated. Because it is a liquid, mercury is sold in steel "flasks" which hold 76 pounds each.

490. Where is mercury mined in the United States? The Coast Ranges of California were the leading source of mercury in the world during much of the latter half of the 19th Century. The early discovery of mercury, because it made possible the easy recovery of gold from its ores—the process called amalgamation (see Question 899)—shares with the gold itself the excitement of the days of '49, and only gold and copper exceed mercury in their total value in

California to date. The New Idria mine (in San Benito County), which has a depth of more than 1,400 feet, has been in operation since 1858, and the New Almaden (near San Jose), with a depth of 2,450 feet, since 1850. These are still the two largest in North America, and California is the chief producing state in the Union.

Nevada ranks second in mercury. Other states have had a very sporadic output, but Oregon, Arkansas, Texas, Idaho, Alaska, Arizona, and Washington have also produced mercury in fair amounts in recent years.

491. Is mercury mining dangerous? Mercury has long been regarded as the most dangerous mineral substance to mine and treat. Handling it or being exposed to its vapors or dust can be highly risky. In medieval days only convict labor could be employed in Spain at Almaden, the world's largest and best-known mercury deposit, which has been worked for more than 2,000 years. The precautions that should be taken, however, at mines, retorts, furnaces, and industrial plants are well known, so that mercury need not be excessively unsafe to work with, but it has a bad reputation.

492. What are the mercury minerals? Cinnabar is by far the principal ore mineral of mercury. Metacinnabar, calomel, and native mercury also yield commercial amounts, but the other 20-some mercury minerals are more noted for their mineralogical interest. The mercury minerals occur in almost any kind of rock, in fractures permitting entry of the solutions. These are deposited at low temperatures and rather near the surface, often by hot springs; they are most typically associated with volcanic activity of Cenozoic geologic age.

493. What is cinnabar like? This is one of the most distinctive of minerals. When pure and rich in grade, it is a vivid vermilion red, which colors the whole countryside where it occurs. It has a good cleavage and is extraordinarily heavy. Occasional specimens are beautifully transparent. Cinnabar is a mercury sulfide, HgS.

494. What is antimony used for? Although the metallurgist considers antimony a nuisance, and ores containing it are often penalized by higher charges, it is a useful base metal in many ways. Its most remarkable property is its ability to expand when cooling, unlike most other substances. For this reason it is used in type-metal and its alloys—printing would look ragged without them. The principal use of antimony altogether is to make lead alloys harder and less plastic; hard lead serves a number of applications. More antimony finds its way into battery metal than into any other use. Antimonial lead for other purposes ranks second in industrial statistics on antimony, and bearing metal and bearings hold third place among the metal products. Antimony also has various nonmetallic uses, especially in ceramic enamels.

495. How is antimony used for fireproofing? Fabrics and paper can be rendered fire-resistant by applying, for example, a mixture of 25 per cent antimony chloride ($SbCl_3$), 25 per cent chlorinated paraffin, and 50 per cent of the petroleum solvent known as Stoddard solvent. Other mixtures are being developed. The material to be fireproofed is first impregnated with sodium carbonate solution, dried, and then impregnated with a 15-per cent solution of the antimony compound in the organic solvent. When tenting, trunk tarpaulins, or industrial paper is set afire, the flames are quickly extinguished because of an automatic chemical reaction as the compound itself is heated. This was the largest single use of nonmetallic antimony during the recent wars.

496. What were the early uses of antimony? Because of the ease with which it can be extracted from its principal mineral, stibnite, antimony has one of the longest recorded histories among metals. As evidenced by a cast vase dating from about 4000 B.C., the Chaldeans were acquainted with the art of reducing antimony from its ores. The ancient Egyptians knew how to plate copper with metallic antimony. In the 15th Century A.D. antimony was used for printers' type and in bells and mirrors. In the 16th Century it was employed in medicine, as had been its natural sulfide in Biblical times.

497. How does antimony occur? Antimony is a common constituent of many minerals, especially the ore minerals of lead, copper, and silver. Stibnite (a sulfide) is the chief individual antimony mineral and one of the most familiar of all minerals. Stibiconite, senarmontite, cervantite, and valentinite are oxidized antimony minerals.

498. What are the properties of stibnite? A metallic-gray mineral, antimony sulfide (Sb_2S_3) in composition, stibnite is characterized by its prominent cleavage. Crystals, especially those from the Island of Shikoku, Province of Iyo, Japan, are often splendidly handsome. Some appear curved or bent, owing to movement along tiny "gliding planes." Stibnite melts readily when heated and is the standard for number 1 in the scale of mineral fusibility (see Question 100).

499. Where is antimony produced?　The Republic of South Africa is currently the largest producer of antimony, now surpassing China, which led both before and after World War II, although Bolivia was ahead during the war. China especially has enormous reserves. Mexico has been the dominant source in North America for many years; the ores are smelted at Laredo, Texas—the world's largest antimony smelter—and hence are not dependent upon ocean transport. Among the lesser producers the Soviet Union and Yugoslavia rank high.

500. How is antimony produced in the United States?　At present the only important yield of antimony in the United States is a by-product of silver, copper, lead, and zinc mining and smelting. The Coeur d'Alene district in Idaho is the outstanding example of this type of operation. A minor production comes from straight-antimony deposits. During World War II the Yellow Pine mine at Stibnite, Idaho, represented an elaborate attempt to obtain a domestic source of supply, and from it developed an open pit mine of considerable size.

501. How is arsenic used?　As a metal arsenic is used only slightly and this mostly for hardening lead shot and in certain copper alloys; usually arsenic is considered deleterious in alloys, reducing their workability. Arsenic compounds, however, are widely used as insecticides, and in such products as weed killers, preservatives, dyes, glass fluxes, pigments, medicine, and fireworks. Like every other element, arsenic is used in the chemical industry. The so-called "arsenic" of commerce is actually arsenious oxide (As_2O_3), also known as white arsenic, and this is the substance referred to in production and marketing statistics.

502. Where is arsenic obtained?　White arsenic comes mainly from the smelter smoke of arsenic-bearing ores of gold, silver, copper, lead, and zinc. It is thus a byproduct, and, in fact, is produced in amounts greatly in excess of the world's needs. It furthermore faces competition for its likeliest uses from synthetic chemicals.

Realgar and orpiment (see Question 503) are sulfide minerals used as sources of arsenic in some countries of Europe and Asia. Arsenopyrite is doubtless the best known arsenic mineral (see Question 24) but is usually mined only for its cobalt or gold content.

503. How are realgar and orpiment related?　Both of these fine minerals are arsenic sulfides, differing vividly in color but closely related otherwise. Bright-red to orange realgar has the formula AsS and alters to lemon-yellow orpiment, having the formula As_2S_3. They are almost invariably associated with each other, and specimens of this sort are surely among the most attractive in the entire Mineral Kingdom. Both minerals are sectile enough to be cut with a knife, unless too powdery in structure.

504. What are the uses of bismuth?　Known since the Middle Ages but often confused with other white metals, bismuth was formerly used mostly in the drug industry and in solder, but during the past two decades its alloys have become of increasing significance and wide-spread use.

The alloys of bismuth are chiefly characterized by their low melting points. Bismuth, moreover, is one of the few substances that expands upon solidification. Bismuth itself melts at 271 degrees Centigrade but some of its alloys melt at as low as 47.2 degrees. Thus they serve such purposes as automatic water sprinklers for fire protection because they melt in hot water or even a hot room.

505. Which metal makes the most enduring magnet?　The "most-permanent" magnet known is an alloy of bismuth and manganese developed by scientists of the Naval Ordnance Laboratory, Washington, D.C. More demagnetizing force is necessary to remove its residual magnetism than for any other substance. It is formed as a powder that can be molded into any desired shape, but no particular form is required, such as a bar or horseshoe.

506. What are the sources of bismuth?　Bismuth is obtained mostly as a byproduct of other ores, such as tin, copper, or silver, and as a refinery byproduct, mainly from lead ores. Native bismuth, however, is not rare. Neither is the sulfide, bismuthinite, which is the most-used ore of this metal where bismuth is mined for its own sake. These minerals both oxidize to bismite or bismuth ocher. The United States, Peru, Mexico, Japan, and Korea are, in that order, the five leading producers of bismuth.

507. What is the nature of bismuthinite? A metallic gray mineral somewhat resembling stibnite, bismuthinite is bismuth sulfide, Bi_2S_3. It has a good cleavage and is fairly heavy, but otherwise it has no particularly recognizable features and must usually be tested for its bismuth content.

VIII. IRON AND FERROALLOY METALS

Introduction. The Industrial Revolution was the marriage of iron and steam. Iron, its alloy, steel, and the several metals known as ferroalloys, which are alloyed or mixed with steel to create artificial metals having new and useful properties—these together form the backbone of modern civilization, an organism powered by water, the fossil fuels, and the promising radioactive materials—mineral substances all.

Iron is the basic metal; modern agriculture, manufacturing, construction, transportation, and armament could not have developed without it. The high standard of today's living has been effected largely by the ready availability of iron ore and its accessibility to the coking coal needed for the making of iron and steel.

508. What are the main problems of the iron industry? Although iron is the second most abundant metal in the crust of the earth, the difficult nature of its compounds delayed its use until much later than that of certain much less common metals. The fundamental techniques of large-scale steel making are only a century old, beginning with the invention in 1856 by Sir Henry Bessemer (1813–1898) of the modern blast furnace. Nevertheless, the approaching depletion of easily accessible high-grade domestic ores has already made necessary strenuous adjustments in the industry, so that a greater reliance upon foreign and lower tenor sources is required. These involve adjustments in transportation and furnace practice, and mean either a higher price or increased efficiency, or perhaps both. The differing location of iron deposits in relation to coal, limestone, the ferroalloys —the requisite raw materials for steel—and, on the other hand, to centers of consumption, is at the heart of the problems of the iron industry. A reliance upon foreign resources can present a serious aspect of national security, entirely apart from the economics involved.

509. What is pig iron? This is the original product obtained from the blast-furnace reduction of iron ore. Smelted with coke and limestone, the ore is turned into molten iron, which always contains some carbon, the amount determining the use to which the metal is put.

This is called pig iron because of the shape of the 40- to 100-pound bars. From pig iron is obtained cast iron, wrought iron, or steel.

510. What is cast iron? Articles that are not subject to shock and do not require high tensile strength are made from cast iron. The pig iron is melted in a cupola furnace. Some castings require further purification of the pig iron or the addition of other ingredients.

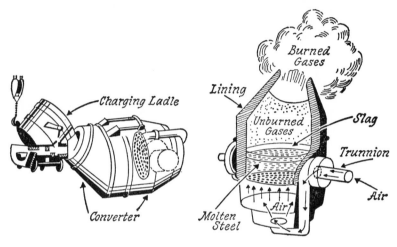

Diagram of the Bessemer process

511. What is wrought iron? Malleable, ductile, and corrosion resistant, wrought iron is a rather pure iron obtained from pig iron in a puddling furnace, where the impurities are slagged off by stirring, after which the red-hot metal is hammered into the desired shape. Before furnace fusion was first accomplished in the 14th Century, practically all iron was what we would today call wrought iron.

512. What is steel? Steel is an alloy of iron and carbon. The content of carbon is usually under 1 per cent, though it may be as high as 1.6 per cent. "Mild steel" has the lowest proportion of carbon. To steel is added one or more of the ferroalloys in order to produce desirable properties not otherwise found in it.

513. What is the function of coke in steel making? Coke—produced from coking coal by the elimination of much of the volatiles in it (see Question 857)—has the dual function in steel making of supplying heat and of combining with oxygen from the ore, freezing the iron to accumulate at the bottom of the blast furnace. This reduction of iron ore by carbon from the coke thus converts it to metallic iron, and is the fundamental principle of both the Bessemer and open-hearth methods of steel manufacture.

514. What is the role of limestone in steel making? Limestone is necessary in the making of steel to reduce the temperature at which the ore melts. This is called a fluxing action, and is aided further by the addition of silica. Limestone is even more essential, however, in forming a slag which serves to remove impurities from the ore.

515. What is taconite? A hard siliceous rock occurring in the Lake Superior region, taconite under favorable conditions contains 20 to 30 per cent iron. It is believed to be similar to the original source rock from which the Lake Superior iron ores were derived by natural processes of leaching and alteration. Slaty and cherty taconite are the two principal classes. With the fast decline in the quantity of high-grade ores available in that most prolific of all the world's iron mining areas, taconite is becoming the most important ore of iron in the United States. Significant changes in mining and beneficiation are accompanying the transition from the mining of rich iron minerals to the mining of taconite.

 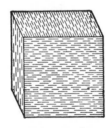

Pyrite crystals

516. Which are the iron-bearing minerals? Hundreds of iron-bearing minerals are known. Of these, four may be regarded as ores of iron, although pyrite, pyrrhotite, and ilmenite have in some places been used for their iron content, and each of the chief minerals has varieties that bear special names. Magnetite is the richest of the iron ores but small in quantity used. Hematite maintains the iron industry in America. Limonite and siderite, of minor value in the Western Hemisphere, are important in Europe.

517. What are the properties of magnetite? A metallic-black, hard mineral, magnetite is an oxide of both ferrous and ferric iron, its chemical formula being Fe_3O_4. It may contain inclusions of

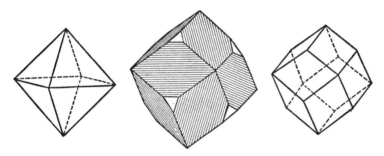

Forms of magnetite crystals

ilmenite, giving it a content of titanium. As the name indicates, this mineral is magnetic; when it acts as a natural magnet it is called lodestone (see Question 91). It often occurs in octahedral crystals, sometimes in dodecahedrons.

518. What is the nature of hematite? A ferric oxide, Fe_2O_3, hematite is a common metallic mineral, either reddish brown or black. A red earthy variety is known as *red ocher*. No matter what its color, it crushes to an Indian-red streak (see Question 86). Fine crystals of shiny black hematite come from the island of Elba; Cumberland, England; and at St. Gothard, Switzerland, where attractive *iron roses* are found (see Question 520). Rounded lumps of hematite are known as *kidney ore*. Hematite crystals that have altered from magnetite are referred to as *martite;* they have the octahedal shape of magnetite but the red streak of hematite.

519. What is specularite? This mineral, also known as *specular hematite,* is really a variety of hematite having a leaflike structure resembling a metallic mica. It gets its name from its mirror luster, from the Latin word *speculum,* "mirror." Because it indicates a high-temperature origin, specularite is sometimes regarded by geologists as a separate mineral.

520. What is an iron rose?   This is a concentric grouping of tabular plates of shiny black hematite. St. Gothard, Switzerland, is a world-famous source of these roses of hematite.

521. What is limonite?   Previously considered a mineral of definite composition, limonite is today thought of as a noncrystalline form of the mineral *goethite* plus a variable amount of water, and impurities of clay, manganese oxides, and hematite. Goethite itself is a recognized mineral having the composition FeO(OH). Once believed a rather uncommon mineral, it has been shown to be exceedingly abundant and to make up most of what used to be called limonite. It seems likely, however, that the term limonite will, because it is so familiar, continue to be used for the brown iron material with a yellow-brown streak.

522. What are the features of siderite?   An iron carbonate, $FeCO_3$, siderite belongs to the calcite group of minerals, named and described in Question 31. It is the heaviest of them. When mixed with clay minerals, it is known as *clay ironstone*. When associated with coal it is known as *black-band ore,* which is interbedded with shale. Siderite is an important ore of iron in Great Britain and Austria.

523. What are the iron ranges?   The bodies of "folded" rocks that contain the hematite ores of the Lake Superior region in Minnesota, Wisconsin, and Michigan are known as iron ranges because of their typically mountainous structure, though they are not mountainous in topography.

Of these ranges the Mesabi is the most important—the largest and richest iron deposit yet known. It lies in northeastern Minnesota. Southeast of it is the Cuyuna Range. To the southeast lie the Gogebic (in Wisconsin and Michigan), Menominee, and Marquette Ranges (in Michigan); while north of the Mesabi is the Vermilion Range (in Minnesota).

524. What are the Clinton ores?   Second in importance in the United States to the Lake Superior deposits are the sedimentary beds of hematite known as the Clinton iron ores. Although named after Clinton, New York, and outcropping the length of the Appalachians, they become of major significance chiefly at Birmingham, Alabama. Owing to the proximity of coking coal and limestone as well, Birmingham has become one of the leading industrial cities of the nation and one of the steel centers of the world. At Red Mountain four beds are present and two are workable, the main production being from the Big Seam.

At Wabana, Newfoundland, are large bodies of iron ore similar to the Clinton ores, though undesirably high in phosphorus. Dipping beneath the Atlantic Ocean, they have been mined 2 miles out from shore.

525. What are the Minette ores? Next in importance to those of Lake Superior among the iron deposits of the world are the limonite beds of northwestern Europe. These, known as Minette ores, occur in France, Luxembourg, Belgium, and Germany, and they change countries with each change in boundaries. They are usually associated with the geographic divisions of Lorraine and Luxembourg. They furnish the nearest ore for the Ruhr steel industry, although much iron needs to be brought in from Sweden.

526. What are the iron ore deposits in Lapland? In Swedish Lapland are the world's largest deposits of magnetite, the richest of the iron minerals. These are situated at Kiruna, on the crest of a long ridge of ancient rock. Across the lake from Kiruna is another iron body at Luossavaara, and 50 miles south is one at Gellivare. These have helped to supply Germany and England with iron ore and make Swedish steel famous.

527. Where are the new sources of iron ore in North America? In addition to the taconite deposits that are being worked under newly devised techniques of beneficiation (see Question 515), American industry has opened up new sources of iron ore in the Western Hemisphere to replace the dwindling high-grade ores of the Mesabi and other ranges.

The most prominent one is along the Quebec-Labrador border. This is of huge size, has varying grades of useful hematite, and is accessible by means of a recently constructed railroad to Seven

Islands on the St. Lawrence River. The Great Lakes–St. Lawrence Seaway is a critical factor in the utilization of these ores.

The Steep Rock or Atikokan district in Ontario, in the Lake Superior region, is another new area of large iron reserves.

528. Where are the new sources of iron ore in Latin America?
At El Pao, Venezuela, is a large body of hematite with some magnetite. At Cerro Bolivar, Venezuela, 65 miles west of El Pao, is a vast deposit of a mixture of hematite and limonite in lenses; this requires a 90-mile rail haul to Puerto Ordaz on the Orinoco River, where transfer is made to ocean-going vessels.

The Itabira district is the most important in Brazil. Two other districts in the state of Minas Geraes and one in the state of Mato Grosso are also of considerable value.

In Chile there are major deposits of iron at El Tofo and Romeral.

Cuba is a potentially immense foreign source of iron. Along the north coast lies one of the largest groups of ore bodies in the world, of the earthy, weathered type known as *laterite*. At present these furnish nickel, but chromium and cobalt are also present, in addition to the iron.

529. Which are the ferroalloys?   Manganese is the most important of the ferroalloy metals because it is essential to the making of all carbon steel. The others are added to give desired properties to steel but they can often be substituted for one another. These metals include especially nickel, chromium, molybdenum, tungsten, vanadium, cobalt, and titanium. The nonmetals silicon and phosphorus are used for certain steels, and there is a very minor use for a number of other elements to function as deoxidizers, desulfurizers and sulfur neutralizers, and agents to improve hardenability, resistance to corrosion, special magnetic and electrical properties, and certain properties desired at high temperatures. Of the major ferroalloys titanium is more valuable in other ways than as a steel alloy.

530. What is the use of manganese in steel?   There will be no substantial substitute for manganese in steel unless the steelmaking process is changed from today's methods. It is employed as a necessary reagent for the purpose of removing oxygen and sulfur in order to produce a clean, solid metal. About 13 pounds is used for each ton of steel. Further amounts are added to produce special manganese steel and other alloy steels, noted for hardness and toughness, as in armor plate, safes, and car wheels. Manganese is employed either in the form of ferromanganese, which has a manganese content of 80 per cent; or as spiegeleisen, with a content of 20 per cent; or as silicomanganese. Some metallic manganese is made electrolytically.

531. What else is manganese used for? In the chemical industry manganese is used as an oxidizing agent and to produce permanganate and other compounds. Manganese is important in dry-cell batteries in the form of manganese dioxide (MnO_2), which is the depolarizing agent in the cell. Furthermore, small amounts of manganese are needed in the production of other nonferrous metals.

532. How does manganese occur? Most of our supply of manganese is obtained from sedimentary deposits and residual deposits derived from the weathering of other manganese bodies. The minerals are mainly oxides, although carbonate and silicate minerals also furnish some commercial material. Pyrolusite, margarite, psilomelane, hausmannite, rhodochrosite, and rhodonite are the most familiar manganese minerals. So intimately are the hydrous oxides associated that they are difficult to separate individually, and the mixture goes under the mining term of *wad*.

533. What is pyrolusite like? Manganese dioxide (MnO_2) in composition, pyrolusite is a soft black mineral. It is the most widespread of the manganese minerals, occurring in masses that commonly soil the fingers. When pyrolusite grows into well-shaped crystals, it is known as *polianite* and is then quite hard—but these are altogether rare. The most interesting form of pyrolusite is the dendritic pattern seen in moss agate (see Question 730) and on the surface of various rocks.

534. What are the features of manganite? More often appearing in crystals than any other manganese oxide, manganite is black but has a brown streak, and its hardness is between those of pyrolusite and psilomelane. Crystals show a good cleavage and are likely to be grouped in bundles. The formula for manganite is $MnO(OH)$.

535. What are the properties of psilomelane?　This rather unusual-sounding mineral name comes from two Greek words meaning "smooth" and "black," and well describes the mineral. It is harder than the ordinary forms of the other manganese oxides. It is found in irregularly rounded masses. The composition is complex, because several elements may substitute for one another in the structure; a common formula is $H_4Ba_2Mn_8O_{20}$.

536. What is the nature of rhodochrosite?　Rhodochrosite is a member of the calcite group of carbonate minerals (see Question 31). It is usually an attractive pink mineral, grading from rose-red to dark brown.

537. What are the properties of rhodonite?　This interesting mineral has been polished as an ornamental stone, as well as serving as an ore of manganese. The material from the Ural Mountains is especially choice. The crystals are usually rough with rounded edges and somewhat resemble feldspar, though heavier. The composition is manganese silicate, $MnSiO_3$. As the name indicates (from the Greek for "rose"), rhodonite is pink, until it alters to black manganese oxide.

538. Where is manganese mined?　The Soviet Union, Republic of South Africa, Brazil, India, China, and Gabon Republic are, in that order, the leading producers of manganese ore. These relative standings change somewhat from year to year, which is true of all production statistics referred to in this book, even when the figures are entirely reliable, as they sometimes are not.

539. Where is the largest manganese mine?　The Nsuta mine in Ghana (formerly the Gold Coast) is reported to be the largest single manganese mine in the world. It is an open pit from which some 3,000 tons of ore are taken daily. Although in a still-primitive country, this mine is equipped with diesel-electric power and both railroad and dock facilities, at Dagwin and Sekondí, respectively.

The largest deposit of manganese, however, is at Chiatura in the Caucasus Mountains of the Soviet Union. This is a stratum 6 to 7 feet thick and continuous over 14 square miles.

540. Where is manganese found in the United States? Gilbert L. DeHuff has listed the largest manganese deposits of the country. The Chamberlain district of South Dakota exceeds all the rest combined, with an estimated 2,500,000,000 tons of raw material. The Cuyuna range in Minnesota (see Question 523) ranks second in ore but is believed to yield somewhat less finished metal than the deposits in Aroostook County, Maine, which are in third place in the amount of available ore. Artillery Peak, Arizona, is fourth, and the others are very much smaller.

541. Where is the nickel industry distributed? Outside of the Soviet Union, about 90 per cent of the world's nickel comes from the Sudbury district of Ontario. The International Nickel Company of Canada, Ltd., operates mines in this district, smelters at Copper Cliff and Coniston, Ontario, and refineries at Port Colborne, Ontario, and Clydach, Wales. The other producer at Sudbury, the Falconbridge Nickel Mines, Ltd., also maintains a smelter at Falconbridge, Ontario, and a refinery at Kristiansand, Norway.

Most of the rest of the Free World's supply of nickel ore comes from Cuba and New Caledonia. New Caledonia was once the principal source; the Cuban deposits are being exploited more intensively as time goes by. New discoveries in northern Manitoba and elsewhere in Canada look highly favorable. Large reserves are indicated in Brazil, Indonesia, and Venezuela. Nickel-bearing iron ores are the largest potential source of nickel, but the grade is low and the product expensive. Manganese nodules on the ocean floor (see Question 477) and discoveries of nickel ore being made in tropical regions promise much future production. The Republic of the Philippines may contain more than 1 billion tons of ore.

The Soviet deposits at Petsamo (formerly in Finland) and in the Kola Peninsula are of major significance.

542. Which is the main nickel mineral? Pentlandite, a sulfide of nickel and iron, $(Fe,Ni)_9S_8$, is believed to be the source of nearly all the Sudbury nickel. The ores there contain pyrrhotite and chalcopyrite, mostly, both of which are sulfide minerals through which pentlandite is disseminated. Interestingly, these ores also yield by-product gold, silver, and platinum—one of the few places in the world where all the precious metals are produced in substantial quantities.

543. What is Monel metal? Monel metal is an alloy of nickel (67 per cent) and copper (33 per cent), discovered by the International Nickel Company for the purpose of utilizing both of the main metals occurring together in the Sudbury deposits. It is used chiefly for household purposes, such as sinks. A plant at Huntington, West Virginia, makes Monel metal from roasted and sintered "matte" shipped from Canada.

544. What is garnierite? This is the nickel-bearing variety of serpentine that occurs in New Caledonia and elsewhere such rocks weather under tropical conditions. Its composition is $(Mg,Ni)_6Si_4O_{10}(OH)_8$. Garnierite has typically an apple-green color and a dull or earthy luster. It is found as crusts and in lumps.

545. Where does chromium occur? Chromium is one of those metals that is found mainly in parts of the world where little is consumed, and so it involves a worldwide commerce. The industrial nations are, of course, the principal users of chromium. Russia is both a large producer and consumer, but the other main sources are the Republic of South Africa, Republic of the Philippines, Turkey, and Rhodesia. Albania, Iran, and Yugoslavia are other large suppliers. Cuba is potentially the largest source in the Western Hemisphere, but satisfactory methods have not yet been devised for using its lateritic iron ore (see Questions 461, 528).

546. What are the uses of chromium? The direct metallurgical uses of chromium account for just over half the total output. Chromium plating on automobiles and household appliances is doubtless the most conspicuous such use, but *stainless steel* involves far larger tonnages. Stainless steel is basically a chromium-nickel alloy of steel. The high-speed tool steel called *stellite* is another important alloy of chromium. The alloys of chromium used in jet airplanes make possible the resistance to high temperature, fatigue, and corrosion necessary in passing the sound barrier.

One-third of the production of chromium enters into the making of refractories (heat-resisting materials) used mostly by the metallurgical industry for lining and patching furnaces. The rest of the chromium inventory is used in the chemical industry, but even here a good deal is employed in metal-treating, plating, and the manufacture of chromium metal.

547. Which are the chromium minerals? Only one ore mineral of chromium is known. This is chromite, which has the theoretical formula $FeCr_2O_4$, but contains variable proportions of magnesium and aluminum as well. Chromite characteristically has a pitchy or submetallic look, not quite the same as most metallic minerals, and it ranges in color from black to brownish black.

548. What is the Bushveld Igneous Complex? This remarkable geologic structure is a vast body of rock in South Africa. It shows a uniform layering of bands of chromite within the enclosed basic igneous rocks (see Question 158); these can be traced for miles across the country. The Complex also contains bands of titanium-bearing magnetite, and it yields valuable platinum ores. Mining is carried on around Rustenburg and Lydenburg.

549. What are the ores of molybdenum? The mineral molybdenite is by far the most important ore of this metal. It grades into *powellite,* which is sometimes treated to recover molybdenum. In years past the mineral *wulfenite* was also used.

550. What are the properties of molybdenite? This is a molybdenum sulfide, MoS_2. It is a greasy, gray mineral that closely resembles graphite. Usually it occurs in narrow ribbonlike veins, but when it is found in distinct crystals it shows the same kind of cleavage as mica.

551. Where is the highest mine in the United States? Although many small mines, a few of which are still working, are situated at a higher altitude in the Colorado Rockies, the Climax Molybdenum Company operates the highest large-scale mine in the United States at 11,300 feet above sea level at Climax, near Leadville, Colorado. By an intensively developed caving system, more than 35,000 tons of ore can be mined daily from two main haulage levels. This is the greatest concentration of molybdenum in the world. However, at Bingham Canyon, Utah, and other porphyry copper deposits (see Question 419), byproduct molybdenum in favorable years becomes a strong competitor to Climax's dominant position.

552. Which is the most familiar use of tungsten?   Tungsten filaments in electric light bulbs were introduced in the early years of the 20th Century, superseding the older carbon-filament lamps and becoming the most common use for tungsten. Later the tungsten filament entered extensively into vacuum tubes in electronic equipment, though it is now being replaced by transistors. This metal otherwise is most used as a steel alloy, especially for high-temperature purposes, and in tungsten carbide for cutting tools and armor-piercing shells.

553. Which are the tungsten minerals?   The ore minerals of tungsten are scheelite, grading into powellite and cuproscheelite, and a series of three "black ore" minerals often classed together as wolframite. These last are properly separated as ferberite, wolframite, and huebnerite (see Question 555).

554. What are the properties of scheelite?   Calcium tungstate, $CaWO_4$, in composition, scheelite is most noteworthy for its ability to fluoresce under short-wave ultraviolet light. As the tungsten is replaced by molybdenum, scheelite grades into powellite. The presence of copper instead makes *cuproscheelite*. Scheelite may occur in double pyramids belonging to the tetragonal crystal system. In massive form it resembles greasy quartz but is unusually heavy for a nonmetallic-looking mineral.

555. What is wolframite like?   Wolframite is the middle member of a series of iron-manganese tungstate minerals, going from ferberite, which is black and has the formula $FeWO_4$, to huebernite, which is brown and has the formula $MnWO_4$. Wolframite covers the middle range—between 20 and 80 per cent $FeWO_4$—is much the most common of these minerals, and is the chief ore of tungsten. Besides the dark color and heaviness, wolframite is recognized by its one direction of good cleavage.

556. Where is tungsten mined? The Orient is the prime source of the world's tungsten. China, the Republic of Korea, and Burma stand among the leaders in production and reserves—China has had a total output at least twice that of any other country. Continuing around the Pacific Ocean are the deposits in the western United States, especially in Nevada, California, Montana, Colorado, and Idaho. The Hamme mine in Vance County, North Carolina, is a large one. Substantial bodies in Bolivia have come into prominence, and the Soviet Union, Portugal, and Australia are responsible for a considerable production. Tungsten has become an important byproduct of the molybdenum mine at Climax, Colorado (see Question 551), and it is a byproduct at a number of tin smelters throughout the globe.

557. Is vanadium a radioactive metal? No, but it occurs so abundantly in certain types of uranium ores that in the United States it has become mainly a byproduct of the radioactive-minerals industry. The carnotite-roscoelite ores (see Question 659) are rich in vanadium, and there is an ample supply of this useful metal in the phosphate rock looked upon as a future source of uranium from large-scale recovery operations.

558. What are the uses of vanadium? As a ferroalloy metal, vanadium is used in metallurgy. About 90 per cent of it is consumed in the form of ferrovanadium. Its essential use is in steel to refine the grain and harden it for alloy tool and high-speed steel, but a little vanadium goes a long way. Many future uses are doubtless awaiting discovery, but meanwhile vanadium, unlike most of the ferroalloys, is in surplus supply.

559. Where are vanadium deposits situated? The United States is the largest producer, as well as the largest consumer, of vanadium. Three other countries share almost all the rest of the world's output. These are Northern Rhodesia, South-West Africa, and Peru. Small deposits are scattered throughout Argentina. The largest single mine is reported to be at Mina Ragra, in the Andes of Peru, which has been an important source since mining began in 1907. The material there is a peculiar association of asphalt, a black sulfide known as patronite, and a red calcium vanadate; extraction is by open-pit methods. In North Rhodesia vanadium is a byproduct of lead-zinc ores at Broken Hill, and in South-West Africa the vanadium is a byproduct of lead-copper-zinc workings in the Otavi region.

560. Which are the vanadium minerals? The principal ore minerals of vanadium are patronite (the Peruvian material, see Question 559), carnotite and roscoelite (in conjunction with radioactive deposits), and vanadinite.

561. What are the characteristics of vanadinite? Its color typically red and orange and its luster brilliant, vanadinite is one of the handsomest of minerals. Its rounded hexagonal crystals, sometimes hollow, resemble those of pyromorphite and mimetite, two related minerals of different color. Vanadinite is an exceptionally heavy mineral. Chemically, it is a lead chlorovanadate, $Pb_5Cl(VO_4)_3$.

562. What is the source of cobalt? Because the minerals of cobalt are seldom found in sufficient quantity to be mined for cobalt alone, the production of this metal is mostly a byproduct or coproduct of other metals, chiefly copper. The cobalt minerals include cobaltite, skutterudite, linnaeite, carrollite, and erythrite, among numerous others.

563. Where is cobalt obtained? The cobalt industry is concentrated in Africa. The Union Minière du Haut-Katanga is much the largest producer in the world, with elaborate facilities in the Congo; final refining is done at Oolen, Belgium, and at Niagara Falls, New York. Although the United States has been only a small producer of cobalt ore, the output is increasing from several parts of the country—Idaho, Missouri, Pennsylvania—and the United States is a major factor in the trade as a refiner of crude cobalt and the largest importer of crude cobalt, metal, and oxide. The laterite deposits in Cuba are the largest potential source of cobalt but they are as yet unworked for this metal.

564. What are the uses for cadmium? Most cadmium is used in electroplating. The next largest uses are for pigments and low-melting-point alloys. Bearing alloys of cadmium were important in World War II. Although of subordinate importance, cadmium is used to make green gold (see Question 372), it hardens copper, and it makes silver tarnish resistant, as well as combining with silver to make an alloy for tableware.

565. How is cadmium found?   Cadmium is recovered solely as a byproduct of zinc mining, because it is so commonly associated with zinc. Cadmium minerals in commercial amounts are rare; the likeliest one is *greenockite,* a cadmium sulfide, CdS. This usually is seen as a yellow coating or stain on sphalerite, the primary ore of zinc (see Question 450).

566. Where is cadmium found?   Nearly one-third of the world's output of cadmium comes from the United States. However, an unknown proportion of this has been imported as zinc ores, concentrates, and flue dust. Although not a large producer of zinc, South-West Africa ranks among the large suppliers of cadmium because the content of this metal in the other ores that are mined is high. The Soviet Union, Canada, and Japan are large producers of zinc and hence of cadmium. Belgium figures high in the statistics, owing to its imported raw materials, and Great Britain and France operate on much the same basis.

567. What is selenium?   Selenium has been described by John D. Sargent as a paradox, "being either a metal or a nonmetal, a conductor or nonconductor, amorphous or crystalline, colorant or decolorant, and a hydrogenator or dehydrogenator." It was discovered in 1817 by the Swedish chemist Baron Jöns Jakob Berzelius (1779–1848) while studying flue dust at the sulfuric acid plant at Gripsholm. Selenium is an acidic element related to tellurium (see Question 571).

568. What are the uses of selenium?   Selenium first came into substantial use during World War I as a substitute for manganese, which was then scarce, for decolorizing glass by neutralizing the greenish tinge imparted by iron impurities. This use proved so satisfactory that it has continued ever since. After World War II selenium began to be used mainly for rectifiers for converting alternating to direct current. Because it conducts electricity only when exposed to light, selenium is employed in photoelectric cells in such products as electric eyes and photographic exposure meters. Selenium is also used in the rubber, stainless-steel, and pigment industries; it has come a long distance since the days before World War I when its presence was the despair of smeltermen and it was discarded wherever possible.

569. What is the universal solvent?   This is a hypothetical substance long considered an academic puzzle by chemists. No such thing can exist, for where could it be kept? But selenium oxychloride is so corrosive that one is tempted to call it the universal solvent— it is the only one for plastics. It dissolves phenolic resin, rubber resin, glue, paint, and varnish.

570. Where is selenium obtained?   Selenium is obtained on a large scale only as a byproduct of copper smelting. The United States is the leading producer. Canada and Sweden are other countries of high rank. Mexico has a major output of selenium but most of it is recovered and refined in the United States. A vast area of North America, from the Rocky Mountains to the Mississippi River and from Canada to Mexico, is a selenium province, containing unusually large amounts of this element in its rocks, soils, and vegetation. The notorious locoweed, which poisons cattle, sheep, and horses, is made undesirable by its selenium content.

571. What is tellurium?   A semi-metal, tellurium is closely related to selenium in its nature. It is more abundant than selenium; consumption has increased of late years but the supply still exceeds the demand. The principal uses of tellurium are in the making of various alloys and as a vulcanizing agent in the rubber industry.

572. What is the source of tellurium?   As with selenium, tellurium is obtained mostly from blister copper (see Question 928), chiefly in the United States and Canada. It does occur, however, as a native mineral, though rarely, and it is the only element that forms, to any extent, compounds with gold—the gold and silver tellurides are described in Questions 380–382.

IX. RARE AND UNUSUAL METALS

Introduction. The metals described in this chapter differ from those in other chapters more in their rarity and limited use than in their fundamental nature. Some of the radioactive minerals of Chapter 10 are certainly uncommon enough in their distribution, but they share a remarkable property which sets them apart. Some of the ferroalloy metals of Chapter 8 were regarded as unfamiliar until quite recently, and some of the structural metals of Chapter 7—such as magnesium, titanium, and aluminum—were not so long ago treated as unusual, even though obviously not rare, and they had restricted application. Thus, it would be no surprise to find some of the "rare and unusual" metals of this chapter turn up in years to come as widely used structural metals, perhaps to be thought of as no better than "base metals."

573. What is the nature of beryllium? Beryllium is assuredly one of the most interesting of all metals in both its industrial uses and its geologic occurrence. It is the only stable light metal with a high melting point. Recent technology has taken it from the stage of a mineral curiosity to one of outstanding importance in the field of nuclear energy, and it has with some justification been included among the "atomic-energy" minerals. Pure beryllium is used mainly— apart from undisclosed applications—in X-ray-tube windows and with radium as a source of neutrons, and as a moderator and reflector of them. Beryllium oxide is a high-temperature refractory. Most of this metal, however, goes into alloys.

574. How is beryllium alloyed? The principal alloy of beryllium is with copper. This artificial metal is of great value for its many virtues, especially its resistance to fatigue. Springs made from it can be stressed several billion times without failure. Machine parts subject to abnormal wear engendered by extreme vibration are profitably made from it. Beryllium is also added to other metals, such as zinc and nickel.

575. Is beryllium a health hazard?   The handling of beryllium and its compounds seems to be one of the most risky in the metals industry. Exposure without due care causes dermatitis and pneumonia, but proper precautions can be taken to make beryllium as safe as other mineral products. Its toxic effects, however, are a serious problem.

576. Which are the beryllium minerals?   Although some other minerals contain a larger percentage of beryllium, the mineral *beryl* (see Questions 577–579) is the only one generally considered an ore of the metal. The puzzling deposit of the Boomer mine in Colorado, for a while the largest producer in America, suggests that phenakite is yielding the chief amount of beryllium, though beryl is also present. Helvite and chrysoberyl are possible future sources of the metal if found in large enough quantities. High-temperature veins in Nevada and elsewhere are revealing unsuspected mineral combinations of beryllium. The invention of the Berylometer, which detects the element by use of radioactive antimony, has greatly increased the chances of finding new deposits.

577. How does beryl occur?   Beryl is, except in isolated and unusual occurrences, recovered entirely from pegmatites, the coarse-grained equivalent of granite (see Questions 181–184). In these bodies it is almost always a byproduct of the mining of feldspar, mica, cassiterite, columbite-tantalite, or lithium minerals. To be recovered economically, beryl must be in crystals large enough to permit hand sorting, because mechanical methods have not been perfected.

578. What is the appearance of beryl?   Six-sided crystals, often of large size, are characteristic of beryl; some have reached a weight of tons. The color is typically bluish green but may vary considerably. White beryl resembles quartz. Transparent specimens of the appropriate color make several of the leading gems—emerald and aquamarine, as well as the less well known morganite and golden beryl (see Question 683). When fresh, beryl is one of the hard minerals, but commercial material is often leached to a somewhat chalky state.

579. Where is beryl mined?   Owing to its occurrence in pegmatites, beryl is associated with large bodies of granite in the heart of mountainous country. In the United States it occurs mostly in the Appalachians, Black Hills, and Rocky Mountains. Brazil is perhaps the leading producer, but figures are not available for the Soviet Union, although the Ural Mountains have long been a principal source. Rhodesia, South-West Africa, Republic of South Africa, Malagasy Republic, Mozambique, and Morocco combine to make Africa probably the most prolific continent in beryl. Argentina and Portugal are other important producers.

580. Do columbium and tantalum occur together? These metals are nearly always found together, for they occur chiefly in minerals that form a continuous series from one element to the other—the columbite-tantalite series. There are also five other principal minerals of these metals, namely the pyrochlore-microlite series, fergusonite-formanite series, samarskite-yttrotantalite series, euxenite, and eschynite—these are all radioactive multiple-oxide minerals (see Questions 620, 641).

581. What is the columbite-tantalite series? This is a series of minerals consisting of two "end-numbers" that grade into each other by a substitution of elements. If the specimen contains more columbium than tantalum, it is called columbite. If less, it is called tantalite. Both minerals also contain iron and manganese, giving the general formula $(Fe,Mn)(Cb,Ta)_2O_6$. They are black with a submetallic luster and often an iridescent look. They are hard and heavy.

582. Where are columbite and tantalite found? The largest share of these minerals is obtained as a byproduct of the placer mining of cassiterite, the tin mineral (see Question 464). The rest comes from pegmatites, from which they are recovered along with cassiterite, beryl, spodumene, feldspar, or mica.

Nigeria exceeds all the rest of the world combined in the production of the columbite that comes to the United States, the largest user; tantalite also comes mainly from Africa but from several countries, as well as from Brazil and Portugal.

583. What are the rare-earths? The rare-earths or rare-earth metals are a closely related group of 15 metals. These are lanthanum, cerium, praseodymium, neodymium, promethium, samarium, europium, gadolinium, terbium, dysprosium, holmium, erbium, thulium, ytterbium and lutetium. It has been possible to isolate the least abundant of these elements for research only within recent years. Some are really not rare at all, except in their obsolete name—cerium is the commonest; others seem not available for any sort of extensive use unless unexpected concentrations are discovered.

584. What are the uses of the rare-earth metals?   Some of the uses for the rare earths are familiar and of long standing. Such is the case with ferrocerium, an alloy of 30 per cent iron, which is brittle and emits sparks when abraded; it makes lighter "flints." Most of the uses, however, are of recent development and involve nuclear energy and a host of new applications, too many to attempt an enumeration. The glass industry uses perhaps the largest quantity of these metals. Another major use is for carbon-arc-electrode cores, which has made possible high-speed photography. Ferrocerium and misch metal (see Question 585) account for a good proportion of the total. And the miscellaneous uses are legion, befitting an array of 15 similar but not exactly alike fundamental substances.

585. What is misch metal?   This is a mixture of all the rare-earth elements in metallic form. Because cerium, the most abundant, predominates to the extent of 45 to 55 per cent, the mixture is often referred to as cerium. Misch metal is alloyed with copper, nickel, zirconium, zinc, aluminum, and magnesium as a structural metal and for other purposes.

586. Which minerals contain the rare earths?   More than 200 minerals contain an appreciable quantity of rare-earth elements in varying proportions. Monazite and bastnaesite are the chief commercial sources today. Cerite and allanite, though not scarce minerals, are generally marginal. Monazite, however, is a radioactive mineral as well (it contains thorium, see Question 639), and its future use may be reserved for that purpose. In turn, the extraction of thorium from monazite on a large scale may provide a surplus of the rare earths from this one source alone. Among the other minerals that seem most likely to furnish future supplies are gadolinite, euxenite, pyrochlore, samarskite, and fergusonite.

587. Where is the largest deposit of bastnaesite?   In April 1949 a huge deposit of bastnaesite, a fluocarbonate of the rare earths, was discovered in the Mountain Pass area of San Bernardino County, California, and production was begun in May 1952. A tremendous tonnage is available by open-pit mining, the main ore body being about 2,500 feet long and 500 feet wide.

588. What are the uses for germanium? The widely advertised germanium transistor has made the name of this metal familiar to many who have not the slightest idea what it is actually like. Together with the germanium diode and rectifier, it is replacing vacuum tubes, being small and light, long lived, shock resistant, and requiring much less power to operate, because it needs no hot filament or cathode. It can, furthermore, perform some functions that vacuum tubes cannot. Germanium—classified technically as a semiconductor—is indeed effecting a revolution in electronics, and it may cease to be considered a rare metal. In 1940 its price was $4,500 per pound, nearly 9 times the price of gold, but it has fallen to a fraction of that.

589. What are the sources of germanium? Although there are several germanium minerals—argyrodite and germanite among them —they are relatively scarce, and so this metal is recovered as a by-product of other minerals in which it occurs as a chemical impurity. Sphalerite, cinnabar, and pyrargyrite seem to contain the largest proportion of germanium. The zinc deposits of the Tri-State district (see Question 150) constitute the principal source in the United States. Africa has large known reserves. Certain coals yield germanium from their ash.

590. What are the uses for zirconium? Unlike germanium (see Question 588), zirconium has not been publicized, but the atomic-powered submarine *Nautilus* was made possible by the use of it. No other material has been found to be as satisfactory as a structural metal in nuclear reactors. Steel alloys and surgery also employ zirconium metal. Zirconium compounds are, however, more extensively used for diverse industrial purposes than the metal itself.

591. Which are the minerals of zirconium? Only zircon (from various parts of the world) and baddeleyite (from Brazil only) are sources of commercial zirconium, although this element is present in other minerals from which it is not extracted. Zircon is also one of the important gems (see Question 725).

592. Where is zirconium produced? Five countries share most of the world's resources of zirconium ore—the United States, India, Australia, Brazil, and Ceylon. The beach sands of eastern Florida are the main deposits in the United States; monazite, rutile, and ilmenite are also mined here. Beach sand is likewise the source of zircon in the other countries. In Brazil, baddeleyite comes from mines at Cascata.

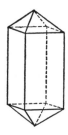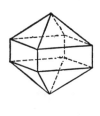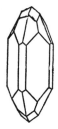

Crystals of zircon

593. Which is the lightest metal? The lightest metal and the third lightest of all the elements is lithium. Although discovered nearly 150 years ago and widely distributed in the earth's crust, including its bodies of water, lithium has become of industrial significance only lately. Intensive research has uncovered many worthwhile uses for this metal and its compounds—such as ceramics, air conditioning, and the new "all-purpose greases"—and lithium is an up-and-coming mineral resource.

594. Which are the lithium minerals? Four minerals yield the bulk of the lithium that is produced. In addition, lithium is obtained from brine at Searles Lake, California, in the form of lithium-sodium phosphate. The minerals are spodumene, lepidolite, petalite, and amblygonite—all are found only in pegmatites (see Questions 181–184).

595. Where are lithium minerals mined? The largest reserves of lithium minerals in the United States are in the Kings Mountain district in North Carolina. Previously, the Black Hills of South Dakota were the principal source; from here have come the gigantic crystals of spodumene mentioned in Question 106. San Diego County,

California; the Harding mine in northern New Mexico; Fremont and Gunnison Counties, Colorado; and Fremont County, Wyoming, have outstanding deposits of spodumene, lepidolite, petalite, and amblygonite.

In other countries the pegmatite localities of the lithium minerals are also in mountainous terrane. Quebec and Manitoba, in Canada, the Republic of Mali, Rhodesia, and Western Australia are important producers.

596. Why is lithium used in air conditioning? Lithium chloride is one of the most hygroscopic of chemical compounds, meaning that it strongly absorbs water. A saturated solution will dry air that passes over it to a low relative humidity, and it also removes dust and odors. In the gas-absorption type of air conditioning, lithium bromide is used instead.

597. Which metal has the widest range of liquefaction? With a melting point of 85.5 degrees Fahrenheit and a boiling point of 3,601 degrees, gallium remains liquid over a broader range of temperature (3,515.5 degrees Fahrenheit) than any other metal. Hence it has been used in high-temperature thermometers, in which the metal is placed under vacuum in fused quartz tubes.

598. Where does gallium come from? Although few persons have heard of gallium, it is as abundant as lead in the crust of the earth. It is recovered as a byproduct of other metallic ores by several methods. Investigations into gallium began in the United States in 1915 when F. G. McCutcheon accidentally discovered beads of gallium-indium alloy sweating from slabs of lead that had been exposed to sunlight. He set about to secure more of the metal and by 1944 had isolated about 15 pounds. Zinc concentrates and aluminum residues have furnished gallium in Germany and the United States. Coal from some localities, especially in England, have surprisingly high percentages of gallium, and the flue dust from this coal is an important source.

599. What is thallium? This is a rare metal, soft, bluish-white, and chemically resembling lead. It is produced by few companies, and is used mostly in rat poison. Four minerals contain substantial percentages of thallium, but they are all too rare to be of commercial importance, and so the metal is obtained as a byproduct of some sulfide ores.

600. What is scandium? Although widely distributed as an impurity in various well-known minerals, scandium is a comparatively expensive element, difficult to extract. The only known mineral that is itself a scandium compound is thortveitite, which has been mined in Madagascar and Norway. This element has at present no appreciable use, but research is being directed toward it.

601. What is cesium? Until 1932 regarded as a laboratory curiosity, the soft, silvery white metal cesium is now important in various interesting optical and detection devices. Among these are the sniperscope and snooperscope, which make it possible to view objects in the dark. Most cesium, however, is used in photoelectric cells employed in infrared photography and television. Pollucite is the only strictly cesium mineral, but other minerals contain small amounts. The largest supply comes from the Jooste lithium mines near Karibib, South West Africa.

602. What is indium? A lustrous, silver-white metal, indium has been used mostly for bearings in the automotive, aviation, and diesel industries. No indium minerals are known, but the element is obtained from the refining of zinc and lead. The supply exceeds the demand, although indium alloys have many promising uses. Very soft itself, indium imparts hardness and strength, as well as corrosion resistance, to other metals.

603. What is rhenium? Rhenium is a metal so scarce that it is measured in minerals as parts per million. Molybdenite (see Question 550) contains the largest percentage—3,110 parts per million is the highest recorded. About half the world production until late years has come from the University of Tennessee, where an extractive process has been developed. Rhenium forms good corrosion-resistant alloys and is an excellent metal for electroplating.

604. What is rubidium? Closely related to cesium (see Question 601), rubidium is a little-known metal used more in compounds (as for medicine) than in metallic form. The principal source is lepidolite, the lithium mica (see Question 169). The United States and Germany are the leading suppliers of rubidium and its compounds. Since mining for this mineral, chiefly as a source of lithium, has practically ceased, rubidium has been processed from pollucite.

X. RADIOACTIVE MINERALS

Introduction. To people of the next centuries the modern world may be thought of as having begun with the utilization of nuclear energy—but we cannot yet be sure. Nevertheless, to people of the present time the radioactive minerals are the most interesting minerals, with the exception of a few others of especial prominence, such as diamond and gold, and the curiosities or freaks, such as asbestos. Here, then, are minerals that spontaneously break down of their own accord, and which, in fact, cannot be prevented from doing so by any known means. Neither pressure, heat, chemical techniques, nor the passage of time seem to have any influence upon their radioactivity. Each radioactive element changes into lighter and less complex ones, emiting heat energy as it does so. Special devices are used to detect the radiation evolved, and upon their use hinges the whole field of prospecting for and identifying the radioactive raw materials.

605. Which are the radioactive elements? The natural radioactivity of earth materials is due to three isotopes of uranium (each has a slightly different atomic weight), to thorium, to the elements that result when these disintegrate or *decay,* and to a certain number of light radioactive elements that are not part of any radioactive series. In addition to these natural elements, all the man-made elements, which are so marvelous a triumph of recent physics, are radioactive.

606. What are the radioactive series? These are groups of elements that originate with a radioactive element, which undergoes changes in a regular fashion, giving rise to other elements known as *daughter elements.* Each of these in turn becomes the parent of other radioactive elements until the final product is reached—this in each case is lead, which is stable, and here the process ceases.

607. Which are the isotopes of uranium? Uranium-238 is by far the most abundant of the three natural isotopes of this metal, constituting 99.28 per cent of the total. The radioactive series that begins with this isotope includes such well-known products as radium and radon, and ends with stable lead-206.

Uranium-235, with a percentage of 0.71, is the progenitor of the so-called *actinouranium family,* which includes actinium and ends with stable lead-207.

Uranium-234 is present only to the extent of 0.0058 per cent of the total uranium, and so is of little significance.

608. What is the thorium family? This is a radioactive series that begins with thorium-232 and concludes with stable lead-208. Thorium is present in the average primary or igneous rocks (see Chapter 2) to the amount of 11.5 grams per ton, compared to 4 grams per ton for the combined uranium isotopes; nevertheless, uranium is more than 3 times as abundant as thorium in sea water.

609. Which are the lighter radioactive elements? About a dozen of the chemical elements having smaller atomic weights than lead possess isotopes that are naturally radioactive. These change into other elements but do not belong to a radioactive series. The most important, because it is so abundant in common minerals and rocks, is potassium-40, which is transformed into calcium and argon. Potassium is present especially in the feldspars, but also in numerous other familiar minerals. Carbon-14, which decays to nitrogen, is of particular interest to students of history, archeology, and the earth sciences because it is being used as a means of accurately dating organic substances up to about 50,000 years old.

610. What is fissionable material? The term fissionable material refers to material capable of releasing substantial quantities of energy through nuclear chain reaction. By means of it weapons are produced and energy which can be converted into power is released. It includes uranium-235, present in natural uranium in the proportion of one part in 140. Although chemically identical with the other uranium isotopes, it can be separated because of its different atomic weight, as is done from uranium hexafluoride in the gaseous-diffusion plants at Oak Ridge, Tennessee; Paducah, Kentucky; and Pike County, Ohio. Fissionable material also includes plutonium (see Question 611) and any material artificially enriched by these fissionable materials.

611. What is plutonium? Plutonium is a fissionable element produced artificially in an *atomic pile* by bombarding metallic uranium-238 with neutrons in nuclear reactors, as is done at Hanford, Washington, and Aiken, South Carolina. Neutrons are the unchanged particles in the nucleus of an atom.

612. Is thorium fissionable?   No, for unlike uranium, thorium does not have a natural fissionable isotope. When, however, it is bombarded by neutrons, it turns into uranium-235, which is a fissionable material.

613. What is radon?   One of the intermediate products of the decay of uranium-238 to lead-206 is a gas called radon. It is highly penetrating and often is a source of confusion, leading the prospector to believe that the radioactivity due to it is actually coming from a uranium deposit, which may be some distance away or buried deeply beneath the soil that contains the escaping radon.

614. What is the relation between radium and uranium?   Radium is one of the most distinctive disintegration products of uranium-238. Until the emergence of the atomic age, radium was the only radioactive substance familiar to the general public. Its use in medicine was spectacular, but even this has been reduced by the development of man-made radioisotopes, of which iodine and cobalt are two of the best known, because these are cheaper and more flexible in use. In mineral deposits that have reached a state of equilibrium (see Question 654), there is a nearly constant ratio between radium and its parent element—one part of radium is present to 3,400,000 parts of uranium. The richest uranium ores contain less than one-quarter gram of radium per ton; some have been worked for as little as 1 gram of radium in 300 tons, so valuable is this rare metal, averaging 1 part in about a million million parts of rock in the crust of the earth.

615. When was radium discovered?   The existence of this element was shown in 1898 at the Sarbonne in Paris by Pierre Curie, Marie Curie, and G. Bemont. Through a complete chemical analysis of pitchblende (see Question 623), polonium was discovered at the same time. In 1902 Mme. Curie isolated the pure salt of radium, and in 1910 she and A. Debierne succeeded in producing radium metal.

616. Where has radium been obtained? The first major production of radium was in the United States, from the carnotite deposits of the Colorado Plateau (see Question 659); processing was carried on mainly in Denver and Pittsburgh, between 1911 and 1923. The mines of Joachimsthal in Bohemia (now Czechoslovakia) furnished the original raw material and were the principal factor in this specialized industry for a number of years. The rich Belgian Congo deposits, discovered in 1913, began to yield radium in 1922 when a refinery put into operation at Oolen, Belgium, dominated the world market. In 1933 a refinery at Port Hope, Ontario, started to produce radium from the Great Bear Lake deposits, which had been found in 1930.

617. What is a radium dial? Watches, clocks, and meters that have dials to be read in the dark are treated with a luminescent paint made from zinc sulfide. A very small concentration of radium salt used to be added, but for the sake of safety this has been replaced by tritium, which is radioactive hydrogen.

618. What are source materials? Virtually a legal rather than a technical term, source material was defined in the Atomic Energy Act of 1946 as "uranium, thorium, or any other material which is determined by the (Atomic Energy) Commission, with the approval of the President, to be peculiarly essential to the production of fissionable materials; but includes ores only if they contain one or more of the foregoing materials in such concentration as the Commission may by regulation determine from time to time."

Minerals of uranium and thorium belong to this classification only if they are present to the amount of 0.05 per cent or more, separately or together.

619. How are uranium and thorium present in minerals? Uranium forms two types of compounds, called uranous and uranyl, which occur in many minerals. Thorium, on the other hand, forms just one type of compound and is an important constituent of relatively few minerals. About 85 well-defined uranium and thorium minerals have been named and described, but new ones are being discovered yearly, and the old ones are in a constant state of being restudied and redefined, so that the matter of nomenclature is in a state of flux and is likely to continue so for some time to come. At least 100 names are currently worthy of serious consideration.

620. What are the primary radioactive minerals? Formed mainly by rising hot mineralizing solutions, the primary minerals of uranium and thorium are dark-colored (black to brown), opaque to semitranslucent minerals. They are classified chiefly as oxides, multiple oxides, and some silicates.

621. Which are the primary uranium ores? There are five primary uranium minerals of economic significance. These are uraninite, pitchblende, davidite, coffinite, and brannerite. Uraninite and pitchblende are fundamentally related; pitchblende may even be regarded as a type of uraninite.

622. What are the characteristics of uraninite? Ideally, uraninite is a uranium oxide with the composition UO_2. As the tetravalent uranium is oxidized to hexavalent uranium—these terms refer to the chemical combining power of the element—the proportion of uranium varies, and it usually ranges from about 50 to 85 per cent U_3O_8, which is the standard for buying and selling uranium minerals. Uraninite often occurs in cubic or octahedral crystals, sometimes of large size. It is grayish black, sometimes with a greenish cast, and is rather hard. Although it is found in various kinds of ore deposits, its most widespread occurrence is in pegmatites.

623. What are the features of pitchblende? The massive variety of uraninite is called pitchblende, from its pitchy luster. It is more typical of vein deposits and is the basis of nearly all the world's high-grade uranium deposits. Pieces weighing 20 tons have been found at Katanga in the Congo Republic. Pitchblende is typically fine grained, having a rounded form and radiating structure, although it takes on diverse aspects from one place to another. Because lacking definite crystallization, pitchblende is not so pure as uraninite, being generally a mixture of UO_2 and UO_3, with about 50 to 80 per cent U_3O_8.

624. What is davidite like? Becoming a source of uranium in 1951 when it was produced at the Radium Hill mine near Olary,

South Australia, davidite is an iron-titanium oxide containing rare earth elements (chiefly of the cerium group, see Question 583) and 7 to 20 per cent U_3O_8, together with up to 0.12 per cent thorium. It is a black mineral, perhaps with a reddish crust; in thin splinters it is translucent and reddish brown or red. It has a glassy to submetallic luster, is moderately hard, and is somewhat lighter than pitchblende. Never occurring in rounded shapes like pitchblende, it favors irregular angular forms, sometimes with crystal outlines.

625. What is the nature of coffinite?　First described as recently as 1955, coffinite has been shown to be a major uranium mineral in the Colorado Plateau region (see Question 659). It closely resembles fine-grained pitchblende and is intimately associated with organic (carbonaceous) material. Except in the finest particles it is black and has a bright luster.

626. What is brannerite?　Significant chiefly for its occurrence at Blind River, Ontario (see Question 661), brannerite is, when fresh, a black to reddish brown mineral, not especially distinctive in appearance. It has moderate hardness and heaviness (specific gravity). Chemically, it is a complex silicate.

627. What are the secondary radioactive minerals?　These are the minerals that have altered from the primary minerals (see Question 620). As different as can be from the brown and black primary minerals, they occur in bright colors easily recognized in the field. E. William Heinrich has listed these as orange, orange red, and amber; yellow and greenish yellow; yellow green; and green. Some fluoresce under ultraviolet light, giving an even more brilliant effect. They are translucent to transparent, and are found as delicate needles, flakes, or as earthy and powdery material. Chemically, they are classed as hydrous oxides, carbonates, sulfates, phosphates, arsenates, vanadates, and silicates, and they contain little thorium.

628. Which are the secondary uranium ores?　Uranium ores (that is, minerals of commercial value) of secondary origin are practically confined to the following: carnotite, tyuyamunite and metatyuyamunite, torbernite and metatorbernite, autunite and meta-autunite, and uranophane. Many more secondary uranium minerals are known but are not mined except incident to the recovery of those named above or of the primary ore minerals.

629. What is carnotite like?   This lemon-yellow mineral is probably the most abundant of all the secondary uranium minerals. In rare micalike flakes it is brilliant, but usually carnotite is found in soft powdery masses or in thin films or stains on various minerals and rocks. Its composition is that of a potassium-uranium vanadate, $K_2(UO_2)_2(UO_4)_2 \cdot (1–3)H_2O$. Its content of U_3O_8 is 50 to 55 per cent.

630. What are the characteristics of tyuyamunite?   In the Alai Range of Russian Turkestan is a limestone hill called Tyuya Muyum, overlooking the gorge of the Aravan River. At this locality—reportedly mined for copper in the Bronze Age—was found the mineral that was to be named tyuyamunite—omitting one syllable, which won't be missed. The mineral is slightly more greenish than carnotite but otherwise looks just like it. In chemical composition it is also similar to carnotite, but has calcium instead of potassium; its formula is $Ca(UO_2)_2(VO_4)_2 \cdot (7–10\frac{1}{2})H_2O$. With 3 to 5 molecules of water instead, the mineral becomes *metatyuyamunite*. The U_3O_8 content of these is between 48 and 55 per cent.

631. What is the nature of torbernite?   This is a bright green mineral growing in flat, square translucent crystals having a pearly luster. It is a hydrous copper uranium phosphate, $Cu(UO_2)_2(PO_4)_2 \cdot (8–12)H_2O$. With a smaller amount of water, the mineral grades into *metatorbernite,* which seems to be the more common of the two. They have about 60 per cent U_3O_8.

632. What are the properties of autunite?   As calcium substitutes for copper, torbernite is replaced by autunite. This is almost always yellow of a lemon or sulfur hue, but with some copper it is apple green. The bright yellow or greenish yellow fluorescence is a most noteworthy aspect of this mineral. With a slightly lower water content, the material is known as *meta-autunite.* Both closely resemble torbernite and metatorbernite in form, occurring in scattered small translucent crystals, which are rectangular, square, or octagonal and flat, or as thin coatings and stains. Autunite has the formula $Ca(UO_2)_2(PO_4)_2 \cdot (10-12H_2O)$, with about 60 per cent U_3O_8.

633. What is uranophane like? The commonest of the uranium silicates, uranophane is found as tiny crystals, fine fibers, or stains and coatings. It is yellow, sometimes pale and sometimes orangish. In composition it is a hydrous calcium uranium silicate, $Ca(UO_2)_2$-$(SiO_3)_2$ $(OH)_2 \cdot 5H_2O$, with a U_3O_8 content of about 65 per cent.

634. What is schroeckingerite? This is a complex uranium mineral that has been mined at Marysvale, Utah, and near Wamsutter, Wyoming. It ranks as a marginal ore mineral and is of little commercial importance. It is yellow to greenish yellow and fluoresces strongly in similar colors. When first found in Wyoming it was named *dakeite* after Dr. Henry C. Dake, then editor of the *Mineralogist,* Portland, Oregon, but the older name of European origin was found to be the proper one.

635. What is gummite? Once thought to be an independent orange-red to yellow uranium mineral, having the general appearance of gum, gummite is now known to be a variable fine-grained mixture of miscellaneous secondary uranium minerals, together with hydrous oxides and silicates. Clarkeite is a common constituent. Fine specimens have come from localities in North Carolina (Spruce Pine) and New Hampshire (Grafton).

636. Which are the thorium minerals? Because thorium does not tend to form secondary minerals, there are fewer thorium than uranium minerals. Yet more than 100 minerals have at least traces of thorium, and this element may be present in any uranium mineral. Uranium, in turn, may be found in any thorium mineral.

Although thorianite and thorite are the only two minerals in which thorium is the major constituent, monazite is the most important source of thorium and the only one that can be regarded as an ore of the metal. The other thorium minerals are natural compounds of the rare earths (see Question 583) and zirconium, in which the thorium is a minor element, as indeed it is in monazite itself.

637. What are the properties of thorianite? Grading completely into uraninite (see Question 622), thorianite is an oxide, ThO_2, and the division between the two members of this series is an arbitrary one, placed at the ratio of 1:1 thorium to uranium. Thorianite is a black to brownish or grayish mineral, rather hard and demonstrably heavy; it is almost identical in appearance to uraninite. It occurs mainly in marble and placer deposits containing gold and tin.

638. What are the features of thorite? A thorium silicate, $ThSiO_4$, thorite is black, greenish black, or brown and occurs in small square crystals with pyramid-shaped ends. It is moderately hard and heavy. When altered by a breakdown of its atomic structure this mineral assumes green and other bright colors more resembling those of the secondary uranium minerals.

639. What are the characteristics of monazite? This, the most abundant thorium-bearing mineral, is a phosphate of rare earths, mainly cerium. Its formula may be written $(Ce,La)PO_4$. The percentage of thorium varies, usually being between 1 and 15 per cent thorium oxide (ThO_2). The colors of monazite are yellow, yellow brown, red brown, and even greenish. It is fairly heavy and hard and makes an ideal placer mineral, being found in such deposits in a world-wide distribution. The original crystals are apt to be tablet shaped. Monazite is obtained mostly as a byproduct of placer mining, and the thorium is a byproduct of the rare earths for which this mineral is principally sought.

640. What is thucolite? A number of strange radioactive hydrocarbons go under the name thucolite, which was derived by H. V. Ellsworth from the symbols of the elements that are present— *th*orium, *u*ranium, *c*arbon, *o*xygen, plus *lite*. The radioactivity is due mainly to uraninite or pitchblende, mixed with one or more hydrocarbons or oxyhydrocarbons. Mineral inclusions are responsible for the titanium, iron, and other metals that show up in analyses.

641. Which are the radioactive blacks? These are a group of dark minerals, mostly having a pitchy or glassy luster, and containing enough uranium or thorium to be radioactive. They are mostly rare-earth minerals and are much alike in their appearance, so that it is easier to classify them as radioactive blacks than to try to name them individually. Allanite, gadolinite, and the samarskite-yttrotantalite, euxenite-polycrase, and fergusonite-formanite series are among the most familiar of these minerals.

642. What radiation is given off by radioactive minerals? Most of the radiation that comes from radioactive minerals is due to the intermediate daughter elements rather than to uranium or thorium themselves, but of course they are the primary source of it all. Three types of radiation exist; these are known as alpha, beta, and gamma radiation. Each has a different nature and behaves in its own distinctive fashion. In addition, heat energy is emitted and the gas helium is also given off.

643. What is alpha radiation? This radiation consists of particles which are atoms of helium stripped of their two electrons (outer negative charges), leaving only the positively charged nucleus. Alpha radiation has little power of penetration and can be stopped by a few inches of air or a few sheets of paper. It is not useful in ordinary prospecting methods.

644. What is beta radiation? Having a higher penetrating ability than alpha particles, beta radiation requires perhaps a foot of air or a thin sheet of metal to absorb it. It consists of electrons and so has a negative charge. These particles can be deflected from their paths by a magnet and they will darken a photographic plate. Some prospecting devices utilize beta radiation for measuring radioactivity.

645. What is gamma radiation? Unlike the other two types of radiation, gamma rays are true rays like those of light and X-rays. Thus, they are not electrically charged. They have a high degree of penetrating power and are the ones employed to detect radioactivity in most prospecting equipment. Nevertheless, they can be stopped by about 3 inches of lead, 1 foot of rock, $2\frac{1}{2}$ feet of water, or several hundred feet of air.

646. Can radioactivity be seen in the dark? No, although fluorescence and phosphorescence can be, but these effects are not due to radioactivity. Many nonradioactive minerals and other substances glow in the dark.

647. Is radioactivity magnetic?   There are no magnetic properties to radioactivity. It does not influence a compass or watch, no matter how many stories are told to the contrary.

648. Are radioactive minerals dangerous?   Inasmuch as radioactive minerals are present in all the rocks of the earth's crust, exposure to them in natural deposits has no danger. If held next to the skin for long periods of time, they can cause radioactive burns. Mining radioactive minerals is scarcely more dangerous than any other kind of mining, which is always a hazardous occupation and requires ventilation under all circumstances.

649. Is radon gas healthful?*   There is no evidence that it is. Some mine tunnels in various parts of the country are operated as places of treatment for arthritis and rheumatism. One should remember that underground openings of any type are apt to be damp, and sitting in such an atmosphere is usually not recommended for these disorders. The slight amount of radioactivity given off by the radon gas is ordinarily less than that of the luminous dial on a watch, unless there is such an abnormally high concentration that an immediate departure for reasons of safety is advisable.

650. How does a Geiger counter work?   The most general means of detecting and measuring radioactivity is through the use of the Geiger counter. Beginning as a bulky laboratory instrument, it has now developed into a portable, lightweight, and relatively inexpensive piece of equipment that is remarkably versatile.

Gamma rays and some beta rays penetrate the walls of the Geiger-Mueller tube, where they collide with a molecule of an inert gas inside it and yield changed particles. Some of these are attracted toward a metal wire running the length of the tube and produce an electrical impulse, which is amplified. This is then recorded on a meter or else it causes an audible click in a set of earphones or a flash in a neon light. In the portable instruments batteries supply the power which does these things as well as creating a high voltage between the wall of the tube and the center wire.

*IMPORTANT: See new Publisher's Note on page v.

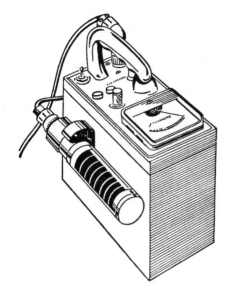

Portable Geiger counter

651. What is a scintillation counter? Newer in its applications than the Geiger counter is the scintillation counter. ("Scintillometer" is the trade name of a particular make.) It is more expensive but also more delicate than a Geiger counter; each has its own advantages. Instead of a Geiger-Mueller tube, the scintillation counter has a crystal (known as a phosphor) and a photomultiplier tube, which is sensitive to flashes of light produced in the crystal by gamma rays from outside. The electrical pulses are amplified and recorded on a meter.

652. What is background count? The presence of some radioactivity in all soils and rocks, in every natural and man-made object—even in the Geiger and scintillation counters themselves—produces the background count which is recorded even in the absence of radioactive minerals. This must be subtracted from the overall reading, in order to arrive at the amount that is due to the uranium or thorium sample. Most of the background count comes from cosmic rays; this radiation from outer space varies from place to place and from time to time. It increases with altitude and latitude. The rest of the background count is also variable and depends to a large extent upon the kind of rock on the ground at a given place.

653. How does mass effect operate?   The total amount of radio-activity that reaches the tube of a Geiger counter or the crystal of a scintillation counter—not the percentage of uranium or thorium in the specimen—is what is recorded by the meter, light, or earphone. Thus, a large specimen will give a higher count than a small one, and surrounding rock material will affect the "reading" obtained. Hence comparison should be made with a sample that has been standardized as to strength, and the specimens should be held at the same distance each time, in order to eliminate the "mass effect."

654. What is equilibrium effect?   When the entire series of radio-active elements is in a state of equilibrium, each member is being formed at the same rate as it decays to the member into which it changes. Otherwise, the radioactivity count will not correspond to the actual amount of uranium that is present. Uranium, for example, be-ing soluble in underground water, may be carried away, leaving its daughter elements which respond well to the counter but have no commercial value. When uranium or thorium are separated from the rest of the series, they immediately begin to form them again. About one million years is required for the elements in each series to ac-cumulate in their original proportions. Owing to the equilibrium ef-fect, the results of a chemical analysis, upon which sales of radio-active materials are made, may be pleasingly good or disappointingly low, in comparison with the indications given by a Geiger or scintilla-tion counter.

655. How can radioactivity write its autograph?   Radioactivity cannot be seen, felt, or heard unless received and recorded by ap-propriate instruments which transform it into other kinds of energy. The simplest way to indicate the existence of radioactivity—the way, in fact, that it was first discovered by accident in 1896 by Henri Becquerel—is by means of photographic film. The invisible radia-tion from uranium and thorium minerals blackens an unexposed film just as sunlight does, producing a *radioautograph*. If a metallic ob-ject such as a key or coin is placed between the film and the mineral, an outline of it will show on the film after it is developed. The strength of the mineral and the kind of film will influence the time required and the sharpness of the image.

656. How is a scintilloscope used? A small cylinder containing a magnifying lens at the eyepiece and a screen coated with zinc sulfide powder at the other end can be used to detect radioactivity by the flashes of light that are produced on the screen in a dark room. This scintilloscope is related to the "radium" dial of a watch or clock (see Question 617).

657. What is the electroscope test? Radiation is detected by the closing together of two metallic leaves of gold or aluminum, which are suspended from a metal rod inside a glass container—the whole device being known as an electroscope. This has previously been "charged" with a rubbed glass or hard rubber rod, which separates the leaves, and the radioactive discharge from a mineral brings them together again.

658. How is the amount of uranium determined? The strength of radioactivity is one thing, but the amount of uranium that is actually present may be quite another. This depends partly upon the amount of ore available—a single rich specimen of pitchblende does not make a mine. Thorium, furthermore, is also radioactive (though about one-third as strong as the uranium series), but it has at present no fixed value in the atomic energy program. Then, as we have seen in Question 654, most of the radioactivity is recorded from the daughter elements while the uranium itself, which is all that is sought for or bought, may have been dissolved away or otherwise be "out of equilibrium" (see Question 654)—uranium is highly soluble in natural subsurface water. For all these reasons, and still others, the only sure determination of the amount of uranium in an ore is by means of a standard chemical analysis.

659. What is the Colorado Plateau? Described as a geologic show-case, the Colorado Plateau is a classic region for the occurrence of uranium in the western part of the United States. It covers about 150,000 square miles in the states of Arizona, Utah, New Mexico, and Colorado—roughly the area of the Colorado River drainage system. It consists of many plateaus, together with a diversity of plains, valleys, mesas, and mountains. The ores are principally of the carnotite-roscoelite type derived from uraninite, coffinite, and sundry vanadium minerals, and they contain vanadium and copper in addition to the uranium. They are present in nearly thirty different geologic formations, of which the Morrison is the most productive. The Ute and Navajo Indians used the bright secondary minerals for paint, and these deposits have within the 20th Century been a source of radium, uranium, and vanadium, separately and together.

Mining uranium in the Colorado Plateau area

660. What is the relation between uranium and organic substances? Apart from the fact that certain types of plants grow in a conspicuous fashion in soil derived from uranium-bearing minerals, there is a close association between uranium and the carbon of organic origin. In the most favorable strata of sedimentary rocks in the Colorado Plateau, the presence of plant debris, accumulated in meanders of former streams, helped to localize uranium deposits in such places. Fossil trees and their parts, ranging from trunks to shredded leaves, have had a strong affinity for the uranium solutions, which settled among them and replaced them with mineral matter. Petroleum products, carbonized wood, petrified wood, fossil shells, and dinosaur bones are among the organic and fossil substances intimately found with the uranium in the deposits of the Colorado Plateau. Buried dinosaur bones, richly endowed with carnotite, have become the site of many a uranium mine in this region.

661. Where is Blind River? About midway between Sault Ste.

Marie and Sudbury, in Ontario, is the Blind River area in the Algoma district. Here are located larger uranium resources than those of all the United States combined. Going against the discouraging results of surface exploration, diamond drilling conducted by Franc R. Joubin proved the existence at depth of large tonnages of low-grade ore, of pitchblende and brannerite, making this one of the most important uranium deposits in the world.

662. Where is the greatest uranium deposit in the United States? First discovered in 1955, the uranium mineralization of Ambrosia Lake, New Mexico, ranks first in the United States in terms of total reserves, making New Mexico the leading domestic source of radioactive materials. An asphaltic substance, derived from petroleum, is mixed with coffinite and served to precipitate the uranium.

663. Where is the Shinkolobwe mine? This, the largest and most noted uranium deposit in the world, is in the Katanga district of the Belgian Congo, near the border of Northern Rhodesia, 80 miles northwest of Elisabethville. A large number of colorful secondary uranium minerals, produced by deep weathering in this tropical climate, come from here; many were first found and named from this locality, which was discovered in 1915 by a British army officer. Mining began in 1921 and this was the foremost source of radium until the Eldorado mine at Great Bear Lake in the Northwest Territories, Canada, was opened in 1933 and proved a strong competitor. The complete exhaustion of the ore reserves of the Shinkolobwe mine was announced in 1960, coincident with the turbulent political events in the newly established Congo Republic.

XI. GEMS

Introduction. Gems are certain natural substances—mostly minerals —and their man-made substitutes, regarded by the human race as desirable for personal decoration or for personal adornment because of their beauty, durability, and rarity. When placed in a suitable setting, a gem becomes a jewel.

Some few gems are of organic origin and so are not minerals. Several gems are rocks. An increasing number of gems are artificial, growing in the laboratory or factory rather than in the earth, and these are members of the Mineral Kingdom only by courtesy—although their identity is not always easy to determine. The term *gemstone* means virtually the same as gem, but obviously it would not be proper to use it in referring to something as unlike a stone as a pearl or piece of amber.

664. What is gemology? Gemology is the science or study of gems. It includes the history and lore of gems, the art of cutting and mounting them, and even the merchandising of gems. Beginning in Europe, the gemological movement has spread to all the continents. In 1913 the Gemmological Association of Great Britain was established in London as an affiliate of the National Association of Goldsmiths of Great Britain and Ireland. In 1931 the Gemological Institute of America was founded in Los Angeles, and associated with it is the American Gem Society. There are similar national organizations in Sweden, Norway, Finland, the Netherlands, Belgium, France, Switzerland, Canada, Brazil, and Australia. Most of the members are jewelers or mineralogists.

665. Which are the precious stones? There is no real distinction between the so-called precious and semiprecious stones. Based upon rarity, diamond is much more abundant, hence less "precious" than many gems costing a good deal less per carat. Some choice qualities of otherwise common gems bring a higher price than the ordinary grades of the rarer ones. The long-familiar precious stones are diamond, ruby, sapphire, and emerald, but some authorities have not hesitated to add opal, cat's-eye, alexandrite, and other gems even less well known. *Semiprecious* should be an obsolete word, although still popularly used for quartz and similar gemstones that can be found by the average mineral collector.

666. Which is the rarest gem?   In gem quality such minerals as brazilianite and sillimanite are known in only a few specimens altogether. Hence, these and others like them are really the rarest gems. From the standpoint of price and a regular market, however, emerald has for some time been considered the most valuable gem, bringing a higher price per carat than any other gem of the same quality, and considerably more than diamond.

667. How are gems weighed?   Some of the less valuable gems are sold by the gram, pennyweight, ounce, or pound. Most gems, however, are weighed in *carats*. A carat (not to be confused with *karat,* which refers to the purity of gold alloys, see Question 371) was originally the weight of a seed of the locust tree growing in Mediterranean countries. Of course, it varied from place to place and time to time. The carat is now internationally standardized at 200 milligrams or $\frac{2}{10}$ gram, and is referred to as the metric carat, having been legalized in the United States in 1913. There are about 150 carats to the ounce. The carat is divided into 100 parts called *points*. A special unit, known as the *pearl grain,* is used for pearls; each weighs $\frac{1}{4}$ carat.

668. What is a cameo?   A cameo is a carved gem in which the design stands in relief. Cameos were first introduced about 300 B.C. They serve only for the purpose of decoration, in contrast to the older form of carving known as the *intaglio,* in which the design is cut into the surface—originally in order to serve as a seal, which was the personal, business, and royal signature in ancient times. Although intaglios are usually engraved in hard stones, such as hematite, cameos appear frequently in soft materials, such as coral, as well as in the more durable gems, including onyx and other varieties of chalcedony (see Questions 727–728).

669. What is a scarab?   A scarab is a carved representation of a beetle. As the symbol of the immortality of the soul, it had great religious significance in ancient Egypt, becoming prominent about the time of the 9th dynasty. It was fashioned out of various gem stones, which were then used both for amulets or charms and for seals.

670. What are birthstones?   The custom of wearing a gem to correspond with the date of one's birth goes back to 16th-Century Germany or Poland. The appropriate sign of the zodiac was first used rather than the month of the calendar. The idea seems to have begun with the Biblical series of 12 engraved gems that adorned the high priest's breastplate of judgment (*Exodus* 28), and then to have been transferred to the foundation stones of the holy city, New Jerusalem (*Revelation* 21). The list of birthstones has undergone many changes in recent centuries. Below is given a fairly well accepted list as used in the United States.

January	Garnet
February	Amethyst
March	Bloodstone, aquamarine
April	Diamond
May	Emerald
June	Pearl, moonstone
July	Ruby
August	Sardonyx, peridot
September	Sapphire
October	Opal, tourmaline
November	Topaz
December	Turquois, lapis lazuli

671. Which is the simplest gem?   In chemical composition, diamond is the simplest gem, for it consists solely of carbon, which has crystallized in the isometric crystal system (see Question 110). Other gems are oxides (as corundum), carbonates (as smithsonite), phosphates (as turquois), and other chemical compounds (see Question 15). Most gems are classed as silicates, some of which are of bewildering complexity. Take tourmaline, for example: $(Na,Ca)(Li,Mg,Fe,Al)_9B_3Si_6(O,OH)_{31}$. No wonder that John Ruskin said, "The chemistry of it is more like a medieval doctor's prescription than the making of a respectable mineral!"

672. Which gems are rocks?   Lapis lazuli, a blue gem of ancient and honorable lineage, is a rock of metamorphic origin (see Chapter V). The primitive mines of lapis lazuli in the Badakhshan district of

Afghanistan, which have been worked for 6,000 years, were visited by Marco Polo in 1271. Other important deposits are near Lake Baikal in Siberia and in several places in Chile. Lapis lazuli consists of haüynite and two related blue minerals of the sodalite group, together with white calcite and brassy-colored pyrite. This is the gem called sapphire in the Bible.

Natural glass, of which three kinds have been used as gems, is another gem-rock. Obsidian (see Question 207) is the best-known natural glass. Tektites (described under Meteorites, Question 237) belong to this group, as does the substance known as silica-glass, which was discovered in 1932 in the Libyan Desert and which cuts into pale yellowish-green gems.

673. Which gems are of organic origin? Pearl, coral, amber, and jet are the four organic gems. Although they contain calcium carbonate, a mineral substance, pearls are the product of certain mollusks which secrete the pearl-stuff to allay the discomfort of an irritation caused by disease, a parasite, or a foreign particle. The result is the "queen of gems," formed inside the protective mantle that surrounds the soft parts of the animal's body, within the shell.

Coral is the accumulated skeletal material of tiny marine animals called polyps, which live in branching colonies. Extracting calcium carbonate from the water, they deposit it in their tissues and build their hard framework of hollow tubes, which remains after their death.

Whereas pearl and coral are of animal origin, amber and jet are derived from plants. Amber is the fossil resin of early coniferous trees (see Questions 737–739). Jet is a compact black variety of lignite coal.

674. What is refraction in gems? The bending of a ray of light when it enters a gem, or emerges from it, is termed refraction. The extent of the bending, which results from the sudden change in the speed of the light, is a measure of the optical density of the gem. It is expressed mathematically as the *index of refraction,* which is the ratio of the velocity of light in air to that in the gem. Several ways may be used to determine this value, but gemologists usually use a handy instrument known as a *refractometer,* which gives a direct reading on a simple scale and helps to identify the gem. The brilliancy so characteristic of a finely cut diamond depends largely upon its

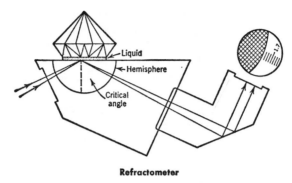

Refractometer

high index of refraction (2.42), whereby light that travels into and through a diamond is made to bend so as to return to the eye with a minimum of loss through the bottom of the stone. In comparison, white topaz (about 1.63) and clear quartz (about 1.55), no matter how well they are cut, will appear glassy and lifeless.

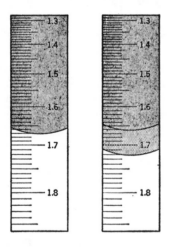

Refractometer readings for singly and doubly refractive gems

675. What is dispersion? When bent or refracted, white light is automatically separated into its component colors—the spectrum, as best seen in the rainbow. In a gem this spread of colors is known as *fire;* technically it is dispersion, expressed as the difference in the index of refraction of the red and violet rays. Of the familiar gems, diamond has the most dispersion (0.044), and it is this fire, combined with the high index of refraction (see Question 674) and the "hard" (adamantine) luster that glorify the "king of gems." Certain other gems, however, have an even greater dispersion—the green variety of andradite garnet (called demantoid), 0.057; cassiterite,

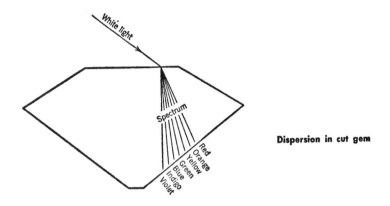

Dispersion in cut gem

0.671; and sphalerite, 0.156. Two synthetic gems, strontium titanate (0.19) and titanium oxide (0.28), exceed even sphalerite in this respect, and the "unnatural" effect of tiny rainbows is readily observed.

676. What is dichroism? When a ray of light enters a gem, it is divided into two rays, unless the gem belongs to the isometric crystal system (see Question 110) or is noncrystalline and hence is *singly refractive* in both cases. Each of the two rays travels at a different velocity, except in certain special directions, and may show a dif-

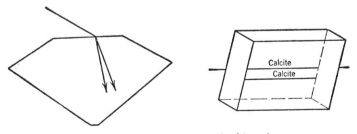

Double refraction in cut gem and calcite prism

ferent color. This effect, which occurs only in the *doubly refractive* gems, is known as dichroism. It can be seen with a petrographic microscope, used by professional mineralogists, but it can be observed even more readily with a simple instrument called a *dichroscope*. A piece of the Iceland spar variety of calcite, mounted with a magnifying

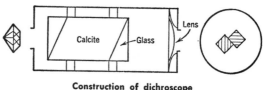

Construction of dichroscope

lens inside a short tube, increases the double image produced by the gem and shows the twin colors side by side. Gems belonging to the orthorhombic monoclinic, or triclinic systems are even more complex, possessing three principal colors, but only two can be seen at a time. The more general term *pleochroism* is often used, nevertheless.

677. What makes the "star" in a star sapphire? As you turn a spool of thread in your hand, a ray of light is seen running at right angles to the fibers. Similarly, a crack in glass shows a beam of light at right angles to it. The effect is called *diffraction,* and it accounts for the star in a star sapphire, star ruby, or any *asteriated* (star) stone. In such gems the cause of the light ray is either an inclusion of a foreign substance, perhaps another mineral or an excess of coloring matter, or else a minute hollow space. A hexagonal crystal, as sapphire (corundum) is, will have three rays meeting in the center, as drawn here. When cut with a rounded top, the gem seems to focus these rays in the starlike pattern.

678. Which other gems are asteriated? Although corundum (ruby and sapphire) is the likeliest gem mineral to show asterism, others do so in some specimens. Asteriated garnet from Idaho is often cut into spheres, so that the star follows the eye as the ball is turned. Unlike corundum, however, garnet has a four-rayed star, because of its cubic crystal symmetry. Rose quartz, beryl (in its aquamarine variety), and green zircon are also sometimes asteriated.

679. What makes the "eye" in cat's-eye? The band of light in such gems as cat's-eye, tiger's-eye, and hawk's-eye is the result of the parallel alignment of mineral fibers, which diffract the light in a manner very similar to the star stones described above, except that there is only one direction to the structure. In the gems mentioned here, the effect is known as *chatoyancy,* which word comes from the French name for cat. The valuable kind of cat's-eye is a rich variety of chrysoberyl; quartz cat's-eye is generally of an inferior quality. Tiger's-eye and hawk's-eye are both quartz that has altered from a previous blue asbestos mineral known as crocidolite, but the iron in tiger's-eye has oxidized to a golden-yellow color which makes this gem preferred to the still-blue hawk's-eye.

These, however, are not the only gems that display chatoyancy. Tourmaline may on occasion show it vividly, and beryl, apatite, diopside, and scapolite also have their cat's-eye varieties. The "Chinese cat's-eye" brought back from islands of the South Pacific during World War II is a common gastropod shell and is entirely unrelated to the gems.

680. What causes the color in opal? The pure rainbow colors that glorify opal above all other gems are due to the *interference* of light rays as they are reflected from extremely thin layers that differ slightly in their ability to refract (bend) the light that strikes them. Unlike the other principal gems, opal is a solidified gel, which is not of uniform composition or structure. This optical effect is like that seen in a film of soap on water, or of oil on water. The color of opal depends upon the direction in which it is viewed and the particular nature of the individual layers.

Moonstone, with its subdued blue sheen, and labradorite, with its spreading sheets of blue or green, also owe their eye-appeal to interference of light, caused by structural irregularities characteristic of feldspar.

681. Do gems form best in warm climates? This used to be believed by nearly everyone, because the finest gems seemed to be those coming from such tropical countries as India, Burma, and Ceylon. Even the natives of these Oriental lands thought that the gems grew in the soil, aided by rain and sun. When the study of geology showed that the original home of most of the gem minerals was in rocks forming deep in the crust of the earth, it was realized that the weather at the surface could have nothing to do with their quality. During recent centuries, moreover, excellent gems have been found in barren lands and inhospitable climates all over the world. Only a few gems, those of shallow secondary origin, are influenced by the atmosphere; turquois, for example, is favored by dryness, as in Iran, Egypt, and the southwestern United States.

682. Are ruby and sapphire related? Although usually thought of as widely different in appearance, ruby and sapphire are about as closely related as two gems can be. Both are color varieties of the same mineral species, known as *corundum*. Red corundum, colored by chromium oxide, is termed ruby. All the other hues of corundum go under the name sapphire, so that, in addition to the familiar blue sapphire, which owes its color to titanium oxide, there are also yellow sapphire, green sapphire, white (really colorless) sapphire, and others. Many confusing names of long standing are applied to colored corundum, such as "Oriental amethyst" for the purple variety, but their use is to be discouraged. A purple sapphire is actually a mixture of alternate red and blue layers, and a pale ruby grades imperceptibly into a pink sapphire, showing clearly how little essential difference there is from one interesting corundum gem to another.

683. Which other gems are related? All gems that are varieties of the same mineral species are intimately related, no matter how unlike they may appear in color, pattern, or other features. Thus the many varieties of quartz, of chalcedony, and of other gem minerals are fundamentally very much alike because they have the same chemical composition and atomic structure. Of the related gems besides ruby and sapphire (described above), and the common quartz and chalcedony gems (see Question 727), perhaps emerald and aquamarine are the best known. These are both varieties of the mineral *beryl,* as also are the rose-red morganite, and the golden-yellow heliodor. Alexandrite and cat's-eye are both varieties of *chrysoberyl* (see Questions 576, 726). Pyrope and almandite are two of the numerous kinds of *garnet* (see Question 723). And there are many other pairs and groups of related gems, proved to be so by the techniques of chemistry and physics—in contrast to pre-scientific times, when gems were classified almost solely according to color, which made all yellow gems topaz, and all green ones emerald.

684. What is a synthetic gem?   A gem that has the same chemical composition and atomic structure as a natural gem is its synthetic counterpart. When the resemblance is confined to superficial appearance only, the substance is referred to as an *imitation* gem, such as glass. A true synthetic gem may, however, be used commercially as a substitute for a quite different gem, as when synthetic purple sapphire (a variety of synthetic corundum) is sold instead of natural amethyst (a variety of quartz) because they look alike. The word *simulated* (most often used for pearls) means the same as imitation. All these are *artificial* gems. In addition there are four other kinds of man-made gems—*reconstructed* gems (applied almost exclusively to ruby, see Question 686), *composite* gems (built up of two or more separate pieces), *treated* gems, which are natural in origin but not in color (see Question 725), and *cultured* gems, which are pearls grown by a mollusk but instigated by man.

685. What is synthetic diamond made of?   Inasmuch as all true synthetic gems have the same chemical composition as the natural gems that they represent, synthetic diamond must be composed of carbon, as is the natural mineral. The source of carbon in the General Electric Company's synthetic diamonds has not yet been revealed, but is likely of simple organic origin, such as sugar. Sugar was used in earlier experiments in synthesizing diamond by Henri Moissan, Sir William Crooks, and Sir Charles Parsons.

686. What is a reconstructed stone?   This term is often wrongly used for any synthetic gem, but it is correctly applied to artificial ruby that is built up by fusing fragments of poor-quality natural stones in an oxyhydrogen flame. The color is restored by adding potassium bichromate to the mixture. Reconstructed rubies of this sort appeared on the market in 1885, but they have been entirely superseded by synthetic corundum made entirely of raw chemicals (see Question 687).

687. Who invented synthetic corundum?   After years of trial, synthetic red corundum, known as synthetic ruby, was first made by

Auguste Victor Louis Verneuil (1856–1913), a French chemist. His equipment, an inverted oxyhydrogen blowpipe called a chalumeau, is still used, with improvements, in the factory manufacture of synthetic gems. The powdered alumina and appropriate coloring matter are melted in the hot flame and dropped onto a pedestal which can be moved as the growth continues. The crystal, called a boule, builds up in cylindrical form, although as Verneuil originally produced it, it was pear-shaped. In attempts to create synthetic sapphire, Verneuil added magnesium but found that he had made an entirely different synthetic mineral, known as spinel. In 1909, however, he succeeded in synthesizing blue corundum, though the true sapphire color came somewhat later.

688. What is paste? Glass imitation gems have been known as paste since this term was introduced in 1662. The raw material consists of fused silica, potash, or soda, lead oxide, lime, and other chemicals, the most important of which are compounds of boron, phosphorus, fluorine, barium, zinc, and titanium. Owing to its content of lead, paste is usually bright (highly refractive) but soft and does not resist wear; it soon tarnishes from the effect of sulfur in the air. Although now becoming obsolescent, the term *strass* (named after Josef Strasser in 1820) is well known in the gem trade as the basis of imitation gems used to simulate diamond. *Rhinestones* are glass gems improved in brilliance or color by the use of foils, which are usually made of metal and placed on the lower facets; sometimes they are coated with mercury or pigment.

689. What is an Oriental gem? Strictly speaking, of course, an Oriental gem would be one that came from India, Burma, Ceylon, China, Japan, or elsewhere in Asia. However, the term is often used —or misused—to refer to the harder or more valuable gems of a given color. Thus, "Oriental emerald" is a green sapphire (a variety of corundum), which is harder than the true emerald, a variety of beryl. Likewise, "Oriental amethyst" is purple sapphire (corundum), harder and also more expensive than true amethyst, which is a variety of quartz. This usage of the word Oriental is a reminder of the days when the best gems reached Europe from the East and the hardest colored gems were distinguished in that way.

690. Where is the highest gem deposit? The Kashmir sapphire mines, situated in a valley at nearly 15,000 feet, are the highest gem locality in the world. Mount Antero, in the Sawatch Range in Colorado, is the highest in the United States. It is also the highest mineral deposit in North America. At an altitude of 14,245 feet are found fine crystals of blue aquamarine, together with rock crystal, smoky quartz, and other gems. This place is accessible only during the summer. It has been worked for its gems and mineral specimens for three-quarters of a century, and for a few years was a commercial source of beryllium. In addition to aquamarine (a variety of beryl), two other beryllium minerals—phenakite and bertrandite—occur in noteworthy quality.

691. Where is the deepest gem mine? The pit of the Kimberley diamond mine, nearly 4,000 feet deep, is the deepest large hole of man-made origin in the world. Hundreds of thousands of oil wells are much deeper than that, and metal mining is conducted in several countries at depths exceeding 12,000 feet, but the Kimberley pit is large in outline. The mines at Kimberley, in the Union of South Africa, were the first place where diamonds had ever been found in solid rocks in which they presumably had been formed, and the rough gems were recovered from open pits which were later merged into large mines. The DeBeers, Dutoitspan, Bultfontein, Wesselton, and Jagersfontein are other famous mines in the Kimberley area.

692. What gems are produced in the United States? A wide range of gems, especially of the less valuable or "semiprecious" kinds, have been found in the United States. Amateur collectors have been responsible for extensive finds of the quartz and chalcedony gems (see Question 727). Thousands of diamonds have come from Arkansas, but their influence on the commercial world has been slight. Sapphire from Montana is perhaps the principal gem that has been mined on an organized basis. The United States ranks among the leading nations in the production of turquois, tourmaline, opal, spodumene (of the kunzite variety), and amazonstone (a microcline feldspar). Variscite is almost exclusively an American gem, as are benitoite, beryllonite, pollucite, thomsonite, willemite, and zincite—almost all of very minor importance, though interesting enough.

693. Which gems have American names? Danburite, named after Danbury, Connecticut, where it was first found; benitoite, named after San Benito County, California, for the same reason; and shattuckite, named for the Shattuck mine, near Bisbee, Arizona, where it has been obtained, are the only gems that bear the names of mineral localities in the United States. In addition to these many American names have been given to local occurrences of minerals or rocks adapted to ornamental usage, chiefly by amateurs, but not recognized on an international scale or in scientific circles.

694. Where are the leading sources of gems? A few countries stand out above all others as producers of gems. From a hobby standpoint the United States doubtless accounts for more gem stones found, cut, and used than all the rest of the world combined. As commercial sources, however, certain other nations have nearly a monopoly. India and Burma, with their yield of diamond, ruby, sapphire, spinel, jade, and other choice gems, are exceptional. Tiny Ceylon rates even higher, considering its restricted area, from which come ruby and sapphire, alexandrite (a variety of chrysoberyl), spinel, zircon, topaz, garnet, tourmaline, and many other gems. Asia altogether produces nearly half of the world's supply of gems, excluding diamond. Diamond, however, amounts to 94.3 per cent of the world total, according to the latest available figures, which vary from year to year. In this market the Republic of South Africa is supreme. Outside of Asia and the diamond fields, the main countries in which gems are a significant product include Brazil, the Malagasy Republic, Australia, Colombia (for its emeralds), and the Soviet Union.

695. Are there any new gems? Apart from new trade names given to familiar gems, and the usual coining of names for stray patterns in quartz and chalcedony, a number of actually new gems have been discovered within the past few years. Several of these are entirely new minerals, previously unknown to science. The rest represent minerals already named, the gem varieties of which were not known. Of the new gems brazilianite, taaffeite, painite, and sinhalite deserve special attention (see Questions 696–699).

696. What is brazilianite? The most important of the brand-new minerals that have been found in gem quality is brazilianite. Named after its country of origin, this is a hydrous sodium-aluminum phosphate with the formula $NaAl_3(OH)_4(PO_4)_2$. Pale greenish-yellow in color, it is attractive but only moderately hard. Two gems, of 23 and 19 carats, have been cut from brazilianite, as well as numerous small ones.

697. What is taaffeite? Taaffeite, a pale mauve-colored gem named for Count Taaffe of Ireland who first suspected it to be a new mineral, was not identified until 1945 and is still extremely rare. It is a magnesium-beryllium aluminate, $MgBeAl_4O_8$, fairly heavy and very hard. The largest specimen, recognized in 1967 after having been found in Ceylon and already cut, weighs 5.34 carats. Like the others, it had been called spinel (see Question 708).

698. What is painite? The newest gem, described in 1957, is painite, a clear deep-red mineral, both heavy and remarkably hard. It was named after A. C. D. Pain, who first recognized its unusual nature from the single specimen available. Its composition is not known.

699. What is sinhalite? For a number of years prior to 1950, certain brown gems that were called olivine had been viewed with suspicion. They were all in cut form and so it was not possible to study the crystals. Finally in 1951 and 1952 specimens in the Mineral Gallery of the British Museum (Natural History) and the United States National Museum were examined with X-rays and found to be a new species of mineral. They were named sinhalite from the Sanskrit name for Ceylon, from where they had apparently come. In 1955 tiny crystals of the same mineral were discovered in rock in Warren County, New York. Sinhalite is a magnesium-aluminum borate, formula $MgAlBO_4$. A gem as large as 158 carats is owned by W. E. Phillips, of Los Angeles.

700. What is sillimanite? An example of a common mineral that entered the ranks of the gems only after being known in its ordinary form for more than a century is sillimanite. Bearing the name of the pioneer American scientist Benjamin Silliman (1779–1864), sillimanite usually occurs in a gray shade of brown or green, somewhat resembling jade but of little interest as a gem. In recent years, however, material having a pale sapphire-blue color has been uncovered in the ruby mines at Mogok, in Upper Burma. Poor examples of the same kind were known for a long while in the gem gravels of Ceylon, but they were mistaken for sapphire or cordierite, another gem that is often pale blue and is known as "water sapphire."

701. Which is the most famous gem? The Koh-i-nur diamond is without doubt the pre-eminent individual gem of history. Resting today in the circlet of the crown made for and worn by the Queen Mother, it was earlier worn as a brooch by Queen Victoria. Its history, however, goes back at least as far as 1304, when it was acquired by the Mogul Emperors, though legend traces it 4,000 years before that date. It probably came from the fabled Golconda mines of Southern India. During its eventful life the Koh-i-nur, which means "mountain of light," adorned the Peacock Throne of Shah Jahan at Delhi. By successive conquests it traveled to Persia, then to Afghanistan, again to India, and finally to London upon the conclusion of the Second Sikh War, when it came into the possession of the East India Company. Unfortunately, this magnificent gem was recut in 1852 to a shallow brilliant weighing 108.9 carats—its original weight in ancient times was reported as 800 carats.

702. What is the largest known diamond? In its original state the Cullinan diamond, found in 1905 in the Premier mine near Pretoria in the Transvaal, was the world's largest diamond, having a weight of 3,106 carats, or slightly more than 1⅓ pounds. Even this giant gem was, as suggested by the shape of its three natural faces, only part of a crystal more than twice its size. From it have been cut the two largest cut diamonds in existence—the Cullinan I or Star of Africa (530.2 carats), now set in the Sovereign's Sceptre of the British crown jewels, and the Cullinan II (317.4 carats), set in the Imperial State Crown. Altogether 105 stones were cut from the Cullinan, named after Sir Thomas Cullinan, chairman of the company that owned the mine.

703. Which is the largest Brazilian diamond? Several huge stones reported to have been found in Brazil are believed by most gem authorities not to be diamonds. One, the Braganza diamond in the Portuguese regalia, is thought to be topaz; it is said to weigh 1,680 carats. The Regent of Portugal, weighing 215 carats, is likewise probably topaz.

An authentic and magnificent Brazilian diamond, which fluoresces bluish-violet under ultraviolet light (see Questions 978–979), is the

Presidente Vargas, weighing 726.6 carats. This crystal was cleaved into several pieces, from which 29 stones were cut.

The best known of the Brazilian diamonds is the historic Star of the South, picked up at Bagagem in the state of Minas Gerais in 1853. A water-clear crystal of 261.88 carats, it was cut into a brilliant of 128.8 carats and was sold to the Gaekwar of Baroda.

704. Which are the historic colored diamonds? The rarity of finely colored diamonds has assured that most of those that are found will be given individual names and a good deal of publicity. Such, for example, is the Hope diamond, the one best known in America (see Question 705). This is, however, not the largest of all known colored diamonds. The Tiffany Yellow, weighing 128.7 carats, is an orange gem, well known to the public for its having been on display in the store of Tiffany & Company, New York, and at various world's fairs. A deep amber-colored diamond, called the Tiger-eye, weighs 61.5 carats. The Red Cross is a canary-yellow diamond cut in a square shape; the unusual feature of this 205-carat gem is the Maltese cross visible through the top facet. The Dresden Green is a 41-carat apple-green diamond of unexcelled quality, formerly in the Green Vaults at Dresden and now reputed to be in Soviet possession. Four brilliant yellow diamonds, the largest weighing 38 carats, were also among the colored Dresden gems. The Austrian Yellow—also known as the Tuscany and the Florentine—was in the Hofburg in Vienna in 1938 but has since disappeared. Paul I is the name given to a certain pink diamond of 10 carats; this has often been described as ruby-red in color, but the stone was backed by coloring matter and a foil.

705. What is the story of the Hope diamond? Weighing 44.4 carats and deep sapphire-blue in color, the Hope diamond is believed to be the main portion of a diamond found at the Golconda mines in India. Obtained in 1642 by the French jeweler and traveler Jean-Baptiste Tavernier, it was sold by him to Louis XIV in 1668, and stolen with the rest of the French regalia in 1792. The gem turned up in its present form in 1830 and was bought by Henry Philip Hope, a banker and gem collector. In 1908 it was bought by Habib Bey, and in 1909 by a Paris diamond dealer named Rosenau, who sold it to Edward McLean, Washington publisher. His daughter, Evalyn Walsh

McLean, made it familiar to the American public. In 1949 the New York firm of Harry Winston acquired it, and in 1958 it went to the Smithsonian Institution.

706. What was the Cuban Capitol?   This was a yellow diamond of 23 carats, probably of South African origin. It was bought in 1928 by money raised among the workmen who were constructing the capitol building at Havana, Cuba. After being elaborately set in the marble floor of the building, it was used as the starting point for measuring highway distances in Cuba. On March 25, 1946, during civil commotion, it was stolen and has not been seen since.

707. Which noted diamond is engraved?   There are several historical diamonds that have been engraved with Oriental writing. Considering the extraordinary hardness of diamond, such a feat is a remarkable one. The Shah diamond, an Indian diamond taken from the Golconda mines in the 16th Century, has engraved upon it the names, in Persian, of three of the rulers who owned it, and the dates, which correspond successively to A.D. 1591, 1641 and 1826. Ultimately this gem of 88.7 carats went into the Diamond Treasury of the Soviet Union, at Moscow.

Another engraved diamond, but not yet known by a specific name, was sold at auction in London in 1954 and again in 1957. It also has the names of two of the Mogul Emperors inscribed in Persian letters upon it.

The Akbar Shah was an engraved diamond until it was recut in 1866, when it lost its Arabic lettering.

708. What is the Black Prince's Ruby?   Probably the most celebrated gem in existence, except certain of the great historic diamonds described above, is the Black Prince's Ruby. It, however, is not a ruby at all, but a red variety of spinel, a mineral with which the true corundum ruby is often confused. This gem first appears in history in 1367, when it was stolen by Dom Pedro, the king of Castile, from the king of Granada. In turn it was given, for military assistance, to the Black Prince, the son of Edward III, and so it went to England. The "ruby" was worn by Henry V in his helmet, which saved his life at the battle of Agincourt. Sold, together with the other crown jewels, by the government of Cromwell, it was later returned as royal property and appears today in its original uncut form in the Imperial State Crown.

709. What is the Edwardes Ruby? Although lacking a history of significance, the excellent crystal of ruby called the Edwardes Ruby, on display in the Mineral Gallery of the British Museum (Natural History), is of interest because it was donated by John Ruskin. This English author, art critic, and social reformer (1819–1900) is one of the few men of letters who was well acquainted with gems and minerals. He gave the ruby in honor of Major-General Sir Herbert Benjamin Edwardes (1819–1868), a military administrator in India.

710. What is the Timur Ruby? No account of famous gems would be complete without mention of the red spinel now known as the Timur Ruby, but long celebrated throughout the Orient as the Tribute of the World. Having a weight of 361 carats, it is the largest stone of its kind in existence. It is engraved in Persian, in two different scripts. The history of this gem, before it was given to Queen Victoria by the East India Company in 1851, is complicated, but it belonged to the conqueror Tamerlane, who seized it in the capture of Delhi in 1398. The inscriptions on the stone tell of five of its subsequent owners; other names had been removed. The Timur Ruby was once attached to the Peacock Throne at Delhi, and since 1612 has always been in the possession of the same owner as the Koh-i-nur diamond (see Question 701).

711. What is the Devonshire Emerald? A huge natural crystal of emerald from Muzo, Colombia, weighing 1383.95 carats, was named after the Duke of Devonshire, to whom it was given in 1831 by Dom Pedro, exiled emperor of Brazil. Far from perfect, it nevertheless has a fine color and is a noteworthy gem specimen. It has been exhibited from time to time at various shows and on other special occasions.

712. What are the principal cuts of gems? The forms of cut gems can be classified into three main groups—cabochon, faceted, and engraved. *Cabochon* cuts are the simplest, consisting of rounded surfaces; the bottom of the stone may perhaps be flat. A completely uniform cabochon gem would be a bead or sphere. *Faceted* gems are cut with flat surfaces called facets. There are a large number of different faceted styles, among which are the *brilliant-cut, rose-cut, step-cut,* and numerous modifications and combinations of them (*mixed-cuts*). *Engraved* gems take all aspects, ranging from simple inscriptions to three-dimensional carvings of the most elaborate design.

713. What cuts are used for diamonds?   A diamond can be cut into almost any shape; there are even engraved diamonds (see Question 707) and carved diamonds, such as cameos. In order, however, to bring out the fire and brilliance of this noble gem, the standard brilliant-cut is most often used. This form evolved from the earlier rose-cut, which usually consisted of a series of triangular facets. The introduction of the brilliant form is ascribed to Vincenti (or Vincenzio) Peruzzi (or Peruggi), a diamond cutter in Venice at the end of the 17th Century. A modern brilliant-cut diamond contains 33 facets above the equator or *girdle* and 25 facets below. The top is called the *table,* the largest of the 58 facets; the bottom, the smallest facet, is the *culet.* Each group of facets has a name of its own. Sometimes, and especially for large diamonds, more facets are added to increase the brilliance, and the girdle may be polished for a smoother appearance. A diamond of good proportions has a carefully contrived ratio of 100 for the diameter of the girdle, 16.2 for the height of the upper part or *crown,* and 43.1 for the depth of the lower part or *base.*

By altering the circular girdle and changing the facets to correspond, other attractive cuts can be created. Among these *modified brilliants* the *marquise-cut*—an elliptical design with pointed ends— is probably the most charming and certainly the most popular. The *pendeloque* is a drop-shaped form.

Diamonds are also cut in various angular shapes, such as the emerald-cut, but these are really more appropriate for colored gems. *Baguette* is the style of cutting used for small rectangular diamonds and other stones.

714. How are diamonds cut?   There are four main steps in the fashioning of a rough diamond so that it is ready to be set in jewelry. First, the crystal or fragment is properly oriented so that *cleaving* can be done in order to remove undesirable portions, such as flawed parts or excess weight. This must be done by an expert because a wrong blow makes further treatment useless. A small diamond mounted in a holder is employed to scratch a nick at the right spot in the stone to be cut, and then a blade is inserted in this nick and struck sharply, causing the diamond to split. The second step requires *sawing* the diamond in directions where cleaving is not possible. This operation is simple, the stone being held mechanically against a vertically rotating disk made of phosphor-bronze. Next, the diamond is subjected to *grinding,* whereby it is roughly shaped to give it a preliminary faceting; another diamond is used as an abrasive. Finally, the diamond goes through the *polishing* process. Soldered or otherwise gripped in a holder called a "dop," the stone is held against a rapidly moving horizontal "lap" made of soft iron and fed with diamond powder. This performs the cutting and polishing at the same time.

715. What is a diamond pipe? Diamond pipes are the only original source-rock of the most important of the gems. All other occurrences of diamond are in secondary rocks, in which it has been incorporated by weathering, erosion, transportation, and subsequent burial by sedimentary action. In the pipes, however, diamond is found in the primary rock in which it was presumably formed. The geology of the diamond pipe is far from being thoroughly understood, and it may be that the diamonds have been brought into the pipes by underground explosive action after they originated at even lower depths in the earth's crust.

A diamond pipe is a somewhat circular or funnel-shaped body of diamond-bearing rock. Maps of the diamond mines at various levels indicate that the pipes are actually enlargements of large fissures or cracks which go down to unknown distances. The rock is called *kimberlite,* a dark rock which is broken and altered, having been derived from a parent rock known as peridotite. Even the kimberlite variety of peridotite is not an uncommon rock, but it contains diamonds as an accessory mineral in only a relatively few of the places where it is found.

716. Where is the Williamson mine? The largest diamond pipe ever found is named the Williamson, after Dr. John T. Williamson (1907–1958), a Canadian geologist whose search for it is one of the classic stories in the long history of mineral prospecting. Under

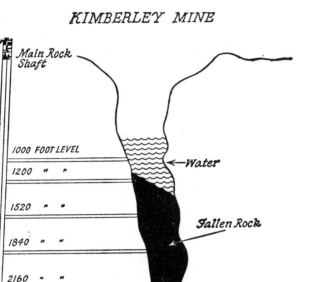

KIMBERLEY MINE

Main Rock Shaft

1000 FOOT LEVEL
1200 "   "
1520 "   "
1840 "   "
2160 "   "
2520 "   "

←Water

Fallen Rock

Discovered 16ᵀᴴ July 1871
Area at Surface 38 acres
Perimeter ⌒ 1 Mile
Surface to Top of Pipe 300'
Surface to Water 845'
Depth of Water 490'
Ground excavated
25 Million Tons

Solid Blue Ground→

3520 "   "
3601 "   "

Diamond pipe

prolonged circumstances of acute poverty and physical hardship that made exploration nearly impossible, Williamson eventually struck it rich in 1940 at Mwadui, which is now in Tanzania. His diamond pipe measures 3,500 feet in diameter. From this mine has come a large production, including the 54.5-carat pink diamond given to Queen Elizabeth II as a wedding present, and a crystal of 240.83 carats found in 1956.

717. What is the oyster line? Along the coast of Little Namaqualand, northeast of Alexander Bay, on the Atlantic shores of the African continent, is found a rich deposit of diamond associated with a particular type of fossil oyster shell, which stretches along the sea front at a definite level above the water. Hence this occurrence is referred to as the Oyster Line. The diamonds from here have included a number of large and fine crystals, but the region is extremely desolate, wind-swept, and inaccessible, and the gems are difficult to recover from the loose debris that lies over them.

718. Is diamond a rare mineral? No. Diamond is a relatively abundant mineral, at best described as "uncommon" but certainly not rare. G. F. Herbert Smith, an outstanding authority on gems, said that "it carpets large areas in Africa and is even scattered, regularly if sparsely, throughout the material filling apparently bottomless vents in the earth." Of the gems recognized without qualification as "precious," diamond is many thousand-fold the most common. Why, then, is diamond so highly regarded? It is expensive to cut, because of its great hardness. Its beauty is unquestioned except by a few connoisseurs who prefer the distinctive richness of emerald, ruby, sapphire, opal, or amethyst. And its output is carefully controlled, so that a virtual monopoly exists in its mining, cutting, and distribution.

719. What is padparadschah? This "fantastic term," as it was called by G. F. Herbert Smith, pertains to the yellowish-red variety of corundum. It is therefore a kind of sapphire. This, and several similar names, are corruptions of the Sinhalese word for lotus-color. The name is most often used for synthetic corundum of the same color.

720. What is the cause of color in emerald? The grass-green variety of beryl which we call emerald owes its unsurpassed color to the presence of a small amount of chromium, although vanadium is thought to play a minor role in the composition of this beryllium-aluminum silicate, $Be_3Al_2(SiO_3)_6$. The color, so characteristic as to be spoken of as emerald-green, has been complimented by descriptions such as "green as a meadow in spring," and "like wet grass in the shadow of great trees after a summer rain." The amount of coloring matter is so slight that it might truthfully be said that it conveys more value for its weight than any other substance known. Incidentally, the chromium that causes it is the same metallic element that makes a ruby red—but in a state of oxidation different enough to account for the complete unlikeness of these two gems.

721. Which gem is favored by the American Indian? Even though the choicest quality turquois still comes, as it has for centuries, from ancient mines near Nishapur in Iran, this gem can without much exaggeration be said to be of as much American significance as Persian. For it is the most highly regarded of mineral substances by the original American, the Indian. Especially in the Southwest, among the Navajos, is turquois a prized possession, an article of barter and a medium of exchange. These people mined it for a long while before the white man arrived on the scene. New Mexico was once the largest producing state, but the deposits near Los Cerillos are exhausted. Arizona, Nevada, Colorado, and California now yield most of the domestic supply.

722. Which gem is often confused with topaz? Probably no gem is more often confused in the public mind than topaz. Most people think of topaz as the typical example of a yellow stone; in earlier centuries, in fact, the name was given promiscuously to any yellow gem. Nevertheless, topaz is likely to be blue, light-green, pink, or colorless; and, of course, there are many yellow gems besides topaz. Yellow quartz, most properly called *citrine,* is the gem that is sold for topaz in most jewelry stores. Even attempts to call it "quartz topaz," however, fail to satisfy, for want of precision and clarity.

723. Which gems are garnets? Garnet is a group of minerals, five of the six subspecies furnishing gem material. The brown and reddish colors come quickly to mind, but garnet occurs in other colors as well. The green variety called *demantoid* is a brilliant gem, resembling a bright emerald and in fact is often sold as emerald when mounted in diamond-set rings.

Pyrope is the magnesium-aluminum garnet, with the formula $Mg_3Al_2(SiO_4)_3$. Almandite is the iron-aluminum garnet, $Fe_3Al_2(SiO_4)_3$. Pyrope and almandite are both known as precious garnet because of their gemmy varieties. The rare *rhodolite* garnet is a chemical mixture of both subspecies. *Spessartite* is the manganese-aluminum garnet, $Mn_3Al_2(SiO_4)_3$. *Grossularite* is the calcium-aluminum garnet, $Ca_3Al_2(SiO_4)_3$, which includes the gem *cinnamon-stone*. *Andradite* is the calcium-iron garnet, $Ca_3Fe_2(SiO_4)_3$, of which demantoid is a variety. Uvarovite, the calcium-chromium garnet, $Ca_3Cr_2(SiO_4)_3$, yields no gems only because its crystals are too small to be cut.

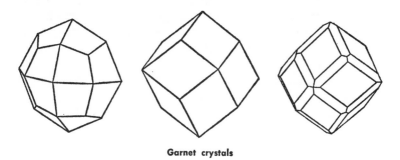

Garnet crystals

724. What are the colors of tourmaline? No two specimens of tourmaline seem to be alike. The color of this gem not only ranges from colorless to black, with all the hues of the rainbow in between, but the colors occur in zones or bands, arranged vertically or horizontally. "Watermelon tourmaline" has a red center surrounded by a zone of white and then by a green outer border. Other tourmaline has the red and green colors reversed. Long crystals may have a bottom of red and a top of green, perhaps crowned with white, or be colorless except where capped with black. The combination of colors is endless, and for this reason tourmaline is endlessly fascinating. In addition, this remarkable gem has a high degree of static electricity, and has the ability to transform pressure impulses into electric current, so that it can be used, for example, in depth gauges in submarines.

725. How is zircon colored? Practically all the cut zircons seen in jewelry and even in private specimen collections have been heat treated in order to give them the desired color. A considerable industry has been built up at Bangkok, Thailand, since World War I for the production of the golden-yellow zircon, the "starlite" blue zircon, and the colorless variety that so much resembles diamond. The process that is now employed heats the ordinary reddish-brown stones, which come principally from Indo-China, to a temperature between 850 and 1,000 degrees Centigrade. In the presence of air, the color turns golden yellow or else is driven away entirely; in the absence of air, the color becomes blue.

726. Why does alexandrite change colors?   "An emerald by day, an amethyst by night"—thus is alexandrite described. This remarkable variety of chrysoberyl changes color according to the kind of light in which it is viewed. The explanation lies in the differing color emission of the chromium that it contains. This is maintained at a delicate balance of red and green, so that daylight tips the color toward the green portion of the spectrum, and ordinary artificial light tends it toward the blue.

Alexandrite was named for the future czar Alexander II, on whose birthday it was first discovered, and its twin colors, those of the Imperial Guard, helped to make it especially popular in 19th-century Russia.

727. Is there more than one type of quartz?   Quartz, the most familiar of the gem minerals, occurs in two distinct types according to the temperature of formation—alpha or low quartz and beta or high quartz are the names usually applied to them. In gemology, however, and for the mineral collector, quartz and *chalcedony* are the two main types of common silica. They differ in the nature of their crystallinity and only slightly in their composition. Many mineralogists consider them the same mineral, while others prefer to regard them as two different species. The varieties of quartz proper are frequently found in crystals, perhaps of large size or high degree of perfection and transparency. Chalcedony, however, never grows as crystals, but instead has a rounded or irregular shape, more like pieces of broken porcelain. Its varieties are opaque or nearly so.

Quartz itself includes such important varieties as amethyst (purple), citrine (yellow), smoky quartz (dark brown to black), rose quartz (pink), and rock crystal (colorless). Familiar varieties of chalcedony include carnelian (red to orange), sard (brown), prase and chrysoprase (green), bloodstone (red spots on a green background), agate and onyx (see Question 728), and jasper.

728. What is the difference between agate and onyx? They are both varieties of chalcedony quartz (see Question 727). Except the kind known as moss agate (see Question 730), and some specimens in which the color is distributed in irregular patches (as in the thundereggs described in Question 132), the term agate is properly restricted to chalcedony that shows wavy concentric bands. These usually conform to the shape of the rock cavity in which the silica was deposited, and they may be of any color or combination of colors. Onyx is agate in which the parallel bands of color are straight and fairly wide, especially if the colors are of contrasting shades. Black onyx is solid black and so this name is not strictly correct; sardonyx should be, not merely reddish *sard* or *carnelian*, but either of these combined with some other color, usually white or black. Onyx is especially desirable for cameos because a head of one color can be carved against a background of a different color.

729. How are the bands in agate formed? The banded pattern in agate is best explained by the theory of *Liesegang rings*. As electrically charged atoms of coloring matter diffuse through the silica, which is at that time in a gelatinous state (a gel), they became supersaturated at intervals, depositing rings of color, between which are clear zones. Experiments to this effect were made by R. E. Liesegang, a German chemist, after whom the phenomenon was named. These rings in gels are in contrast to the evenly dispersed deposits of color in a water solution.

730. What are dendrites? Mossy or treelike patterns on the inside of a mineral or on the surface of a rock are known as dendrites. These are the branching designs that make *moss agate* the distinctive gem it is, showing "eternal landscapes in stone." Mineral matter, usually manganese oxide in the form of pyrolusite, or sometimes iron oxide, is deposited where it can spread out and crystallize in the way that frost forms on a window pane. Dendrites in moss agate are typically black or brown, but fibers of chlorite are green, resembling seaweed, and some *plume agate* splashes an array of colors. Moss agate from India has long been known as *Mocha stone*.

731. What is jasper? Almost any dark, opaque chalcedony may be called jasper if no more specific name can be found for it. Having an excess of coloring matter, jasper usually appears dark red, brown, a characteristic yellow, or dark green. Sometimes the colors are in swirling patches, sometimes in bands, to which the name ribbon jasper is appropriately given.

732. What is black opal? Black opal is the dark variety of opal— typical of the gem fields of Australia and Nevada—in which the background color is dark blue or gray. Iron and other impurities are the cause of the darkness. Against this favorable background the wonderful fire that flashes so freely from the gem can be seen to best advantage. Prior to 1905 black opal was unknown. The opal from Hungary and less important localities had, since ancient times, been what we now call *white opal*. In that year the prolific deposits of Lightning Ridge in New South Wales, Australia, were discovered, and opal took on a new meaning for lovers of fine gems.

733. How did amazonstone get its name? The green variety of microcline, a kind of feldspar, is known as amazonstone or amazonite, deriving its name from the Amazon River in South America, in spite of the evidence that none of it has ever been found there. This mineral has evidently been mistaken for jade or some other green mineral. The Pikes Peak region of Colorado is by far the world's most important source of amazonstone. The Colorado material was first made known to the public in 1876 when it was exhibited and sold at the Centennial Exposition in Philadelphia, in such quality and size that mineral dealers from Russia, formerly the leading producer, were put out of business.

734. What is jade? Two clearly separate minerals—nephrite and jadeite—constitute the gem material we know as jade. Neither the Chinese, to whom jade was the most precious of stones, nor any other peoples ever tried to make a distinction between nephrite and jadeite. It was not until about a century ago that the dual nature of this substance was recognized. Jadeite is the least common of the two kinds of jade, and it generally has a richer look than nephrite, but the colors of both have a rather similar range and it is not an easy problem to tell them apart without testing them.

Nephrite is a member of the amphibole group of minerals (see Question 170). More specifically, it belongs to the tremolite-actinolite series, which also furnishes important asbestos minerals (see Question 137). Jadeite is a member of the pyroxene group of minerals, which parallels in many respects the amphiboles (see Question 171). Besides these two kinds of true jade, there are many compact greenish minerals that pass for jade—such as californite, a variety of idocrase; bowenite, a variety of serpentine; amazonstone, a variety of microcline feldspar; steatite or soapstone, a soft and inexpensive jade substitute; pectolite, grossularite garnet, prehnite, zoisite, sillimanite, hornblende, quartz, and a mineral-mixture known as saussurite—all used on occasion for ornamental purposes.

735. Which is the toughest gem? Doubtless the gem most resistant to breakage is jade. Although no harder than quartz in its ability to scratch other minerals or be scratched by them (see Question 87), jade has a matted structure that makes it nearly immune to being broken. A Chinese jeweler in San Francisco was reported in the newspapers as using a jade anvil that had been in his family for that purpose for three generations. If a green jadelike mineral is dropped on a wood floor and breaks, it almost certainly is not jade!

736. What is alabaster? As mentioned in the Bible, alabaster was a glistening white variety of calcite, which is calcium carbonate. It was used for ointment vases of a form known as alabasters. Today, however, the name means a compact variety of gypsum, which is calcium sulfate. These two ornamental stones can be readily distinguished from one another by the effervescence of calcite in acid (see Question 32), whereas gypsum is completely inert. Ancient carved objects labeled alabaster in the large museums of the world prove almost always to be calcite. Jewel boxes and vases of white Italian alabaster of the gypsum kind are familiar in the market. In the United States, alabaster (mostly from Colorado) usually has a brown or gray veining; it is made into lighthouses, ash trays, and other small articles.

737. What has amber to do with electricity? At least as early as 600 B.C. the ability of amber to attract light bits of material after being rubbed was noticed. We now refer to this as developing negative electricity, in contrast to the positive electricity developed by gems such as tourmaline, topaz, and diamond. Because of this property and from the Greek word for amber, *elektron,* our word electricity was coined by Sir William Gilbert, personal physician to Queen Elizabeth I. Even for amber, however, which reveals it so well, static electricity is not a reliable test, owing to the many other substances that also display it, including the various resins that resemble amber and the plastics that imitate it.

738. Is there any modern amber?   Yes, even though all amber is the fossil resin of ancient trees. These trees flourished during the Oligocene epoch of the Tertiary period—nearly 40 million years ago (see Question 258)—and were a species of pine, *Pinus succinifer*. Most properly speaking, amber is a fossil resin containing succinic acid; other fossil resins, such as gedanite and burmite, do not contain this acid. Recent discoveries disclose the existence of true amber both older and younger than Tertiary. Some of it originated during the Pleistocene epoch, the Ice Age.

739. What are the insects in amber?   Hundreds of kinds of insects and other invertebrates of Oligocene age are found beautifully preserved in amber, caught in the sticky sap as it dripped down the bark of the trees. These animals include centipedes, ants, spiders, beetles, moths, flies, and many others—some of which are true insects and others of which are not—together with plant remains blown against the fluid by the wind. Even the most delicate structures of the organisms can be studied today, so perfectly protected have they been during the millions of years that have elapsed since they were caught. Most of the amber "insects" are of species now extinct, though some still flourish today. The oldest fossil ant, and social insect of any kind, was found in amber in New Jersey in 1965 by two mineral collectors, Mr. and Mrs. Edmund Frey.

740. What is ambergris?   This curious waxy substance, the valuable ingredient of the most expensive perfumes, is a morbid secretion in the intestines of the sperm whale or cachalot. It is found floating in tropical seas. Although the word means "gray amber" in French, ambergris has nothing whatsoever to do with amber and is neither gem nor mineral.

XII. INDUSTRIAL MINERALS AND ROCKS

Introduction. An enormous range of nonmetallic substances constitutes the other part of the Mineral Kingdom—more commonplace than the metallic minerals and ores and more widely distributed. Yet, often lacking a certain glamour, these nonmetallic minerals and rocks are not always as well known to the general public, though they are more universally used. The oldest mineral industries were those that involved the nonmetallics, and their uses, which today are numbered in the thousands, have kept pace with the growing complexity of civilization. From gems to water resources—both of which are given special consideration in separate chapters—from abrasives to fertilizers, from building stones to soaps, the nonmetallics present a fascinating array of raw materials. The general term "industrial minerals and rocks" is the modern way of referring to them all.

741. Which mineral expands when heated? This mineralogic curiosity is called *vermiculite,* a name applied commercially to a number of closely similar micalike minerals that expand or exfoliate upon being heated to temperatures between 1,400 and 2,000 degrees Fahrenheit. They uncoil like an accordion or the movement of worms, hence the name, from the Latin *vermiculus,* "little worm." These are hydrous silicates of aluminum, magnesium, and iron, mostly, but differ considerably in composition as well as in physical properties. The exfoliation is due to the expansion of water as it changes into steam between the layers. The original color of black, brown, or yellow alters to a silvery or golden hue, according to the degree of heat and conditions of exposure to air.

742. What are the uses of vermiculite? The coarsest vermiculite is marketed for chicken litter. The medium sizes are used as loose-fill insulation, as a lightweight aggregate for plaster and concrete, and as a soil conditioner. The finer material is employed as a carrier for agricultural chemicals and as an agent to combat caking in fertilizer. There are many minor uses, also, such as for packing and other purposes, even for making imitation marble. The material may be used in its loose state or it may be bonded with any one of numerous binders (casein glue, synthetic resin, waterglass, etc.), so that it can be fabricated into shape.

743. Where is vermiculite produced? The world's biggest vermiculite mine is at Libby, Montana. It is marketed as Zonolite, the company also having an operation in South Carolina. Mines formerly were active from time to time in Colorado, Wyoming, North Carolina, Georgia, Texas, and Pennsylvania, and about 50 exfoliation or "popping" plants are now working in the United States. The Loolekop deposit in the Palabora district in the Transvaal is a huge occurrence of vermiculite.

744. What is the alkali industry? The production of compounds of sodium carbonate and sodium sulfate makes up the so-called alkali industry. Baking soda is sodium bicarbonate ($NaHCO_3$). Soda is the same thing or, more accurately, the oxide or carbonate of sodium. The purified salts are marketed as soda ash (see Questions 745–746), bicarbonate, natron, trona—these are carbonates—salt cake (See Question 747), Glauber's salt, and niter cake—these are sulfates.

745. What is soda ash? Sodium carbonate (Na_2CO_3) is known as soda ash because it was once obtained from the ashes of seaweeds and marine plants, which were burned to recover this product for use in soap, lye, and glass making. Such was common practice from early history until about 1791, when LeBlanc in France developed a means of producing it from salt, sulfuric acid, limestone, and coal. The Solvay process, discovered in the 1860's in Belgium, superseded it and is now employed to yield most of the world's soda ash.

746. How does natural soda ash occur? Although less than 10 per cent of the total supply of sodium carbonate is obtained from natural sources, this substance is taken from solution in brines and as the mineral trona. Even the early Egyptians recovered it from incrustations around dried lakes, and in the United States both Searles Lake and Owens Lake, in California, have large reserves. Trona is produced in the United States mostly from a huge deposit near Green

River, Wyoming, which was discovered through the drilling of an oil well.

747. What is salt cake? This is crude sodium sulfate (Na_2SO_4), used in producing many chemical compounds. Pure anhydrous sodium sulfate is used in the manufacture of glass, but salt cake, because it is cheaper, is important in making kraft pulp in the paper industry. Sodium sulfate also enters into the processing of textile fibers such as rayon and wool. Dyes, coal tar, soap, drugs, and other products use it extensively.

748. Where is Searles Lake? This playa or dry desert lake in southeastern California is a world-famous source of chemicals obtained from its brines. It is the most important lake source of potash in the United States, one of two such sources of borax, and is rich in other saline minerals, including six sulfates, six carbonates, four triple salts, two chlorides, and a borosilicate. Bromine and lithium compounds are recovered, along with salt cake and the potash and borax. Searles Lake consists of beds of saline minerals to a depth of 60 to 90 feet, extending over an area of 20 square miles or more. The porous nature, to the amount of 25 to 45 per cent of the total volume, permits the accumulation of the valuable saturated brines.

749. When were the Death Valley borax deposits worked? One of the more interesting mining operations in American history was the extraction of borax in Death Valley during the period 1883 to 1890. Following the initial discovery of borax in California in 1864 in Borax Lake and Hachinhama Lake, the center of the boron industry shifted to Nevada in 1872, and then back to California when crusts of borax began to be worked in Death Valley. Scraping up and refining the borate material was a laborious process, and the hauling to Mojave by the famous 20-mule teams constitutes a picturesque chapter in the story of the Far West. These operations ended when beds of colemanite were mined in the Calico Mountains.

750. What are the historical uses of salt? Known today as a table food but used in far greater amounts as one of the basic chemicals of industry, salt has had many strange uses during its long history, which goes back as far as man has been upon the earth.

Salt has been used as currency. Our word salary comes originally from "salt money" because the Roman soldier was paid in salt. Salt has been a traditional source of tax revenue. It has caused wars and revolutions. It was the basis of some of the earliest industries.

The many sayings and superstitions involving salt suggest its importance in human affairs. It has been symbolic of such ideals as friendship, purity, faithfulness, hospitality, and destiny.

751. What is the main use for salt? Salt is one of the major raw materials for the preparation of chemicals, and this is its largest use, accounting for about 70 per cent in the United States. The most important use, in terms of quantity, is in manufacturing soda ash (see Question 745). Other large-scale chemical uses are in making sodium metal, chlorine, bleaches, chlorates, hydrochloric acid, and other products needing sodium or chlorine.

752. What are the other uses for salt? Immense amounts of salt are used in manufacturing soap and dyes and in processing textiles and leather. In the food industry—its most familiar use—salt is employed in meat packing and the curing of fish, in dairy products, refrigeration, and livestock feed. It removes snow and ice from roads and stabilizes the adjacent ground and gravel surfaces. It is used in purifying water supplies and in heat-treating, smelting, and refining metals. Thousands of direct and indirect applications are credited to this miracle substance, so essential to life itself.

753. How does salt occur? Rock salt is one of the distinctive kinds of sedimentary rocks, found in beds of most geologic ages. The interesting salt domes of Texas and Louisiana are a special type of body, described in Question 20. Salt also occurs in solution in underground brines contained within sedimentary rocks, and in springs, lagoons, and lakes. The principal reservoir of salt is, of course, the ocean, in which it has accumulated by weathering and erosion of the land and from the contributions of volcanoes.

754. Where is salt produced in the United States? About 95 plants produce salt in the United States, which has an abundance of this mineral, though certain areas do not have local deposits of adequate size. The largest producing area is in the region of the

Great Lakes, with concentrations of rock salt and brine near Detroit and at Manistee and Ludington in Michigan, west-central New York, and northern and central Ohio. Louisiana, in the vicinity of Weeks, Avery, and Jefferson Islands on the Intercoastal Waterway and at Winnfield, is another center of the industry, which operates here from salt domes. Central and southern Kansas and an adjacent area in Oklahoma constitute another region of salt-producing bedrocks. Other important sources of salt are the beds of eastern Texas, the salt lakes of Utah (at Salt Lake City and Redmond), and in California, where it is obtained at Saltus, San Diego, and around San Francisco Bay.

755. How is garnet used as an abrasive? The hardness and sharp fracture of garnet make it a good abrasive. When it is adhered to paper and cloth the product becomes garnet paper and garnet cloth. These are used primarily for woodworking, finishing leather and plastic, and grinding miscellaneous materials. The loose grains are used to grind expensive glass, to polish metal, and for sand blasting.

756. Where is abrasive garnet mined in the United States? The oldest and largest garnet mine in the United States is on Gore Mountain near North Creek in Warren County, New York. It is operated by the Barton Mines Corporation and has at times yielded huge crystals. The garnet is of the almandite subspecies (see Question 723), surrounded by shells of hornblende, which is decomposed near the surface of the earth. This is an open-pit, mechanized mine.

On Emerald Creek in Benewah County, Idaho, almandite garnet is recovered from alluvial deposits, and some garnet is obtained as a byproduct of gold dredging near Warren, in Idaho County.

757. Why are jewel bearings important? Millions of tiny jewel bearings are employed each year in instruments that measure, regulate, and control every conceivable kind of industrial operation. Why a 21-jewel watch is superior to a 15-jewel watch lies not in the presence of six additional valuable gems—for most such jewels are synthetic stones of no intrinsic value—but in the smoother operation of the mechanism, minimizing friction and wear between small moving parts. Some of these jewels are so small that 18,000 can fit in a thimble, and they are made in so many shapes and sizes that they are difficult to stockpile in event of national emergency.

758. What are the uses for jewel bearings? Widely used in civilian and military equipment, jewel bearings are expanding their market rapidly with the trend toward more complex instrumentation. The use of spheres and cylinders in making ball and roller bearings has opened up a new horizon in this field. Watches and electrical measuring instruments were formerly about the only users of jewel bearings, but now a larger variety of gauges, meters, and indicators is being turned out, together with textile thread guides, range finders, and other instruments that can benefit from the presence of the smooth, hard surface of a jewel bearing.

759. Which materials are used for jewel bearings? Jewel bearings are made mostly from corundum—ruby and sapphire (see Question 682). The synthetic mineral has largely replaced the natural. Where extreme hardness and shock resistance are not required, glass and synthetic spinel are used. In earlier years natural Montana sapphire was a fairly popular material for jewel bearings in the United States, but this source is no longer producing for industrial purposes.

760. Where are jewel bearings made? Switzerland is the home of the jewel-bearings industry, using synthetic corundum. Even there the various operations are conducted separately, and only a few firms go all the way from raw materials to finished bearings. Much of the work is done in small companies of the "cottage" type.

In the United States, the Linde Air Products Company makes carrot-shaped "boules" and cylindrical "rods" of synthetic corundrum by the Verneuil process (see Question 687). Its output, however, does not go into the manufacture of jewel bearings but into gems and other articles.

Occasional jewel bearings have been made in other countries, including Italy, France, Germany, Japan, Canada, Russia, and England.

761. What is the Turtle Mountain project? Under the supervision of the Army Ordnance Corps a jewel-bearings plant was established in 1952 by the Bulova Watch Company at Rolla, North Dakota, for the purpose of providing a nucleus of skilled labor for the production of finished jewel bearings and to teach others to pass along this vital knowledge in case of national necessity. The trainees and workmen are Chippewa Indians from the Turtle Mountain Indian Reservation. Their finger dexterity and muscular coordination are the skills that they bring to this task.

762. What is the main use of diatomaceous earth? Of the many uses for diatomaceous earth—the fossil remains of one-celled plants called diatoms—the major one is for filtration. Through this material go acids, chemicals, petroleum compounds, polluted water, antibiotics, and a host of other substances to remove undesirable constituents or unfavorable properties. Further uses are as a mineral filler (see Question 766), insulating material, absorbent, abrasive, and for other purposes.

763. How does diatomaceous earth accumulate? Three types of occurrence of diatomaceous earth have been described: (1) ancient marine beds, sometimes seamed with clay; (2) more recent fresh-water deposits next to rivers and lakes; and (3) deposits in lakes and swamps, associated with decaying vegetation, where the accumulation is still taking place.

764. Where is diatomaceous earth found? Deposits are known in many parts of the world. The United States is the leading producer, most of it coming from California, Oregon, Nevada, and Washington. The 700-foot-thick beds near Lompoc, California, are the most intensively worked and the best known. The Soviet Union and France supply large amounts of diatomaceous earth. The Caucasus Mountains in Russia are said to hold vast reserves.

765. What is mountain meal? One of the many names given to diatomaceous earth is mountain meal, from its powdery grainlike appearance.

766. What is a mineral filler? To supply bulk and to impart desired physical properties, such as strength, mineral fillers are added to manufactured products. A low-priced shirt or bar of candy has a certain amount of useless though harmless filler in it because this costs less than the merchandise. The fillers are finely ground, usually inert chemically, and preferably cheap. Some are nothing more than adulterants. Many are made from waste products, although a few are made artificially for the purpose. Scores of different ones are used and they turn up in paper, rubber, paint, tooth paste, and nearly everything sold. Apart from the instances of dishonesty involved, fillers do furnish toughness, elasticity, flexibility, opacity, and other worthwhile features.

767. What is fluorspar? This is the commercial name for the mineral fluorite, which is calcium fluoride, CaF_2. Crystals are often beautifully formed and attractively colored cubes. Masses are usually purple or green, filling veins, often with lead and silver ores, or else occurring in sedimentary beds of limestone and dolomite. This is the chief mineral of fluorine.

768. What are the uses of fluorspar? The largest use of fluorspar has long been as a flux in the making of steel. However, the use for the production of hydrofluoric acid is nearly as great; this important chemical helps to make high-octane gasoline, as well as other fluorine compounds. A third use is in glass and enamel. Thus, there are metallurgical-grade, acid-grade, and ceramic-grade fluorspar. For none of these is there any adequate substitute.

769. Where does fluorspar occur in the United States? The largest deposits of fluorspar in the United States are in the Illinois-Kentucky district, along the Ohio River. Rosiclare and Cave-in-Rock, Illinois, are noted localities for specimen material. Arizona is of next importance. Most United States fluorspar is, however, imported from Mexico, Spain, and Italy.

770. Which mineral element was extracted from seaweed? Iodine was first recovered from the ash of burned seaweed. It was discovered in France by Bernard Courtois, who was trying to obtain potash for use in gunpowder during the Napoleonic wars. Until recently seaweed, especially drift kelp, was the main source of iodine, because it has the ability to extract it from sea water; this variety grows so that it is always submerged by the tide.

771. What are the present sources of iodine? Between about 1868 and 1929 iodine was obtained principally from the so-called caliche beds of Chile (see Question 789). Then natural brines became the leading source and remain so today. Oil-well brines from near Long Beach, California, and Shreveport, Louisiana, contain remarkably high concentrations of iodine. The other leading producing countries, except Chile, also secure iodine from similar brines and mineralized waters; Japan is an especially large exporter.

772. What are the industrial uses of iodine? Apart from the medicinal and nutritional uses of iodine, which are more or less familiar, including its use as a radioactive tracer, this nonmetallic element is employed in wet-plate photoengraving (though this is a declining process) and in film emulsions. Iodine also has various applications in metallurgy, rubber, and dyes.

773. How is perlite used? This "champion of the lightweight aggregates"—a volcanic rock related to obsidian (see Question 207) —finds its major use in construction, but numerous specialized uses have been discovered for it as well. Like vermiculite (see Question 741), perlite expands within a certain temperature range, enlarging from 400 to more than 2,000 per cent of its original volume, as its contained gases and liquids volatilize. The result is a glassy, inert, white material, ideally suited for plaster (in which it replaces sand as an aggregate), concrete, and loose-fill insulation.

774. Where does perlite occur? Although widely distributed among the Western states, no perlite is known to occur east of the Rocky Mountains. Owing to high freight rates, expanding plants generally locate in the centers of construction activity, bringing in the raw material from the West. California is the leading user of perlite; by far the largest deposits are in Nevada and New Mexico, though five other Western states have perlite mines.

775. What are fertilizer minerals? These are a group of otherwise unrelated nonmetallic minerals that are used for plant food or perform various beneficial functions in the soil. Some furnish direct food for plant life, perhaps special food for special kinds of vegetation, and they replace the elements leached or otherwise depleted from the soil. Some supply substances originally deficient in certain soils. Others transform insoluble substances into a form that can be absorbed by the plants. Others neutralize acid or alkaline soils and help to bring about a better balance. Some eliminate organisms or undesirable ingredients in soil.

776. Which are the fertilizer minerals? Compounds of potassium, phosphorus, nitrogen, calcium, and sulfur are the most essential fertilizer materials, although almost any element may have specific application for this purpose where it is individually needed in the soil.

Potassium is most generally added in the form of potash, glauconite, or feldspar. Phosphorus is supplied by mineral phosphates, slag, and organic substances. Nitrogen is furnished by nitrates or compounds obtained from coal or the atmosphere. Calcium is added as lime, limestone, marl, or gypsum. Sulfur is added as gypsum or native sulfur.

777. What is potash? Commercially, potash is a general name for compounds of potassium, although chemically it means only potassium oxide (K_2O) and so refers to the relative potassium content of various minerals and other substances. The word potash is derived from "pot ash," which was obtained by evaporating in iron pots the leachings of wood ashes for soap making—this product was mostly potassium carbonate, but the term has since been more broadly applied. Wood ashes were the principal source of potash in the United States until 1872, when potash minerals were introduced for fertilizers, but they were used later than that for chemical and other purposes.

778. Which are the potash minerals? There are many dozens of potassium-bearing minerals; this element is estimated to make up 3.11 per cent of the crust of the earth. Most of these minerals have no present economic value. The mineral sylvite is the most available and exists in the most usable form. Other soluble chlorides and sulfates are also of commercial use, and these include carnallite, polyhalite, and langbeinite.

779. What is sylvite like? Sylvite is the mineralogic name for potassium chloride, KCl. It is very similar in appearance to halite or common salt, to which it is closely related, but it has a bitter taste. It is much rarer than halite because it remains in solution long after the halite has been deposited. Sylvite is found mostly in granular aggregates of crystals showing cubic cleavage (see Question 93). It is usually colorless or white, but impurities impart blue, yellow, or red areas of color.

780. What are the properties of carnallite? Occurring in granular masses, carnallite is usually milk-white or reddish, and has a bitter taste. It absorbs moisture and tends to dissolve in its own liquid. Carnallite is a hydrous chloride of potassium and magnesium, $KMgCl_3 \cdot 6H_2O$. An outstanding locality for it is the saline deposit at Stassfurt in Prussia.

781. What are the features of polyhalite? Gray or red in color, translucent, and having a bitter taste, polyhalite is a hydrous sulfate of potassium, calcium, and magnesium, with the chemical formula $K_2Ca_2Mg(SO_4)_4 \cdot 2H_2O$. Other than the frequent red color, polyhalite is not easily distinguished from numerous other saline minerals deposited from solution.

782. Where does potash occur in North America? The Permian Basin of New Mexico and Texas is the center of the potash industry of the United States, and Carlsbad is the capital. The second most important area is Searles Lake, California (see Question 748). New discoveries, ranking among the world's largest, have been made in Saskatchewan, Canada. Potentially valuable though deep beds in the Williston Basin of North Dakota and Montana—an extension of the Canadian deposits—and the Paradox Basin in eastern Utah have been outlined. Small production is won by solar evaporation from Salduro Marsh, near Wendover, Utah; from the wells of the Dow Chemical Company at Midland, Michigan; and from various by-product operations.

783. What are the Stassfurt deposits? Although little mined now, the Stassfurt beds of saline minerals in Germany supplied most of the world's potash before World War I. This locality is famous, furthermore, as having the only complete sequence of deposition of oceanic salts known anywhere. Some 30 minerals are represented, though many of them have been formed by secondary reactions. The most important potassium minerals are carnallite, kainite, langbeinite, polyhalite, and sylvite. There are three potash-bearing zones. These are of the same geologic age, Permian, as the American potash deposits near Carlsbad, New Mexico (see Question 782). Apart from the declining Stassfurt beds, Germany is still, nevertheless, the largest producer of potash in the world.

784. What is phosphate rock?   Any natural rock containing enough phosphate minerals to permit their commercial use is termed phosphate rock. This embraces limestone, sandstone, shale, and igneous rocks, and it occurs as nodules, vein deposits, residual material from the weathering of phosphatic limestone, and either loose or consolidated phosphatic sediments. The most important substance of phosphatic deposits is tribasic calcium phosphate; the mineral is a form of apatite (see Question 59). The processors of phosphate treat the rock with sulfuric acid to yield several kinds of "acid phosphate," which in this form are more readily absorbed as plant food.

785. Where are phosphate deposits located?   The United States produces about one half of the world's phosphate, North Africa about one third, and the rest comes mainly from Russia, France, Spain, Sweden, and islands of the Pacific. By far the bulk of the phosphate rock is from the Northern Hemisphere, the land hemisphere of the globe, yet most phosphate deposits are of marine origin. French Morocco has the largest reserves, an estimated 21 billion metric tons. The United States is second in this respect, the Soviet Union third, and Tunisia and Algeria fourth and fifth—each with more than a billion tons. The discovery of phosphorite nodules on the sea floor may increase world reserves by 100 billion tons.

786. Where is phosphate produced in the United States?   Of the 23 states in which phosphate rock has been reported, Florida, Tennessee, Idaho, Montana, Utah, and Wyoming are commercial producers. Florida and Idaho have enormous reserves, followed in third place by Tennessee. The Florida material is classified as *hard-rock phosphate, land-pebble phosphate rock* (the main kind), and *soft phosphate rock,* which is associated with the other two. In Tennessee the phosphate rock is described as *brown-rock* (the important one), *blue-rock,* and *white-rock,* but these are defined more by the nature of the material than by the actual color. In Idaho, and extending into

Montana, Nevada, Utah, Wyoming, and into Canada is the Western phosphate field, in which the phosphate beds are contained in a shale member of the marine Phosphoria formation.

787. Where are the guano deposits?   Guano, which is a phosphatic material derived from bird manure, is obtained in quantity from certain coral islands of the Pacific and Indian Oceans. The phosphate reacts with the calcium carbonate of the coral to form a usable fertilizer. Among the principal sources are Ocean, Nauru, Angaur, and Makatea Islands, on which the deposits are as much as 65 feet thick. A little phosphate rock is brought into Hawaii from Makatea, although the United States is otherwise self-sufficient in this mineral product except for some low-fluorine phosphate rock obtained from Curaçao.

788. How is nitrogen obtained?   Prior to the development of nitrogen "fixation" early in the present century, the mineral deposits of Chile were almost the sole source of this element. Today coal and the atmosphere supply most of the world's needs for this essential plant food, although the Chilean nitrate deposits manage to compete continually though somewhat feebly. Natural nitrates supply minor or trace elements that the artificial material does not have.

789. What is caliche?   This is the nitrate-bearing material of Chile. In the narrow strips called the deserts of Atacama, Antofagasta, and Tarapaca, in one of the driest regions of the world—"rainless, treeless, fuelless," as described by Alan M. Bateman—are thin beds of gravel held together by sodium nitrate and related saline products, lying at a shallow distance beneath the surface of the ground. Besides nitrates, these deposits contain valuable amounts of iodine (see Question 771). Their origin is subject to dispute, though the nitrogen may be the result of volcanic emanations.

790. How were the Chilean nitrate deposits developed?   Production of nitrates was begun from the Atacama Desert in the 18th Century, but on a small scale until Chile gained control of the deposits after its wars with Peru and Bolivia from 1879 to 1882. British and German capital was sought and the industry expanded to become a world monopoly until World War I, when trade was disrupted and the vast requirements for nitrogen for fertilizer, explosives, and chemicals were met synthetically.

791. Which are the nitrogen compounds? Ammonia is the most important industrial compound of nitrogen. It is used directly and serves as a basic chemical for the production of many other compounds. Nitric acid, urea, and the cyanides are other major nitrogen products.

792. What is dimension stone? The term dimension stone is applied to slabs or blocks of natural rock that are cut to definite sizes and shapes. It includes cut, carved, sawed, and roughhewn blocks of building stone. It includes cut and polished memorial stone, roofing slabs, paving blocks, curbstone and flagstone, and specially formed products such as tanks, sinks and tubs, steps, floor tile, and baseboards. Dimension stone is used for constructing buildings or as a facing stone or trim. It builds bridges, monuments, and statues. Granite, basalt, limestone, sandstone, and marble are the principal rocks used.

793. What is crushed stone? Crushed and broken stone is the term given to all other rough rock products besides dimension stone (see Question 792). These may be of any size, from finest grinding powders to coarse bouldery material. Included are large pieces of irregular shape, used for their bulk, as in spillways at dams and for shore and harbor protection—such material is known as riprap. Crushed stone is used as concrete aggregate, for highway construction and railroad ballast, and in many chemical, metallurgical, and industrial processes.

794. What factors limit the stone industry? The weight of natural stone limits the distance to which it can be shipped economically, with the exception of certain fancy stones that bring high prices, or certain well-known varieties, such as Indiana limestone (see Question 811), that are much in demand by architects. Stone is, furthermore, difficult to work and is not adapted to mass-production methods. The proportion of waste is high, as can be seen at any building-stone quarry. Several substances of a structural nature have invaded the market previously occupied by dimension stone (see Question 795).

795. What are the competitors of stone? Artificial products—such as brick, terra cotta, and novel materials—have increased in utility and attractiveness within recent years, serving as a substitute for stone, especially in facing material and in floors and partitions. The most significant competition to stone, however, was the introduction of concrete on a large scale in the early 1890's. Both in cost and convenience, though certainly not in appearance, it had many advantages. Just preceding the advent of concrete, and participating with it in making inroads upon the stone market, was the invention of the steel-skeleton-frame building of the skyscraper type. This frame took the place of stone in carrying the burden of the superstructure, and reinforced concrete became an essential part of such a building. Stone, when still used, becomes only a decorative sheath on the outside, although it serves many useful purposes in the interior of many fine buildings today.

796. What is the strength of building stone? Structural stone that is sound in other respects will be found strong enough to withstand any use to which it is likely to be put. Quartzite from Montana has been tested to stand a compressive strength equivalent to a building more than 10 miles high! The pressure on the base of the Washington Monument is less than 700 pounds per square inch, yet good-quality building stone will sustain crushing loads of 10,000 to 25,000 pounds per square inch.

797. What is larvikite? This is a handsome building stone from Larvik, Norway. It is often sold under the name Norwegian Pearl Gray granite. Its main mineral is orthoclase feldspar (see Question 162) having a structural peculiarity so that it possesses a rich blue sheen resembling labradorite, which it was once thought to be. This rock is properly a variety of syenite (see Question 186), and its best known installation is on the lower outside of the Chrysler Building in New York City.

798. What is trap rock? Trap or trap rock refers to any dark volcanic rock, most of which is basalt, and even to a fine-grained

igneous rock not of lava origin, most of which is diabase. Trap rock
is rather widely used in the northeastern and northwestern parts of the
United States, where it is abundant.

799. Of which stone is the Lincoln Memorial built?   The beautiful
white marble of the Lincoln Memorial in Washington, D.C., came
from the Yule marble deposits of central Colorado, which at that
time were in active operation; today they furnish marble only for
chemical purposes. From here also came the main block for the first
Tomb of the Unknown Soldier in Arlington National Cemetery. For
cutting the columns the largest diamond-toothed drum column-cutter
on record had to be constructed; it had 80 diamond teeth and fashioned the columns in sections 58 inches long and 7 feet 5 inches in
diameter. The "transparencies" in the roof of the building are translucent slabs of clouded and veined Alabama marble.

800. Of which stone is the Roman Colosseum built?   This stupen-
dous structure, begun by Vespasian in A.D. 75 and dedicated by Titus
in A.D. 80, was erected from travertine (see Question 36) occurring
near Tivoli, 16 miles east of Rome. During the 15th and 16th Centuries the abandoned Colosseum was itself used as a quarry, and
stone was removed for the construction of many churches and palaces,
notably the Piazza di San Marco in Venice and the Palazzo Farnese
in Rome. After this use was stopped, the structure was partly restored.

These same quarries, situated between Rome and Tivoli, also supplied stone for the magnificent St. Peter's in Rome and the Pennsylvania Railway Station in New York, which popularized the stone
in the United States.

801. Which is the most famous English building stone?   Four zones
of a limestone deposited during the Jurassic period of geologic history (see Question 258) constitute the most important building stone
in Great Britain. These zones are known as the Portland, Oxford,
Bath, and Inferior Oölite. Of these, the Bath stone quarried in Wilt-
shire is the most important; the chief workings are in the Somerset
Hills near Bath. The blocks must be "seasoned" by underground
storage during the first winter to avoid the effects of frost action.
Among the fine buildings built of this stone are the Abbey Church

of Bath, Glastonbury Abbey Church, and Wells Cathedral, erected in the 11th and 12th Centuries and still well preserved in the unfavorable climate of western England. The Portland stone was widely employed for the rebuilding of London after the great fire of 1666, and the quarries on Portland Island were controlled by Sir Christopher Wren during the erection of St. Paul's Cathedral, begun in 1675.

802. What is Caen stone? This, a French limestone of oölitic texture (see Question 302), is one of the most notable building stones of Europe. Shortly after the Norman conquest it was shipped to England in large quantities and employed in such superb structures as the Cathedral of Canterbury and Westminster Abbey. This soft, fine-grained, light-colored rock is quarried in Normandy near Caen, Falaise, and Bayeux.

803. What is the Tyndall limestone? Perhaps the best building stone in western Canada is the Tyndall limestone. It occurs about 30 miles northwest of Winnipeg, Manitoba. The Parliament Building and other public buildings in this city and elsewhere are of Tyndall stone. The rock, which is of Ordovician age, has a characteristic mottled appearance because of dark patches evenly distributed through it.

804. Which is the Granite City? Aberdeen, Scotland, is so known because its architecture is dominated by the granite from nearby quarries. Gray to light-blue stone from Aberdeen and red stone from Peterhead were the first granites to enter international trade extensively and so became familiar as Scotch granite; granite even from Scandinavia is consequently marketed through Aberdeen.

805. What are durex blocks? These are small paving blocks about 3 by 4 inches in size that are produced from Swedish granite occurring on the western coast of the Göteborg district. They are cut into shape with splitting machines. Millions of them have been shipped to North America, Argentina, Australia, and elsewhere.

806. Which are the Italian marbles? As a center of art and architecture Italy has also been a leader in the production of marble since the days of the Roman Empire. The best known of its marble is the white Carrara, the yellow Siena, and the colored varieties from Verona and Vicenza. Yet the colors are so variable that they are difficult to describe. Even the Carrara stone—which comes from between Genoa and Pisa—is usually divided into three general groups —statuary, ordinary white, and colored. The fine grain, purity of color, and translucency of the statuary type are especially prized. The industry flourished when the Emperor Augustus stated that he found Rome a city of brick and would leave a city of marble.

807. Where is the greatest variety of marble produced? More kinds of marble are quarried in France than in any other country. The industry dates to the period when Gaul was a Roman province. Among the best known varieties are Sarancolin, a banded and mottled marble; Griotte d'Italie, an expensive decorative stone; and Rouge Français, esteemed for monuments in France and Italy. Le Grande Diable and Le Petit Diable are black and white marbles. Rosso Antico is a famous stone, blood-red in color with white veins and dots.

808. Where is black marble obtained? Although black marble is found in 13 Departments of France, in Italian Lombardy, in Greece, Ireland, and in other places throughout the world, no black stone equals in quality the choicest of the Noir Belge from Belgium. This occurs northwest of Namur and is largely responsible for the high place held by Belgium in the stone industry, for, in general, its marble resources are not extensive, but they have been intelligently developed and skillfully promoted.

809. What are the marbles of Greece? The availability of high-grade marble in that land doubtless contributed to the perfection reached by the sculpture of ancient Greece. Parian marble, quarried on the Island of Paros and Pentelic marble, obtained on Mount Pentelicus near Athens and used in the Parthenon, are the best known of Greek stones.

This industry was largely superseded by the workings in Italy many centuries ago.

810. Where is the largest slate industry? Wales maintains the most important slate quarries in the world. The deposits were worked as early as the days of the Roman occupation, but attained importance toward the end of the 18th Century. The chief product is roofing slate. The stone is trimmed to a sequence of sizes, among which are those that used to be called ladies, countesses, duchesses, princesses, and empresses.

811. Which is the most widely used building stone in the United States? Indiana limestone is the best known and most widely employed natural building stone in America. Scarcely a city of any size does not have one or more buildings constructed of this excellent material, which is often referred to as Bedford limestone. It is easy to work and carve, is unusually attractive in buff and gray colors, is durable when dried, and is readily available from the largest quarries in the nation. This rock belongs to the Salem formation of Mississippian geologic age, and its texture is spoken of as oölitic because of its resemblance to fish eggs, although the "oölites" are mostly fragments of shells of foraminifera and other marine animals.

812. What is Barre granite? This, the best advertised of all dimension stone, comes from Millstone Hill and Cobble Hill, around Barre, Graniteville, and Williamstown, in Vermont. Monument stone is the chief product, and quarrying and manufacturing are done by a number of companies. Elsewhere in Vermont are prominent deposits of building stone, including one variety, Bethel White (from Windsor County), which is so white that it is often mistaken for marble.

813. What is cement? Fundamentally, cement is an adhesive substance made from limestone and clay or shale. When mixed with water it becomes hard, either in air or under water. *Hydraulic cement* is the kind used to bind mineral aggregates and stone in buildings and engineering works; it hardens or "sets" under water. *Nonhydraulic cement* does not set when used under water. There are many varieties of cement in every-day use, and the industry ranks sixth in value of output among the mineral industries of the United States.

814. What is natural hydraulic cement? Made of limestone that contains the right proportion of shale to set under water, natural hydraulic cement is not common enough or sufficiently uniform to be a reliable source of cement. Nevertheless, large quantities were found in the United States at the right time and place to aid in constructing the locks of the Erie Canal, America's first great project of internal improvement. A large industry got under way around Rosendale, New York, and Lehigh, Pennsylvania.

815. What is Portland cement? This is now the principal type of cement, so named in 1824 by its discoverer because it resembled the noted Portland stone of England (see Question 801). It is the product obtained by calcining to incipient fusion a finely ground mixture of oxides of calcium, silicon, aluminum, and iron in selected proportions and grinding the resulting clinker with a small amount of gypsum.

816. What is puzzuolan? The Romans discovered that quicklime (calcium oxide, CaO) added to the volcanic ash at Puzzuoli yielded a cement that set under water. The Pantheon, aqueducts, baths, and other structures were made from it. In the United States puzzuolan is generally made with blast-furnace slag instead of volcanic ash, and is often referred to as slag-lime cement.

817. What is concrete? Cement, when mixed with crushed rock and sand, binds them together into a strong rocklike material known as concrete, which can be poured in place or cast or molded into any desired shape. *Reinforced concrete* has embedded in it steel or other metal in such a way that the two components act together in resisting forces.

818. Which rock is used to make plaster? Just as limestone is the basic raw material for the manufacture of cement (see Question 813), gypsum is the source-rock for plaster. As with cement, an impurity is desirable to improve the process, especially when wall plaster is being made—a retarder, such as cattle hair, horns, or hoof meal treated with caustic soda and lime delays the setting to a convenient rate. In fact, gypsum is, for maximum economy and effectiveness, the most favored retarder in cement. As with cement, gypsum is heated and then mixed with water to make the finished product.

819. What is land plaster? This is the use of gypsum to supply calcium or sulfur, or both, to soil as fertilizer (see Question 775). Its use is not extensive but is economically feasible in areas surrounding gypsum deposits. It is a preferred soil additive for the peanut crop in the southern states.

820. Which are the varieties of gypsum? Depending upon their purity and structure, there are five varieties of gypsum. The typical material is known as *rock gypsum*. *Gypsite* is an impure earthy form. *Alabaster* is a compact variety suitable for carving (see Question 736); *selenite* is transparent and occurs in crystals; *satin spar* is fibrous and silky. These last three have some ornamental uses; the first two are employed commercially. All are hydrous calcium sulfate.

821. What is plaster of Paris? The outstanding characteristic of gypsum is its unique ability to lose three-quarters of its water of crystallization when heated to relatively low temperatures; this is called *calcining*. Then when mixed with water it resets to a rocklike substance (plaster) in any desired shape. Plaster of Paris is the pure calcined product of the gypsum industry, given its name from the Paris Basin in France, where there are extensive deposits of gypsum.

822. Where is gypsum mined in the United States? California has the largest number of gypsum mines and also produces the largest tonnage, and New York has the largest output of calcined gypsum. Michigan is the second largest mining state. Gypsum is a bulky product, costly to ship long distances. Other major gypsum states are Iowa and Texas.

823. How is pumice used? The cellular, glassy lava known as pumice (see Question 209) has come into substantial use in recent years in the United States as a lightweight aggregate for concrete. Its applications for abrasive and polishing purposes were known a long time ago but have declined recently. Because commercial deposits of pumice are not found east of Kansas, the construction industry rarely uses them in the East in competition with more available substances. After the pumice is mined it is crushed, dried if necessary, and screened into usable sizes, which are mostly less than one-fourth inch.

824. What is mineral wool? A general term embracing various heat and sound insulating materials, mineral wool includes such substances as rock wool, slag wool, glass wool, glass silk, and silicate cotton. These consist of extremely thin silicate fibers resembling wool in appearance. The low-heat conductivity is due to the countless tiny air pockets between the nonconducting fibers or plates. By various techniques the molten silicate is cooled rapidly enough to keep it from crystallizing, and at the same time is subjected to shearing forces.

825. Which is the oldest mineral industry?   The clay industry, involving brick, tile, and clay tablets, for constructing cities, irrigation works, writing materials, and household utensils was the first of the mineral industries, at least on any considerable scale. Buildings in Asia and Africa seem to have been erected of brick made from clay before they were constructed of quarried stone, though possibly scattered boulders (field stone) were used as soon as man emerged from caves. Aurignacian relics, dating back 20 to 30 thousand years, include burned clay figures. Egyptian pottery older than 10,000 years is known from the Solutrean period of Paleolithic times. Much of the course of civilization can be traced in the artistic and useful objects of pottery created by man from clay.

826. What is clay?   Clay is any one or a mixture of many hydrous aluminum silicate minerals containing various proportions of impurities. No two clays are alike nor can they be substituted for one another, as a general rule. Commercially, clay is an earthy substance that is plastic when wet and becomes hardened in any fabricated shape when it is "fired." Clay is the basis of the ceramic industry, although other substances are used as well, and in turn clay has other uses apart from ceramics.

827. What are the kinds of clay?   This is a highly complex subject. Since the introduction of the electron microscope, X-ray diffraction, and thermal-analysis techniques, the individual clay minerals are beginning to present a more meaningful picture to the mineralogist. Names such as kaolinite, montmorillonite, and illite have some real significance at last, but we are far from the final word on this subject. Residual clay is often called *kaolin,* but this word has little actual reality as a specific subject.

As to use, the United States Bureau of Mines classifies clays as kaolin or china clay, ball clay, fire clay, bentonite (see Question 317), fuller's earth (see Question 833), and the inevitable "miscellaneous" clays. C. W. Parmelee and C. R. Schroyer have subdivided clay by ceramic properties into 28 classes and numerous subclasses.

828. What are the uses of clay?　Apart from the ceramic industry, which uses practically all the ball clay and fire clay that is mined, clay is used in paper, rubber, and refractories. Over half of the United States consumption of kaolin or china clay goes into paper making, either as a filler to give it body (see Question 766) or as a coating to give the desired character of surface. Bentonite and fuller's earth have their own special uses outside ceramics. Miscellaneous clays are used for cement and heavy clay products.

829. What is ball clay?　Soft and pliable, ball clay was named in England where it was extracted from open pits by cutting it into rounded lumps weighing about 30 pounds. The clay mineral in it is principally kaolinite, but ball clay contains more iron and organic matter than kaolin or china clay.

830. What is fire clay?　Clay capable of withstanding high temperatures is known as fire clay. Their softening point is above 2,900 degrees Fahrenheit. The constituents are mainly the clay minerals of the kaolinite group, which includes such names as dickite, anauxite, and halloysite. *Flint clay* is a variety of fire clay that is hard and develops a weak plasticity only when finely ground in water; it is typically associated with coal and in the United States occurs most abundantly in Pennsylvania, Ohio, Kentucky, and Missouri. Other kinds of fire clay are much more widespread.

831. How is brick made?　Ordinary building brick is made from miscellaneous surface clay of low grade and from shale. These must be plastic enough to be shaped and must burn to a hard, strong brick between 1,800 and 1,900 degrees Fahrenheit, and must not warp during drying or firing. Brick for facing brick should be of a pleasing appearance and so color is an important factor.

832. How does clay originate?　There are two main origins of clay. One type is produced by the residual weathering of rocks rich in aluminum but low in iron and free quartz. The other type is sedimentary, being transported and deposited under marine, lake, stream, or other conditions. The residual type is more important; the silicate minerals (chiefly feldspar) decompose to form hydrous aluminum silicate, while the soluble silica and so-called alkalies are carried away in solution.

833. What is fuller's earth? This is a variety of bleaching clay which is highly adsorptive of oil, fats, and grease, and is used to filter and decolor them. Montmorillonite is the dominant clay mineral in most fuller's earth, but other minerals can occur, and there is nothing in the composition to indicate the powers of absorption which make it so useful in industry, especially with animal, vegetable, and mineral oils, to absorb and refine them. The requirements of the oil-refining industry are being increasingly met by other materials, including bleaching clay that is "activated" by acid treatment, but fuller's earth is expanding into other markets. Georgia, Florida, and Texas are the major producers in the United States.

834. What is mountain soap? A soapy-feeling variety of halloysite, one of the clay minerals, has been known as mountain soap.

835. What is the role of mullite in refractories? Mullite is an aluminum silicate with the composition $3Al_2O_3 \cdot 2SiO_2$, but it is rare in nature. When certain aluminum silicate minerals are heated to the right temperatures they are converted into mixtures of mullite and free silica. These minerals include kyanite, andalusite, and sillimanite —all having the same chemical formula (see Question 16), dumortierite, and topaz. The resulting product makes an excellent refractory material, used for special ceramics, particularly spark plugs, because it is strong, corrosion resistant, and a good insulator at high temperatures. The mullite-forming minerals are not abundant in the United States in economic concentrations, but kyanite is imported from India.

836. What are the properties of dumortierite? Not an easy mineral to identify without optical tests, dumortierite has often a fibrous appearance. It is of moderate weight but is as hard as quartz. The color may be blue, greenish blue, violet, or pink. In composition this mineral is an aluminum borosilicate, $Al_8BSi_3O_{19}(OH)$. In the United States it comes from Nevada.

837. What is lithopone? First produced in the United States in 1892, and the first commercial use for barite, lithopone is the most common white pigment, used chiefly in paint, and acts as a filler. It is an intimate mixture of 70 per cent barium sulfate—which is the composition of barite—and 30 per cent zinc sulfide. Lithopone is undergoing severe competition from titanium dioxide (see Questions 483–484). Precipitated barium sulfate, used for paint, is known as blanc fixe.

838. What is oil-well mud? The largest use for barite is in well-drilling fluids known as oil-well mud, in which it serves as a weighting agent because of its high specific gravity (see Question 88). This product lubricates and cools the bits employed in the rotary type of drilling; it plasters the wall to prevent caving; it carries the broken fragments or "cuttings" to the surface; and it reduces the high gas and oil pressures found, in the United States, in parts of Texas, Louisiana, and California.

839. Which is the most essential filter? Altogether a long list of natural minerals and rocks are used for a wide range of filtering purposes, such as clarifying beer, decolorizing varnish, and extracting vitamins. The most important use, nevertheless, is for filtering water supplies, and the mineral material used is sand. This kind of sand is obtained from deposits that also yield sand for glass making; it contains a small amount of soluble substances and a certain favored ratio of fine to coarse grains.

XIII. THE FOSSIL FUELS

Introduction. Coal, petroleum, and natural gas are the fossil fuels, so called because they represent energy originating in organic activity of the geologic past and stored for long ages in the rocks of the earth's crust. To these may be added oil shale and tar sands, both of which will doubtless be made to yield on a commercial basis a product serving the same purposes as petroleum. These substances are believed to be forming in the earth today, but they can be of no use until they accumulate in large enough reserves to be worth extracting —an eventuality that will take many millions of years and unforeseen geologic changes. At the current rates of destruction the known fossil fuels will be exhausted by the 21st Century A.D. and will then be available, not for power and fuel, but only as raw materials for the chemical industries.

840. What is coal? Technically, coal is a combustible sedimentary rock which had its origin in the accumulation and partial decomposition of vegetation. Like wood, it is composed of carbon, hydrogen, oxygen, nitrogen, and sulfur, together with small amounts of other chemical elements. The chemistry of coal is extremely complex, and the proportions of the main elements vary considerably according to the particular kind of coal. "Coal is one of the shortest words in the English language," says Edson S. Basten, "but one packed with enormous import, for no other word means so much in terms of industrial power and domestic comfort." It also signifies a splendid pageant of life in those periods of the remote past when plants reached their most luxuriant growth.

841. What is the beginning of coal? All coal, regardless of kind, has a plant ancestry, having formed from the remains of ancient vegetation. This plant life grew during prolonged intervals of uniform warm and moist (but not tropical) climate favorable for the development in forested swamps of a lush foliage. During many centuries the vegetation thrived and died and, after partial decay by micro-organisms, was buried beneath new generations of plants.

246

Increased burial helped to transform the organic material to peat, which looks like tightly packed rotted wood.

842. What further changes occur in peat?   Burial continued under the intermittent loads of mud and other sediment brought in by streams in flood, and invading seas depressed the ground still further under the weight of their water and of the sediment depositing out of it from time to time. Progressive changes carry peat through the successive stages of true coal—*lignite, bituminous, anthracite*—and on until the mineral *graphite* is produced. These changes due to decay and burial may be greatly hastened by pressure from the sides, of the type that produces so-called folded mountain ranges, and by contact with molten rock rising from below.

843. What kind of plants turn to coal?   More than 3,000 species of land plants (including fresh-water and stagnant water species) have been identified from coal beds of the Carboniferous—the Mississippian and Pennsylvanian periods of the Paleozoic era—the Age of Coal. None of them grew in salt water. There seem to be no essential differences among these plants in regard to the various ranks of coal; furthermore, they are not too much different from the vascular vegetation (dominantly conifers) growing at the present time in peat-forming swamps. During the Carboniferous era, however, they rose to astounding sizes. Ferns stood like 50-foot trees, and rushes, such as *Calamites,* with its jointed stalks, grew 100 feet tall. Lycopods, which today are small shrubs known as clubmosses, also reached 100 feet above the ground. *Lepidodendron* and *Sigillaria* are so-called scale trees, with distinctive scars marking the places where the leaves were attached to the branches.

844. How rapidly does coal form?   Volney Lewis estimates that 125 to 150 years would be necessary to accumulate enough material for 1 foot of bituminous coal, and 175 to 200 years for 1 foot of anthracite, but the rate depends upon the climate as well as the vegetation.

845. What chemical and physical changes occur to plants as coal is formed?   Certain of the original plant materials are more resistant than others to decay by the action of bacteria, and so decomposition takes place unequally. Waxes and resin, for instance, are very slow to break down, whereas the protoplasm, sugars, and starch alter readily. Vegetation dries as it is buried and compacted; this is one of the most significant changes that occur in the process of "coalification," the metamorphosis of plants to coal. The other volatile constituents (besides water) also are slowly vaporized, thereby reducing the content of hydrogen, oxygen, nitrogen, and often sulfur, while the percentage of carbon and ash or waste increases in the residue. Important physical changes—in color, luster, density (specific gravity), and manner of breaking—accompany the chemical changes.

846. How is coal analyzed?   The percentages of carbon, hydrogen, oxygen, nitrogen, and sulfur are determined by standard chemical means, giving the so-called *ultimate analysis* of the coal. Usually, however, a more useful *proximate analysis* is sought. This yields four items of information: (1) Water content, termed moisture; (2) ash, which is the total of the mineral impurities (silt, clay, silica, pyrite, marcasite, etc.) left after the coal is otherwise completely burned; (3) volatile matter, consisting of the gases driven off when dry coal is heated to stated temperatures, and (4) fixed carbon, the residue that burns after the volatile matter is expelled. The amount of heat produced by a weighed sample of coal is found by burning it in a closed container called a bomb, which is made of stainless steel, filled with compressed oxygen, and immersed in a measured quantity of water. The increase in temperature of the water after the coal has been entirely burned indicates the heating value of the coal. It is expressed in British thermal units (abbreviated B.t.u.); one B.t.u. is the amount of heat required to raise the temperature of 1 pound of water 1 degree Fahrenheit, from 60 degrees to 61 degrees.

847. What are the ranks of coal?   Coal is classified by rank according to the degree of transformation that it has undergone from its earlier plant and peat stages. Lignite or brown coal is the lowest rank of coal, having been least changed. Bituminous or soft coal is of next highest rank, though frequently subbituminous coal is placed in between as a separate rank. Anthracite or hard coal is the highest rank of true coal. When its volatile matter is thoroughly driven off, anthracite turns to graphite, which is no longer coal but a mineral composed solely of carbon. Below is a table comparing the percentage composition of lignite and anthracite:

	Lignite	Anthracite
Moisture	41	3
Volatile matter	26	5
Fixed carbon	33	92

The lower ranks of coal are further subdivided on the basis of their heating value in British thermal units, as well as their weathering and fusing properties; whereas the higher ranks are subdivided according to their maximum and minimum limits of fixed carbon.

848. What is grade of coal?   The grade of coal, as contrasted with the rank (explained above), depends upon the content of ash and sulfur and the temperature at which the ash fuses. The softening of iron in the ash makes troublesome clinkers, and too much sulfur excludes coal from the making of coke or gas. For this reason an inferior coal may be of high rank but low grade. On the other hand, most anthracite has a somewhat lower heating value than the highest grade bituminous coal, but it is more desirable for residential use because it burns longer without attention and without soot.

849. How else is coal classified?   The commercial grading of coal also involves the size of the pieces and any special treatment that the coal may have been given. Anthracite is screened into usable sizes called grate, egg, stove, chestnut, pea, buckwheat, and the smaller "steam" sizes, rice and barley, leaving the finest material for the silt plant. Bituminous coal is sold in several large or lump sizes, as well as smaller ones, referred to as stove, egg, nut, pea, slack, and pulverized coal. Coal may also be classified according to its principal uses; thus are recognized coking, gas, and steam coal.

850. How do natural fires begin in coal mines?   Apart from the more numerous man-made fires, often set by failure to observe safety rules, fire of natural origin is only too common in coal mines. Spontaneous combustion is usually the result of heating of the coal by its absorption of oxygen, which goes on whenever coal is exposed to the air, as in the outcrops of coal beds and in the shafts and tunnels of mines. Various factors, such as pressure and the pyrite, moisture, and gas content, are involved. Prehistoric fires are known to have occurred in coal deposits long before mining took place; evidence for many of these has been described in central Europe. The famous "burning mountain" near Dudweiler, in the Sarre Basin, was afire more than 150 years; the adjacent shale was baked to a blue and red porcelain jasper and to a red slate. Fires along the outcrops of coal beds at Planitz, in the Zwickau district, which lasted several hundred years, were used in the 19th Century to heat greenhouses. New minerals, including sulfur and realgar, are sometimes formed from the vapors of burning coal just as they are from volcanoes. The lower-rank coals, once brought to the surface, deteriorate rapidly when stored in large piles in a hot place, especially when in fine sizes.

851. What are the properties of peat?   Although peat and coal grade into each other, peat can usually be distinguished from coal in three ways: (1) Many tissues and fibers are recognizable in peat, but few or none in coal. (2) Water can be squeezed out of fresh peat by pressing it in the hand. (3) Peat can be cut. In order to make a good fuel, peat must usually be compressed. Although peat has a widespread distribution, it is best known as domestic fuel in Ireland. In the United States peat is used chiefly as a soil conditioner, in fertilizers, and as a packing material for fruits, vegetables, and plants.

852. What are the properties of lignite?   Typically brownish black in color, lignite is banded and cracked (jointed). It slacks or falls to pieces as it dries in the air and is subject to spontaneous combustion. In use, it is generally turned into gas or powdered to make briquettes. In Germany it supplies synthetic petroleum.

853. What are the properties of bituminous coal?   Black and banded in structure, bituminous coal is well jointed, breaking into cubical or prismatic blocks. It ignites easily and burns with a smoky yellow flame. This is the world's principal industrial coal for heating, power, gas, and coking purposes.

854. What are the properties of anthracite?   The uniform texture and the high luster are characteristic of anthracite. It breaks with a shell-like (conchoidal) fracture. Because it is clean to handle, smokeless when burning with its short, pale-blue flame, and has an excellent heating value, anthracite is the most desired residential fuel of the several kinds of coal.

855. What causes the bands in coal?   The banding in coal is due to the alternating layers of bright and dull material, as well as of smooth and rough material. The smooth-textured glossy layers are composed of *anthraxylon,* formed from the woody parts of plants— trunks or stems, limbs, branches and twigs, and roots. The rough, dull layers consist of *attritus,* which is the finer debris left after the plants have decayed—seeds, spores, and resin. Many coal scientists recognize four ingredients and hence four layers of different names in so-called common banded coal, which is mostly a bright bituminous coal. According to the relative amounts of the constituents that are present, banded coal is generally classified into "types" as bright coal, splint coal, and semisplint or block coal.

856. What furnishes the heat when coal burns?   Both the volatile matter and the fixed carbon supply the heat energy of burning coal, but the slow oxidation of fixed carbon is much more effective in giving economical, long-lasting heat than the more spectacular flames that issue from the escaping gas.

857. What is coke?   Coke has the same relation to coal as charcoal does to wood. In other words, it is coal (mostly bituminous) that has been heated to drive off the volatile matter in the forms of gas, water vapor, light oil, and tar. This process is one of destructive distillation, known as *carbonization.* Before the coal breaks down in this manner, but when it is nearly hot enough to take fire, it softens and tends to swell. Coal having this property is called coking coal; it becomes a hard, gray, porous mass after the volatile matter has been expelled by sufficient heating in a sealed oven made of silica brick. The coke then consists mostly of fixed carbon.

858. What are the uses for coke?   The one indispensable use for coke is for smelting iron ore in blast furnaces, where it must be strong enough to support the weight of tons of ore and limestone. Modern processing of coking coal also results in seven main byproducts— gas, coal tar, ammonia, benzol, toluol, xylol, and naphthalene. From these primary chemicals are made thousands of diverse things ranging from aspirin tablets to nylon stockings, from cosmetics to fertilizers, from synthetic rubber to sulpha drugs. The new coal-hydrogenation process is another step toward the fuller industrial use of coal.

859. What is cannel coal? Originally known as "candle coal" because it ignites readily and burns vividly with a long yellow flame while it yields much illuminating gas, cannel coal (as the Scottish called it) is a special type of bituminous coal composed largely of the golden-colored spores of plants. These are the reproductive organs of the lower plants that do not grow seeds. Younger cannel coal also contains abundant pollen grains, likewise blown by wind onto the stagnant water of coal swamps. In addition, cannel coal consists of coarser parts of plants. All this vegetable matter floated until it became waterlogged and sank to the bottom where it changed into coal having a dull, waxy look. Cannel coal usually occurs in lens-shaped bodies within beds of other coal. It is used mostly in fireplaces as a cheerful fuel, and, owing to its relative scarcity, has been referred to as the aristocrat of coals.

860. What are coal balls? Rounded bodies of mineral matter found in coal are known as coal balls, coal apples, and sulfur balls. These concretions consist mostly of carbonates, iron oxide, sulfides, and clay, shale, or sand. They usually range in size from that of a pea to that of a human head, and they often grow together in clusters. One single coal ball, found in a mine at Shore, England, was about 4 feet across and weighed about 2 tons. Coal balls are noteworthy for their content of plant remains so well preserved that the most delicate organs and cells are clearly visible in all their details. They seem to have originated during the early or peat stage of coal making. Another kind of coal ball occurs especially in the Walsenburg field in Colorado, where shiny, rounded lumps of good-quality coal occur in great numbers. These "natural briquettes" seem to owe their shape to the invasion of molten rock into the coal seam, heating and drying the already-formed coal.

861. Which minerals are found in coal beds? Pyrite and marcasite are the minerals responsible for the "sulfur balls," "sulfur diamonds," and "coal brasses," which in Pennsylvania have frequently been set into souvenir jewelry. Impure siderite (iron carbonate) is common as "ironstone," often useful (especially in Great Britain) as an ore of iron, and often merely a nuisance to the coal producer. Many other ordinary minerals occur in coal beds, together with less familiar ones such as millerite (nickel sulfide), which were evidently brought into the beds at a relatively late date. Coal balls are described above (see Question 860), and boulders of foreign rocks are well known in many places.

862. Which fossils are found in coal beds? Beautifully preserved plant fossils are extremely abundant in coal beds, as may be expected from the vegetable origin of coal. Animal fossils are rare but some curious examples are known, such as the impressive dinosaur footprints in the Thomas mine near Grand Junction, Colorado, and the bones of *Iguanodon,* a gigantic dinosaur, found filling cracks in a mine near Bernissart, Belgium.

863. Where has coal been formed? Although coal is found on all the continents—even on Antarctica—the most important deposits are in the Northern Hemisphere, constituting a belt around the earth in about the same temperate latitudes as present-day peat bogs. The formation of coal has been much less common in the tropics and subtropics, not only during the Carboniferous but in all geologic ages since then.

864. Where does coal occur? The United States has 34.4 of the world's reserves of coal and the major share of its production; hauling coal from American mines to markets is the biggest materials handling job in the world. The Appalachian field, extending from Pennsylvania to Alabama, is much the most important, including the uniquely valuable 484-square-mile anthracite area in northeastern Pennsylvania and the largest continuous bituminous area in the world. Western American coal is of generally lower rank than Eastern because most of it was formed one whole era later, during the Cretaceous period, and so has been involved in considerably less earth movement. The deposits, further, are of less value because they are farther from centers of industry. The Soviet Union (24.0 per cent), China (20.2 per cent), and Germany (7.0 per cent) have great coal reserves, and Great Britain, though with a smaller supply (3.4 per cent), is one of the leading producers.

865. Why are the coal deposits of the following states and provinces especially interesting: Nova Scotia? The coal beds in the Sydney field dip beneath the Atlantic Ocean and have been mined under the sea more than 3½ miles from shore. The deepest coal mining in America is at Springhill, at a depth of 3,750 feet.

866. Rhode Island? The coal in this state is of interest mainly because it has been so compressed by intense mountain-making forces that some of it has been changed into graphite and hence does not burn. No coal is produced in any of the New England states.

867. Pennsylvania? The anthracite beds of northeastern Pennsylvania are of outstanding importance; the noted Mammoth seam reaches a thickness of 50 to 60 feet, nearly all good coal. The Pittsburgh seam of bituminous coal is exceptionally widespread.

868. West Virginia? Currently the leading producer of coal in the United States, West Virginia mines much bituminous coal from the well-advertised Pittsburgh and Pocahontas seams.

869. Illinois? Nearly three-quarters of this state is underlain by coal beds, covered with glacial rock from the Ice Age.

870. North Dakota? The largest reserves of coal in the United States are in North Dakota, estimated at 633,329,800,000 tons, but nearly all of it is lignite and only about one-third is believed recoverable.

871. What is petroleum? Petroleum is a natural mixture of various liquid hydrocarbons. With them are so intimately associated the gaseous hydrocarbons known as natural gas that the two products, having usually the same origin, are generally considered together. The petroleum industry, therefore, includes the search for and utilization of deposits of both petroleum or oil and natural gas. This oil is so-called rock oil, which is the meaning of the word petroleum (from the Latin *petra*, "rock," and *oleum*, "oil"). In its original state it is referred to as crude oil or simply crude, to distinguish it from the refinery product. It contains some dissolved solid hydrocarbons as well as the gases mentioned. Typical metallic elements occurring with petroleum are vanadium, molybdenum, and nickel.

872. What is the composition of petroleum? Thousands of compounds of hydrogen atoms and carbon atoms are found as hydrocarbons in petroleum. The heavier hydrocarbons, consisting of the most complex molecules, are unstable and tend to decompose when heated, making it impossible to analyze crude oil in terms of its original compounds except for the lightest ones that can be separated. Hydrogen and carbon are also combined with sulfur, oxygen, and nitrogen, all characteristic of organic substances, such as coal (see Question 840). In addition, nickel, vanadium, and phosphorus seem always to occur in small amounts. No two oils are alike in properties because they vary so extensively in the kinds of hydrocarbons that they contain and the proportions of each that are present.

873. What are live and dead oils? Crude oil that has a substantial amount of natural gas dissolved in it is known as live oil because of its lightness and mobility—the gas acting to propel it along beneath the ground. After most of the gas has escaped, the petroleum becomes dead oil and is considerably less vigorous. This happens as the oil rises toward the surface where the pressure is less and the liquid and gaseous phases tend to separate. The gas is then found on top of the oil and may be extracted independently. However, it is then no longer able to bring the oil up with it, and so the total recovery is less than is required by good conservation practices. The fluidity of petroleum at depth is also aided by the higher temperatures there.

874. Which minor gases occur in natural gas? Although natural gas consists principally of methane, other interesting gases besides carbon dioxide (see Question 875) are sometimes found with it. Of these, helium is the most important; it occurs in New Mexico, Texas, Colorado, and Utah, though nowhere else in the world in commercial volume. Nitrogen, also a noninflammable gas, is another unusual product of some wells, and hydrogen sulfide is a fairly common but obnoxious one.

875. What is an ice cream well? Carbon dioxide, which is known as dry ice when it "freezes" solid, is an occasional associate of natural gas. If an appreciable amount of carbon dioxide is present, the surface pipes and metal fittings—the so-called "Christmas tree"— of a well may become coated with frost as a result of the rapid evaporation and drastic cooling effect of this substance. Owing to its curious appearance, such an installation is spoken of as an ice cream well.

876. What is the origin of oil?   No permissible doubt remains that all petroleum, like all coal, is of organic origin. Whether its source is animal or vegetable is not certain; many kinds of animal and plant life are capable of yielding oil and gas under appropriate conditions, but the transformations that petroleum undergoes during its complex history cause it to lose its earlier identity. Oil can also be produced by inorganic chemical reactions, but the geologic evidence is overwhelmingly against such an origin. More than 99 per cent of the world's oil and gas has to date come from sedimentary rocks (see Chapter IV) typically rich in organic material. Marine invertebrates, such as the one-celled foraminifera, and one-celled plants, such as algae and diatoms, seem to bear the likeliest responsibility for the creation of the substances that gradually evolve into crude petroleum as we know it. After accumulating in a suitable environment (chiefly marine and near shore), the hydrocarbons must be buried for preservation, change from a solid state to a liquid or gas, move (migrate) to a favorable reservoir rock—because oil and gas do not occur commercially in the same rocks in which they probably formed—and end in a favorable structure or trap, from which they can be extracted.

877. How does petroleum exist in the earth?   Oil and gas occupy openings in the soil and bedrock exactly as does subsurface water (see Question 934). These openings may be primary, having formed at the same time as the rocks themselves, or they may be secondary, having formed later. Usually they exist as pore spaces between the mineral grains. Sometimes they are cracks or fissures of various kinds. Only in soluble rocks, such as the carbonates limestone and dolomite —where there are actual caverns beneath the earth—is such a thing as a "pool of oil" possible. Otherwise, there is nothing resembling an underground lake of oil anywhere.

878. What is an oil seep? An oil seep is actually an oil spring. From it may come a few drops of petroleum or a considerable quantity, together with water upon which it floats as an iridescent film of rainbow colors. A few seeps have been profitable to exploit. Many, instead, have been the direct means of discovering some of the most prolific oil deposits of the world, though in other places they seem to be too far removed from the original source of the oil to serve as useful indicators. The accidental escape of gasoline or fuel oil from a pipe line or storage tank has touched off many a false oil "boom," as has the excessive oiling of pumps on water wells. Some frauds have been committed in such ways on purpose.

879. What is an oil structure? The reservoir rock into which petroleum has migrated from its place of origin, called the source rock, must be enclosed if the oil and gas are not to escape still farther. Such a closed reservoir, in which the petroleum is confined between impervious rock, is spoken of as a trap. *Structural traps* or, simply, *structures* are the result of movements of the earth's crust, resulting in fissures, faults, or folds. A common example is an anticline, into which the oil rises, having (typically) a zone of lighter gas above and of heavier water beneath. Traps that contain petroleum in certain spots but not in others because of differences in the permeability of the rock are called *stratigraphic traps,* and these are becoming increasingly important.

880. When was the first oil well drilled? The enormous petroleum industry had its birth in June 1859 when the first well ever drilled purposely for the sole recovery of rock oil was begun near Titusville, Pennsylvania, near an old oil spring on the banks of Oil Creek. August 27th it began to produce at a depth of 69½ feet. This historic place is known as the Drake well, because the enterprise was under the immediate direction of "Colonel" Edwin L. Drake, a former railroad conductor, who was given his title by the promoters to impress the local residents.

Oil had, however, been obtained nearly 2,000 years ago in China, from wells drilled for natural gas, and in Burma before the 10th Century. Other ancient wells drilled for water or salt brine also obtained oil, but mostly it was regarded as a nuisance and was wasted, because its uses were limited to an amount that could be met by oil from natural seeps. When the supply of whale oil for illumination declined in the 19th Century, kerosine or "coal oil" derived from the distillation of coal was substituted, but it too was expensive. Oil wells met the challenge of lighting the nation, and then went on to furnish lubricants and fuel, as well. Today they yield a vast array of ultimate products ranging from aviation gasoline to candles and drugs. If the meat packers use "everything but the squeal," the ingenious petroleum industry would probably find a market even for that.

881. How are oil wells drilled?   Since machinery was first applied to the sinking of wells, two distinct methods have developed. The older one is known as standard, cable tool, churn, or percussion drilling. Particles of rock, called cuttings, are broken off by the repeated dropping from a derrick of a heavy "string of tools" which ends in a metal bit, having a V-shaped edge; the cuttings are removed at intervals to deepen the hole. This method has been largely superseded, especially in deep wells, by the more expensive rotary drilling. Its basic technique involves a rotating bit which shaves and grinds off pieces of rock as it turns. These cuttings are removed continuously by a stream of "mud" pumped down from the surface and brought back up (see Question 838). Instead of loose cuttings, a solid cylinder of rock, known as a core, may be extracted intact in order to study the rock structure; diamond-studded bits are the most satisfactory for this purpose. Nearly a million oil wells have been drilled to date, the deepest reaching 25,515 feet.

882. Where are the principal oil fields?   Most of the petroleum fields of the world are situated in basins of sedimentary rocks, generally in structurally low areas and often along the margins of the continents. The richest deposits are concentrated in three great intercontinental depressions in the earth's crust, and a fourth such location—which includes Alaska—seems indicated by the geologic evidence. One region is situated within and adjacent to the Gulf of Mexico and the Caribbean Sea, between North and South America. Here are the Gulf Coast oil fields of Louisiana and Texas, and those in Mexico, Colombia, Venezuela, and Trinidad. A second region lies between Africa, Europe, and Asia, overlapping all three continents where they border the Persian Gulf and the Red Sea, Mediterranean, Black Sea, and Caspian Sea. Here are Southern Russia and the Middle East of Iraq, Iran, Kuwait, Saudi Arabia, Bahrein Island, and their neighbors, all so prominent in today's news. The third region surrounds the shallow waters between Asia and Australia —the Far East islands of Sumatra, Borneo, Java, and New Guinea. A fourth region, of enormous potential, rims the Arctic Ocean, touching North America, Asia, and Europe. Smaller oil-producing basins rest on the edges and within the interiors of all the continental masses. Even the Sahara Desert seems to be underlain by oil-saturated rock.

883. How is petroleum refined? Refining is the manufacturing stage of the petroleum industry. Nearness to oil fields, centers of consumption, and water transportation determines where refineries will be established. In these plants the crude oil is separated into various groups or "fractions" of hydrocarbons, according to their different volatilities or boiling-point ranges. This is accomplished by heating the oil in rows of steel tubes and thereby vaporizing part of it. The vapors then condense at varying temperatures in a closed vertical tower called a *fractionating column,* while the remaining liquid is drawn off as the *residue.* This *fractional distillation* produces "straight run" products, among which are gasoline, naphtha, kerosine, and fuel oil.

In order to create a larger yield of gasoline (and better gasoline, at that) from crude oil, thermal and catalytic ("cat") cracking processes have been introduced, which break down the heavy molecules of hydrocarbons into simpler and more volatile ones. Besides these basic methods, many other complex refining techniques (including polymerization, hydrogenation, alkylation) are currently employed in this extraordinary industry.

884. What are light and heavy oils? The physical property of petroleum most often considered is density or gravity, and much crude oil is priced on this basis. These technical terms, however, do not mean the same as they do in mineralogy (see Question 88); in fact light oil is said to have a higher "gravity" than heavy oil. Light oil contains more of the volatile hydrocarbons, which boil at lower temperatures and yield more of the profitable gasoline constituents; it is also usually lighter in color, such as the amber-colored high-grade Pennsylvania oil. Medium-gravity oil, typical of the Mid-

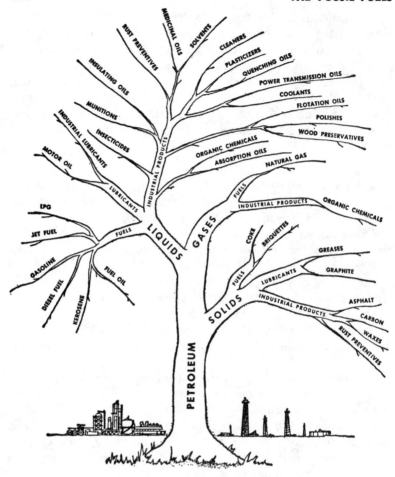

Petroleum and its products

Continent region of the United States, is chiefly green. Heavy oil, having a low gravity, contains more of the undesirable substances which increase refining expense, and it is generally black. The gravity of petroleum is measured by the Baumé scale, in which pure water stands at 10 degrees Baumé. In current practice the American Petroleum Institute (API) scale is used, in which the formula $141.5 +$ (degrees Baumé $+ 131.5$) calculates the actual specific gravity.

885. What are tar sands? Deposits of sand impregnated with heavy oil which serves as a binding or cementing agent are known as tar sands. This oil may have come from a hidden seep or it may be a normal component of the rock formation. The extensive Athabaska tar sands of northeastern Alberta are the greatest of their kind. After years of abandonment, they are once again being investigated as a future major source of petroleum products, ranking second in reserves only to the oil shale of the Western United States (see Question 890). The Athabaska oil is not fluid enough to flow by itself or be pumped from wells, and so it will have to be extracted by mining the sand and treating it with steam, hot water, solvents, or some other method still to be devised.

886. What is a pitch lake? Large deposits of asphalt, a plastic residue left by the evaporation of the more volatile constituents of petroleum, are often called pitch lakes. The most noted example in the world is on the island of Trinidad. Pirates calked their ships with asphalt from there during the days of the buccaneers, as also did Sir Walter Raleigh in 1595. Production has been continuous since 1867, but the millions of tons that have been taken from the nearly circular lake, ⅓ mile in diameter, have lowered its level only about 16 feet. It is believed that the supply is being replenished by fresh seepage of heavy oil from below. Most commercial asphalt, however, is one of the many artificial products of oil refining (see Question 883).

887. Why is Rancho La Brea famous? An exposed accumulation of tarry (semi-solid) hydrocarbons in the city of Los Angeles, California, is a noted burial ground for Pleistocene (Ice Age) animals which were attracted to its shiny surface and became trapped in the sticky stuff. Other animals coming to observe or feed upon them were likewise caught, until this spot became the best outdoor museum of prehistoric mammals in existence. Formerly known as Rancho La Brea, the locality is now referred to as the La Brea tar pits and is an easily accessible city park. Among its relics are the skeletons of the mammoth, mastodon, ground sloth, saber-tooth tiger, and dire wolf.

888. What is gilsonite? A naturally occurring solid hydrocarbon, gilsonite is found in vertical fissures in the Uintah and Green River beds of sandstone and shale in the Uintah Basin of eastern Utah and western Colorado. Some of these veins run for miles across a desolate countryside. When heated to between 250 and 500 degrees Fahrenheit, this black, shiny, brittle substance softens; in this state it has been used for insulation and a myriad of other purposes, from ink to moulded products. The discovery of feasible methods of converting gilsonite to high-octane gasoline and pure coke led to the construction of a refinery near Grand Junction, Colorado, which opened in 1957. The gilsonite is mined at Bonanza, Utah, by utilizing jets of water under high pressure, sometimes combined with a mechanical rotary cutter. The raw material is then carried under pressure through a remarkable pipeline 72 miles long. On the 27-hour journey it crosses 8,500-foot Baxter Pass in the Book Cliffs and spans two deep canyons across the White River and Evacuation Wash, following the earlier route of a curious narrow-gauge railroad in this region.

889. What is mountain tallow?   A yellow, waxy hydrocarbon generally stated to be hatchettite, goes under the name mountain tallow.

890. What is oil shale?   Oil shale is a rock containing an organic substance, a waxlike bitumen, known as kerogen, which consists mainly of plant spores and pollen. From it a petroleum-like product can be generated by heat, though not by pressure or chemicals. The same thing, incidentally, can be done with coal (see Question 858). Except by coincidence, oil shale does not occur with the usual kinds of petroleum-bearing rocks, inasmuch as they have formed under unlike conditions. "Shale oil" has been produced commercially in Scotland and Estonia, as well as in lesser amounts in Manchuria, Sweden, France, and elsewhere. Probably the greatest reserve of oil in the entire world exists in the oil shale of the Green River formation of Colorado, Utah, and Wyoming—the largest-scale mineral resource on earth, apart from the oceans. This sedimentary rock was deposited about 60 million years ago in an inland lake. Oil shale in Alaska is older and of marine origin.

XIV. MINING AND MILLING

Introduction. The recovery of rocks and minerals from the earth has undergone vast changes since primitive man extracted them with his hands and by means of crude tools. The techniques that are used play an important part in determining whether a given deposit can be operated profitably—the term ore, it will be recalled, has both a commercial and a scientific connotation. With further improvements in recovery, still leaner deposits can be expected to be worked economically, until eventually, no doubt, all the world's mineral needs will be met by the bulk use of common rocks, from which will be taken everything that is required. Mining terms are known by the thousand because they originated in various areas of the world and have been transplanted elsewhere; hence, there are similar names from various languages for the same processes, according to whether the miners came from Saxony, Wales, Cornwall, or other places.

891. What is strip mining? Flat-lying sedimentary rocks that are at or near the surface may be excavated by *stripping* operations. Large power shovels remove the overburden and then extract the useful mineral material. Often parallel strips are worked and the waste rock from one strip is dropped into the previous opening. Coal, bauxite, clay, and phosphate are commonly subject to strip mining.

892. What is an open cut? Surface mining of large-scale, usually low-grade mineral deposits is done by means of an open cut. Iron ore, "porphyry" copper (see Question 419), asbestos, clay, and bauxite are among the products likely to be worked by open-cut methods. In the largest operations, such as those involving Lake Superior iron and Western "porphyry" copper, enormous benches descend like great steps into the earth, and ore trains that look like toys from the top slowly wind their way from one level to another.

893. What is a glory hole? This is a combination of open-cut and underground mining. The mining itself goes on within a surface opening, where the cost of operating is less than it would be underground. But when the pit is deep and the sides cannot be set back sufficiently, the rock is removed by being dropped into underground passages, from which it is later removed. Some of the great diamond mines of South Africa are the best examples of glory holes.

894. What is a quarry? Building and other stone and certain other rocks, such as those of pegmatite deposits, are mined in quarries, which are open excavations more or less straight-sided in outline. A quarry may vary from a small opening, worked with hand tools, to a highly mechanized operation.

895. What are pits and trenches? These are small shallow holes from which scattered surface deposits are removed. Pits are generally rounded and trenches are elongated. Placer sand and gravel is an example of material taken from typical pits and trenches.

896. What is hydraulicking? Powerful jets of water wash down loose material, especially from placer deposits, and direct it into traps in which it is caught for the necessary cleaning or separation. Hydraulicking is associated most distinctively with early California gold mining. It is used today in tin mining in Southeast Asia and in limited ways elsewhere.

897. What is a dredge? A dredge is a floating mine, the most elaborate method of placer mining. Set in position in the placer area, the flat-bottomed boat digs itself into an artificial pond; the water is supplied or diverted from somewhere else. As the dredge extracts material from one side of the pond and rejects the waste on the other side, it moves along and advances the pond with it. The loose sand and gravel is washed, screened, and separated on the dredge itself. Row upon row of symmetrical piles of waste gravel characterize the distinctive appearance of a dredge's operation.

898. How is placer gold recovered? The fundamental device for separating native gold from placer sand and gravel is the *sluice* or sluice box. It is a trough, usually made of wood, through which the sediment is washed by a stream of water. Obstructions called riffles— these are usually slats of wood—are attached to the bottom on the inside, where they interrupt the current and provide a protected spot for the gold to settle. Mercury may be put in the riffles to help catch the gold.

899. How is vein gold recovered? For vein gold the methods of *amalgamation* and *cyanidation* are employed. In amalgamation, the ground ore is passed over copper plates coated with mercury, with which the native gold alloys and adheres to the copper, and from which it is separated by scraping off the amalgam and heating it. In cyanidation, the ore is finely ground and leached in tanks containing a solution of sodium cyanide, which dissolves the gold; the metal is then precipitated by adding zinc dust. Preliminary gravity separation (whereby the heavy minerals sink, see Question 923), flotation (whereby the valuable minerals float on a froth of oil, see Question 925), or roasting (which involves heating with access of air but without fusion), may be employed for gold ores before amalgamation or cyanidation. Each deposit presents its own problems of recovery.

900. What is a prospect? A mineral property, the value of which has not yet been proved by exploration, is referred to as a prospect. It represents the intermediate stage between prospecting and mining. Further drilling, testing, and sampling are needed before a prospect can be regarded as a working mine.

901. What is an adit? A tunnel that penetrates a hill from the outside is properly termed an adit, although the word tunnel is often misused for this kind of entry. Ore cars on tracks may haul out the broken rock that is being extracted within the mine.

902. What is a shaft? A vertical opening into a mine is called a shaft. Shafts likewise may be inclined, though these are less common. Some shafts are used solely for lowering the miners to work, some for hoisting the ore to the surface, and some for both purposes.

903. What is a level? This is a tunnel extending from the shaft of a mine (see Question 902). Levels are usually opened at definite intervals, perhaps 100 feet apart. In this case they would be referred to as the first and second level, etc., or the 100-foot and 200-foot level; occasionally they are given letters or even names.

904. What is a drift? A drift is a horizontal opening from a mine level (see Question 903), paralleling the ore veins, hence following or drifting along in the same direction.

905. What is a cross-cut? Unlike a drift, which proceeds with the trend of the ore (see Question 904), a cross-cut is a horizontal mine opening that cuts perpendicularly or at a large angle to the ore. Perhaps it intersects a number of parallel veins.

906. What is a raise? A raise is the vertical upward opening from a regular mine tunnel or level (see Question 903). It may enable the miners to approach the ore from the nearest position.

907. What is a winze? Opposite to a raise (see Question 906), a winze is a vertical opening that drops downward from a mine level.

908. What is a stope? This important term refers to the opening at the actual place where the ore is being excavated. From the typical stope in a modern mine the ore is drilled into and blasted downward. Then it is drawn off through chutes, moved in cars to the hoisting shaft, carried rapidly to the surface in "skips," and dumped into ore bins.

909. What is an apex? The apex is the surface exposure of a vein where it outcrops on the ground. According to American mining law, the position of the apex is of vital importance in conferring rights to mine at depths beyond the actual surface limits of one's own property. This can be done by following the vein from its apex downward within the end lines of a mining claim.

910. What is the hanging wall? The rock surface on the upper side of an inclined vein is called the hanging wall, because to a miner working along the vein it hangs above his head.

911. What is the foot wall? In contrast to the hanging wall (see Question 910), the foot wall consists of the rock surface under an inclined vein. Thus, it lies beneath the feet of a miner standing within the vein area.

912. What are strike and dip? These important terms are useful to describe any body or structure in three dimensions. The strike is the trend of a bed, vein, or other inclined surface, as measured by a compass on a horizontal plane. Thus, a vein or bed of rock may be said to strike northeast. The dip is the angle at which these bodies or surfaces are inclined from the horizontal. Thus, the same vein or bed of rock may have a 45-degree dip. The dip is always perpendicular to the strike; therefore, this one will dip either southeast or northwest at the stated angle.

913. What is a sump? This is an excavation made underground, often at the bottom of a shaft, for the purpose of collecting water, which may be pumped to the surface or to a higher sump. Underground water (discussed in Chapter XV) is a constant nuisance and hazard in virtually all mining activities.

914. What is tramming? Transporting ore underground in cars that run on tracks is known as tramming. The tracks are usually laid so that the empty cars are pushed slightly upgrade, and the heavy filled cars move downgrade in the opposite direction. Where profitable to do so, hand tramming is superseded by animal (mule or horse) and mechanical haulage. Belt conveyor systems are increasing in number.

915. What is room and pillar mining? Flat-lying coal seams, in which support of the roof is a major problem, may be mined by the room and pillar method. From a series of rooms the coal is removed, leaving isolated pillars of coal to hold up the ceiling. As the exposed "face" of coal is undercut, the roof pressure cracks it off, so that the coal gradually retreats toward the end of each room. Some of the coal pillars may be replaced by artificial supports, but considerable loss of coal results nevertheless.

916. What is longwall mining? More efficient than room and pillar mining for coal (see Question 915), but likewise used for flat beds, the longwall method involves extending tunnels from a central shaft to the outward limits of mining. From these limits mining takes place inward, the roof settling into the excavated areas.

917. What is a captive coal mine? Mines owned by steel and utility companies, railroads, and other direct consumers of the coal that is produced are spoken of as captive mines. In 1963 they mined 64 million tons of bituminous coal, or 14 per cent of the total United States output of 459 million tons. The largest single coal mine in the country, the Robena mine in Pennsylvania, is a captive mine, owned by the United States Steel Corporation; its 1955 tonnage was 4,914,741.

918. What is ore dressing?   The object of ore dressing is to prepare the crude ore for more economical transportation and for further processing to recover the metallic contents. It is thus related to milling (see Question 919) and some of the techniques overlap. Ore dressing, however, is specifically the cleaning of ore by the removal of valueless portions. Physical, rather than chemical, methods are employed. Jigging (shaking), cobbing (hammering), and vanning (winnowing) are among the processes utilized.

Rod mill for crushing ores

919. What is the purpose of milling?   To mechanically enrich a low-grade mineral deposit for further treatment, to separate various metallic minerals from one another, or to yield a desired product in finished form—these are the several purposes of milling. Preliminary crushing to a suitable size is almost always required. Milling includes amalgamation and cyanidation (see Question 899) and various concentration processes.

920. What is free-milling gold?   When native gold can be recovered by picking it up with mercury (amalgamation) or by dissolving it in solutions of cyanide (cyanidation), it is said to be free milling, in contrast to its occurrence in minerals that are difficult to treat and must be concentrated and smelted by more expensive methods.

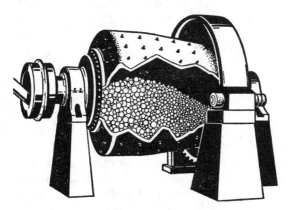

Ball mill for crushing ores

921. How is concentration effected? Various methods of concentration are employed in order to separate the valuable minerals from the undesired ones, when the useful constituents are thinly dispersed throughout the entire body or else make up a fairly substantial proportion of the whole. First, crushing and grinding sets free the wanted minerals; sometimes roasting in a furnace is necessary to aid in the process. Then the valuable minerals are collected, while the waste material is discarded. Concentration helps to reduce the volume of rock to be treated further and hence keeps down the cost of milling. Many ores that could not be worked commercially if shipped in the raw state may be profitable if concentrated before shipment.

922. Are some minerals sorted by hand? When the price of a mineral is high enough to justify hand sorting, this method is used. Usually the valuable mineral is selected from conveyor belts or revolving tables, though on occasion the waste rock is removed and the rest passes along for later treatment. Gem stones, mica, beryl, high-quality asbestos, and other expensive or fragile minerals are often sorted by hand because there is no other means of separating them.

923. What is gravity concentration? This process depends upon a difference in the relative weight (specific gravity, see Question 88) between the useful and the waste minerals. Generally, valuable minerals are enough heavier than the waste or gangue to make it feasible to separate them by devices that cause the broken rock to vibrate or pulsate. The heavy minerals settle to the bottom or move to one side, where they can be recovered for additional treatment.

924. What is sink-and-float?   Crushed ores immersed in a heavy solution, or in a mineral suspension that acts like a liquid, will separate according to their specific gravities—the heavy particles sinking, the lighter (and usually valueless) ones floating.

925. How can heavy minerals float?   The entire principle of gravity in mineral separation is defied by the process known as flotation, which has now become the principal means of separating most metallic minerals and some nonmetallic ones. In "flotation cells" the finely ground ore adheres to a froth of air bubbles which have been coated with a special oil. The minerals for which the oil has been selected then float upward and can be skimmed off. Sulfide minerals are the most amenable to flotation.

926. What is leaching?   Minerals that are soluble in certain inexpensive solvents may be dissolved out of their host rock in an easy manner. Copper, especially, is soluble in acids; sulfuric acid is widely used, and in some places it is even produced by the natural action of water on the ore bodies. Ammonia is used for leaching in some operations, and water in others. Potash, nitrates, and underground salt are leached merely with water.

927. What is smelting?   The melting of ores in furnaces is called smelting—the two words have a common origin. Both blast and reverberatory furnaces, fueled by natural gas or coke, are used. The ore (perhaps concentrated or hand sorted) is referred to as the "feed." To it is added a flux for easier fusion; this also forms a slag in which the waste material collects. While the slag rises, the molten metal settles to the bottom of the furnace, where it is tapped off.

928. What is blister copper?   So called because of the rough surface caused by escaping gases, blister copper is the original metallic copper as it comes from the "converter" in the form of castings. Still too impure for use, blister copper must be further treated in a holding or casting furnace, where it is cast into blister cakes or anodes for shipment to the refinery (see Question 929), or else it is poured molten into a reverberatory furnace, where it is fire refined and then cast into commercial shapes such as cakes, billets, or ingots.

929. What is refining? Usually the last step in the treatment of metallic minerals, refining is of two kinds, fire and electrolytic. It has for its purpose the purification of metal, getting rid of harmful ingredients and recovering the small amounts of valuable "impurities" that are present. Gold, for example, may be of considerable worth in a copper deposit, yet not recoverable until the copper is electrolytically refined, using acid tanks through which an electric current is passed.

930. What is a complex ore? An ore containing minerals of two or more metals is a complex ore. An example is the lead-zinc-silver ore of many Western states. Frequently such an ore can be exploited economically only if the different metals are separated before smelting, as by flotation, and the processes for recovery are always complicated.

XV. WATER RESOURCES

Introduction. Water falling from the heavens as rain and snow; flowing across the surface as bright (or tarnished) ribbons of brook and stream and river; and coursing slowly through the soil and bedrock beneath the ground—"the waters under the earth"—is our one indispensable mineral, our most precious mineral resource. Yet so all-pervading is it that we take it for granted most of the time, until threat of shortage makes us realize with an incredulous shock how much we need water and how very much of it we actually do need.

Civilizations have risen and fallen and been arranged in their peculiar ways largely because of the distribution of underground water; no physical aspect of nature other than the basic patterns of climate itself—upon which water so largely depends—have been so effective in guiding man's role on the earth. The somewhat-near future seems to present an opportunity for the first time in history for converting our principal supply from mineral-laden sea water to salt-free water, transported where we will; but the use of nuclear energy for this purpose has not yet been perfected. Until then we shall be more dependent than ever before upon our ordinary water resources, because irrigation for agriculture and the water requirements for air-conditioning and industry are increasing with the world's expanding economy and burgeoning population.

931. What are the chief uses for water? The principal uses of water are irrigation, industrial supply, and municipal use. Industries developing their own supply rather than buying it from a city make up 46 per cent of the total water use in the United States, exclusive of water employed to develop electric power, which is nonconsumptive because it does not involve withdrawal from rivers or the ground. Irrigation, the main consumptive use of water, accounts for another 46 per cent. Water use for public supplies constitutes 7 per cent, and rural use other than irrigation 1 per cent. Public water-supply use and industrial use are only partly consumptive.

932. What are the industrial uses of water? The most important requirement for industrial water is for processing. Among the largest industrial consumers of water, however—and a relatively few account for the biggest aggregate use—the most important need is for cooling. Other significant uses are for sanitary and service purposes and for boiler feed. A substantial number of industrial plants reuse their intake two or even three times. About half of the companies surveyed by the National Association of Manufacturers and the Conservation Foundation have their own facilities for treating water, the rest relying upon municipal water systems or else not requiring a high degree of purity. More of the larger plants have their own water-treating equipment because it is more economical for them to do so. These large firms are fairly evenly distributed among the industrial metropolitan areas of the United States, the East North Central region being of course the most important.

933. What is the water supply of the United States? On the average about 30 inches of precipitation occurs annually over the United States, according to the Weather Bureau. Records of the United States Geological Survey show that about 21.5 inches of rainfall returns to the atmosphere through *evaporation* and the *transpiration* of vegetation. This varies considerably from place to place, as do the rainfall and snowfall themselves. About 8.5 inches flows across the surface of the land to the sea through the many systems of streams that appear on maps—this is termed the *run-off*—or percolates through the ground into the streams, eventually to reach the ocean by that route. About three-fourths of an inch of this total water supply is intercepted for direct use by man and his industries.

The ocean is the grand reservoir of water from which comes most of the atmospheric precipitation. This came originally from within the earth during the passage of geologic time. Water in lakes and ponds, streams, and the soil is forever returning to the ocean by the continually recurring *hydrologic cycle,* and under normal conditions water of some kind or quality is present at some distance beneath the earth in every spot on the globe.

934. How does water occur beneath the ground? *Ground water, underground water, subsurface water*—these are names for the same thing, the water that fills pore spaces, fissures, and other openings in soil and bedrock below the visible level of the earth's horizon. Water does not—contrary to popular opinion and the claims of fakers or fiction writers—it does not exist as "veins," "domes," "streams," "lakes," or "pools." The occurrence of underground streams or pools is of very limited extent, being possible only where limestone or other soluble rocks have been dissolved to form local caverns, and these supply little water for dependable use.

935. What is the water table?　This vital concept is the boundary that separates the upper *zone of aeration* or *vadose zone* from the lower *zone of saturation,* in which all the air spaces have now been filled with water and from which water can be obtained in reliable amounts. The water table follows somewhat generally the contour

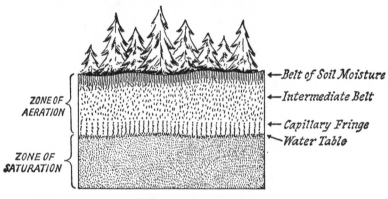

ZONE OF AERATION

ZONE OF SATURATION

←*Belt of Soil Moisture*

←*Intermediate Belt*

←*Capillary Fringe*

←*Water Table*

Underground water zones

of the land surface, being, in humid climates, higher beneath hills and lower beneath valleys. It rises and falls according to the seasonal precipitation—that is, upon how much is supplied to it from above, as the water soaks through the higher levels in its descent to the water table. Where the water table reaches the surface, the ground is swampy, or there will be a pond or lake if a closed depression extends beneath it. If the depression is open at the far end, a spring-fed stream begins to flow. To be sure of a permanent supply of water, a well must penetrate the water table deeply enough so that it will not be stranded by seasonal variations in the height to which the water rises from time to time.

936. What is an artesian well?　Many farmers and ranchers call any deep well artesian, but this term applies properly only to a well in which the water rises higher than its immediate outlet, due to the pressure behind it of water at a higher altitude. The water must have its point of intake at a superior elevation; the difference in altitude—called the "head of water"—will (allowing for some frictional resistance) furnish the pressure that will move the water along to its point of discharge. In some artesian wells the water will rise to the

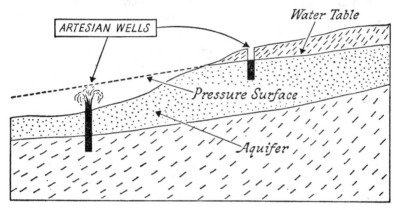

Artesian water system

surface; in others it will rise only part way and has to be pumped the rest of the way. An artesian system can occur only when the ground water is confined within a layer of inclined rock that is both porous and permeable, overlain and underlain by impermeable rocks —the whole resembling, except in shape, a natural water main.

937. What is the difference between porosity and permeability?
Porosity is the amount of water and other fluids (such as oil and natural gas) that a rock will hold in its pore spaces, cracks, solution cavities, and other openings. But a rock, no matter how porous, will not transmit fluids unless it is also permeable—its permeability being its capacity to enable these fluids to move under pressure. A volcanic rock may be porous, as pumice most certainly is (see Question 209), but the separate gas cavities will prevent any movement of water through it, and so its permeability is nil. Clay, among the sedimentary rocks, may be extremely porous and more than half of its volume may consist of water; but the pore spaces are so close together that the water is gripped by surface tension and the droplets do not flow. A

much less porous gravel, in contrast, will transmit water easily because it is so much coarser.

938. What are the impurities in water?　Water impurities consist of contamination and pollution. Pollution by bacteria is at a minimum because of the filtrating action of sand and rock material, although water that flows through porous limestone may be quite unsafe to drink. It is not true that water automatically purifies itself in one hundred yards or any specified distance of movement through sand or any other natural substance. Contamination of water is produced by the presence of dissolved gases, iron and manganese, sulfates, carbonates, and common salt. Gases, such as hydrogen sulfide and methane, may be obnoxious, but aeration removes them. Carbon dioxide makes a natural soda-water and, although it can be driven out readily, is often considered an advantage and is used to concoct palatable soft drinks. Iron and manganese leave stains on porcelain and cause other undesirable effects, but chemical means are often necessary to take out these mineral elements. Sulfates and carbonates produce "hard water" (See Question 940), and common salt or sodium chloride produces "salinity."

939. How is salinity measured?　Sea water averages 35,000 parts per million of sodium chloride. Dr. Alan M. Bateman has listed some of the standards of salinity that govern the use of water, as follows:

Parts per million	Affect
400	No salty taste
500	Slightly salty taste
1,000–2,500	Strong taste
3,300	Suitable for domestic use
3,500–5,000	Almost unbearable
5,000	Unfit for human use
6,250	Horses live on it in good condition
7,800	Horses can live on it
9,375	Cattle can live on it
15,625	Sheep can live on it
16,000	Beyond tolerance for most grasses

940. What is hard water?　Water that suds with difficulty when soap is added, and that leaves deposits of "scale" in boilers and the kitchen kettle is said to be "hard." Water that does not do these unpleasant things is "soft." Hardness may be "temporary" or "permanent."

Calcium and magnesium carbonate yield a temporary hardness, so known because it can be removed by a water softening process which involves "ion exchange," whereby sodium goes into the water to replace the calcium or magnesium.

Sulfates yield a permanent hardness which can be removed only by elaborate chemical means, using silicates such as the zeolites and greensand (see Question 313). This is also an ion-exchange technique.

Hardness in water is measured in parts per million of mineral matter. Hard water contains more than 200; moderately hard water, 101 to 200; slightly hard water, 56 to 100, and soft water, under 55.

941. What is the unusual feature of ground water in Holland?
The Netherlands presents many problems of ground-water utilization. Lying close to the sea are water-saturated wind-deposited sands of dune origin. In them are confined "floating" deposits of fresh water, isolated from the surrounding floods of salt water, which is not potable. Fresh water, being lighter, floats on salt water, but it is a curious fact that the fresh water falling on the land depresses the underlying salt water by an amount proportional to the height of the water table above sea level. This is how fresh water can occur, even below sea level, on a relatively small island in the middle of the ocean if there is enough rain.

942. Where else does fresh water float on salt water?
The situation in the Netherlands is similar to that existing on coastal plains and islands all over the world. In the United States it is particularly acute in New Jersey and Long Island. According to the Glyben-Herzberg law and the Herzberg formula used to calculate this effect, if the water table stands 20 feet above sea level, it overlies a thickness of 800 feet of fresh water below sea level. But when pumping lowers the water table 5 feet (one-fourth of the total altitude), sea water rises 200 feet higher. Therefore it is necessary to see that the rate of recharge keeps pace with the rate of pumping. When this did not happen near Brooklyn, New York, contamination by rising salt water

required a deliberate recharge of water into wells to maintain the supply.

943. What is a perched water table?   Natural earth material is rarely of uniform permeability. An impermeable zone may separate a lens or other body of ground water from the main water table beneath, leaving it suspended or "perched" above the general level of saturation. If large enough, such an isolated body may furnish a good deal of water, but it is not part of the main water zone below and must be replenished independently.

944. How fast does water travel underground?   Depending upon the head of pressure and the permeability of the soil or rock, water has an extremely variable rate of flow. Oscar E. Meinzer (1876–1948), long the chief water expert of the United States Geological Survey, determined the slowest movement in laboratory experiments to equal 1 foot in 10 years, and the fastest movement in field tests to be 420 feet per day. The complete range in nature is probably wider than that, but its normal amount seems to be between 5 feet per day and 5 feet per year. The velocity of ground water varies with the slope of the water table and the permeability of the material.

945. What is the cone of depression?   Withdrawal of ground water from a well lowers the water table in the shape of an inverted cone, pointing downward toward the center of the well. This is known as the cone of depression. As pumping continues the cone deepens and spreads outward, so that inflow becomes slower as the water has a farther distance to travel. Shallow wells nearby may dry up unless the rate of removal is balanced by the rate of new additions to the immediate water supply.

946. What is connate water?   Connate water is the original water that is trapped in sediment as it accumulates and stays there until withdrawn, even long after the loose material has changed into solid rock. Inasmuch as most sediments are deposited under marine conditions, most connate water is salty. The chemical composition of connate water of marine origin is somewhat different from that of water in present-day oceans, but whether it was different to start with is impossible to say. Later mineral matter may be added by percolating ground water, or this water may carry away some of the primary salts. When a well is drilled, perhaps for petroleum, the ancient water comes to the surface with the salt that was dissolved in it many millions of years ago. Some salty underground water may have become so by contact with beds of rock salt or have seeped in from the ocean along the shore line.

947. Do lakes and rivers add to underground water? This idea is correct for semi-arid regions and wrong for humid regions. In humid areas the lakes and streams are fed by ground water, rather than the reverse. In arid regions, where the intake is small because of the climate, the water table is low in most places and rather flattened in comparison to the topography. Runoff is large because of the sparse vegetation. Consequently, the water table is higher under the few streams that do exist, and water flows toward it from the stream bed.

948. What is a water witch? A water witch is a person who tries to locate underground water by means of a divining rod and his alleged innate (usually inherited) extrasensory perception. The equipment is usually a forked willow stick, though it has assumed a hundred aspects. Water witching is known in England as dowsing, and there is an enormous bibliography on it.

The writer on earth-science subjects faces no more embarrassing task than trying to tell what he feels to be the truth about water witching. There are just too many honest people who sincerely believe that they can "witch" water. They cannot be reasoned out of their belief by logical scientific explanations, because water witching is based upon phenomena that are neither logical nor scientific. The best explanation of water witching has come from psychologists who study related aspects of emotional behavior more akin to hysteria than to extrasensory perception.

The first water witch—so-called because his activities were looked upon as a kind of sorcery—is said to have been hanged as a fraud in 16th-Century Germany, though the information cannot now be verified. Most geologists regard this punishment as having been too mild. In fact, the distribution of ground water being what it is, water is easier to find than to miss, virtually everywhere in the world. When, in addition, the water witch undertakes to seek buried treasure, hidden deposits of ore minerals (these were its earliest historically recorded uses), or to detect criminals, the claims become more open to suspicion. Most water witches, furthermore, are as poor as ordinary folk, whereas anyone who can locate with assurance this most valuable of all mineral resources would become a millionaire, and, in doing so, be a benefactor to all mankind, so that deserts as well as babies would be named after him.

Many water witches do have plenty of common sense, however, and some knowledge of water occurrence, and this is of value to them in their search, which is not always fruitless—nor would it be to other individuals not so gifted. Otherwise, such "learned rubbish" as Rossiter W. Raymond called it, belongs with palmistry, astrology, and other superstitions, and not with either science or normal religion.

949. How is ground water discovered?   Sound geologic training is the best guaranty of success in finding reserves of underground water. The nature, distribution, and structure of porous and permeable sedimentary formations should be studied and mapped. The largest branch of the United States Geological Survey is its Ground Water Division, and its Water-Supply Papers are its most numerous publications. Maps of water-bearing strata are available for most parts of the country, and these form the starting place for the careful working-out of water problems.

Not everywhere have maps been made or are they always accessible. Records of nearby wells may give helpful information, especially if there is not too much irregularity in the subsurface structure. Then surface sand and gravel should be observed to see if natural charging has occurred. Alluvial fans and alluvial cones, brought down from the mountains by stream wash, usually provide ample water. The larger cities of Utah are situated in terrane such as this. Basins of substantial catchment, not entirely drained by streams, are likely sources of supply. In igneous and metamorphic rocks, fractures and fissures are the most dependable features to look for. Various geophysical techniques—not in any way involving the personal equation —include conductivity, resistivity, seismic, magnetic, and gravitational methods.

950. How much does water cost?   The average cost for water is about 5 cents per ton, purified and delivered at the tap. Water is more than "dirt-cheap" because dirt delivered to the home will cost more than 10 times as much. Thus it is our least expensive mineral product.

951. How do plants indicate ground water? Certain kinds of plants serve as a clue to the presence of hidden water in arid and semi-arid regions. Their roots grow only in ground water or in the narrow capillary fringe which draws moisture up from the water table. An alignment or concentration of trees, such as clumps of cottonwoods or stately palms, in an otherwise barren landscape likewise indicates the presence of underground water and is especially useful in guiding the desert traveler to watering places because trees are visible from a distance. Even the humble salt grass, however, suggests to the experienced eye the proximity of ground water, which will be found where roads and animal trails converge in dry country.

Inhabitants of deserts usually have an almost instinctive appreciation of the value of plants as indications of subsurface water, as had primitive man before the dawn of history. Marcus Vitruvius Pollio, a Roman engineer and architect of the 1st Century, described the use of small rushes, willows, alder trees, and other vegetation for this purpose. Plants that habitually grow where their roots can penetrate to a secure supply of water are called phreatophytes, in contrast to the xerophytes, which can maintain themselves in a nearly dormant condition during prolonged periods of drought. The former type of plant is literally a natural well with built-in pumping apparatus for lifting water from the zone of saturation; this lift is generally limited to a height of about 50 feet. For this reason alfalfa, for example, continues to grow through the driest season when other field crops not so equipped perish. The value of a species of plant as an indicator of ground water depends upon the extent to which it is absent from places where it cannot reach such water. Some plants indicate not only the occurrence of ground water but also its quality and, to a greater extent, the depth at which it lies.

952. What is a spring? Water that flows more substantially than a mere seepage constitutes a spring. Springs are of all sizes and temperatures. Some are intermittent, others are fed continuously, and some ebb and flow in shorter cycles. Some springs give forth nearly pure water, others are highly mineralized. The study of springs is one of the most fascinating phases of ground water.

953. What are periodic springs? Whereas ordinary intermittent springs flow in wet seasons and disappear in dry seasons, an ebbing and flowing or periodic spring waxes and wanes without regard to the weather. Some such springs have periods of a few minutes or hours; others are counted in days, though some are irregular in their timing. Oceanic tides have nothing to do with them, for most are remote from the sea. In their cyclic action they resemble geysers, but there is little gas involved and no increased temperature. The explanation for this strange performance is that periodic springs behave like natural siphons, and that their air-tightness results from seasonal variations in water supply.

Only 23 springs of this kind are known in the United States, scattered from Virginia to Nevada. All are in limestone. The Tide Spring, near Broadway, Virginia, is a well-known example, but the Geyser Spring, near Afton, Wyoming, is the most spectacular, and has recorded a flow of 17,000 gallons a minute.

954. What are thermal springs? Springs whose water is enough warmer than the rest of the ground water in that locality to attract attention are known as thermal springs. More than 1,000 have been listed in the United States, including places where numerous closely spaced springs are grouped together under one name. In Yellowstone National Park, for instance, several times that number would appear if they were counted individually. Altogether these American thermal springs yield perhaps 500,000 gallons per minute. The largest of them all is probably Warm Spring, in Montana, with a discharge of about 80,000 gallons per minute, but its temperature is only 68° Fahrenheit.

955. What is the source of heat for a thermal spring? Heat is acquired by thermal waters in two ways. One is original heat from still-cooling bodies of magma (see page 43), resting within the shallow crust of the earth. (Lavas seem to cool too readily to furnish much heat in this way.) Heat, or the hot water itself, rises along faults and fissures from these masses. The thermal springs of the Western mountain regions derive most of their water from surface precipitation, but their heat comes mainly from magmas and former magmas.

The other source of heat is due to depth alone, for rocks have a normal increase in temperature as they go deeper. Water that penetrates these depths from above is automatically warmed before it returns to the outside world. The thermal springs of the Appalachians and Ozarks are heated in this fashion, the water being of surface origin.

956. Where are thermal springs in the United States? Of the 1,059 thermal springs and groups enumerated in the United States by Norah D. Stearns, all but 55 are situated in the West, behind a line extending through eastern Wyoming and Colorado. Three are in the Black Hills of South Dakota, 6 in the Ouachita Mountains of Arkansas, and 46 in the Appalachian Mountains from Massachusetts to Alabama, with a heavy concentration along the Virginia–West Virginia border. Every Western state has scores of thermal springs, indicating the recency with which the geologic features have been created—the igneous bodies have not yet thoroughly cooled. Idaho has 203 thermal springs, California 184, Nevada 174, Wyoming 116 (counting the Yellowstone springs in clusters), and Oregon 105.

957. What is a geyser? A geyser is an intermittent thermal spring that erupts water and steam at intervals with considerable force. Because water boils at a higher temperature as it goes down farther into the earth, it must be heated more at depth than at the surface in order for it to come to a boil. When the pressure above is finally relieved, the superheated water then erupts into steam and escapes with explosive violence. The elaborate underground plumbing system of the geyser, necessary to restrict the free circulation of water by convection, must then be filled again in preparation for another eruption. The heat is supplied by hot igneous rocks or the gases given off by them.

958. Where are geysers found? Isolated geysers may occur almost any place where there is volcanic activity or recent volcanism so that the buried rocks have not entirely cooled. Three regions of the world, however, are outstanding for their concentrations of geysers—Yellowstone National Park, New Zealand, and Iceland.

The word geyser itself comes from the name of a particularly noteworthy one, Geysir, in Iceland. Water from the Icelandic geysers and hot springs is used for residential and industrial heating, especially at Reykjavik, the capital. In New Zealand the geysers are confined to

North Island, in the midst of which live the Maoris, the Polynesian natives of the country. Yellowstone contains more than 3,000 geysers. Old Faithful is surely the best known, although its regularity is not so precise as many visitors expect; 30 to 90 minutes may elapse between eruptions, an hour being perhaps a good average.

959. What is a large spring?   Oscar E. Meinzer, who accumulated data on the capacity of all large springs in the United States, noted the difficulties he had in compiling such statistics for useful classification. When is a spring a single spring and when is it really a group of nearby springs?—in some places they have separate names, elsewhere not. How do you compare the flow of fluctuating springs?—minimum, maximum, and average discharges show up variously in the figures. Some records require years of measurement to give reliable results. Allowing for these differences, and using the average discharge as the values were available, Meinzer classified springs according to the following degrees of magnitude:

First	100 second-feet or more
Second	10 to 100 second-feet
Third	1 to 10 second-feet
Fourth	100 gallons per minute to 1 second-foot
Fifth	10 to 100 gallons per minute
Sixth	1 to 10 gallons per minute
Seventh	1 pint to 1 gallon per minute
Eighth	Less than 1 pint per minute

A second-foot is 1 cubic foot per second or 448 gallons per minute; this would fill about a dozen barrels in a minute, equal to about 646,000 gallons a day, or enough to supply a town of about 5,000 inhabitants.

960. What are the characteristics of the large springs in the United States?   Springs of the first magnitude occur mainly in limestone and extrusive volcanic (that is, lava) rock. The Portneuf Springs, a group in Idaho, issue from gravel but probably come originally from basalt; two large springs in Montana come from sandstone, probably from large fissures in that rock; and the Ana River Springs in Oregon come from lake beds overlying volcanic rock.

The water of large springs is only slightly mineralized, with the sole exception of Salt Springs in Marion County, Florida.

Most of the large springs have temperatures virtually the same as the mean temperature of the surrounding air, partly because the large amount of heat required to warm them up is not available, and also because they consist of recently precipitated water that has not penetrated more than a few hundred feet below the ground. Warm Spring, in Montana, and Ana River Springs, in Oregon, have the highest temperatures of any of the large American springs, and so are presumed to have the deepest sources. Some large springs that are fed by streams or lakes have seasonal fluctuations in temperature corresponding to those of the surface water.

961. Where are the large springs in the United States? First-magnitude springs are found in several regions of the United States. Silver Spring, in Florida, the largest in that state, is perhaps the largest limestone spring in the country; the water, after emerging through several openings into a large basin, becomes a navigable stream. North-central Florida, the Ozark region of Missouri and Arkansas, the Snake River Basin in Idaho, the lava-covered areas of the Sacramento River Basin in northern California (counting three huge springs on Fall River) and the Columbia Lava Plateau of the Deschutes River Basin in western Oregon, are noteworthy for their extraordinary springs. Other springs of the first magnitude are in central Montana; along the Balcones fault belt in south-central Texas; and Big Spring, at Tuscumbia, Alabama.

962. What are the ground-water regions of the United States? The United States can be divided into four principal ground-water regions—(1) the East-Central, (2) Coastal Plain, (3) Great Plains, and (4) Western mountain region.

963. What is the East-Central region like? The East-Central ground-water region of the United States includes about one-third of the area and two-thirds of the population. Most of this region is underlaid by rocks of Paleozoic age, including water-bearing sandstone and limestone and unproductive shale. The deep water from these rocks is heavily mineralized. The parts of this region that are underlaid by Pre-Cambrian rocks (older than Paleozoic) or Triassic rocks (which are younger) have meager supplies of water. The superficial glacial deposits in the northern part, and the outwash sands and gravels beyond the margin of these glacial beds yield large amounts of water. (For the ages of these geologic periods see Question 258.)

964. What is the Coastal Plain region like? The Coastal Plain of the United States borders the Atlantic Ocean and Gulf of Mexico in a wide belt that occupies one-seventh of the country. It extends from Martha's Vineyard, in Massachusetts, to the Rio Grande, and embraces Florida and the Mississippi Valley as far as the mouth of the Ohio River. This well-populated region is underlaid by Cretaceous, Tertiary, and Pleistocene formations, which include prolific water-bearing beds of sand and limestone.

965. What is the Great Plains region like? The semi-arid to semi-humid plains lying east of the Rocky Mountains contain extensive Tertiary and Pleistocene deposits of water-bearing sand and gravel, as well as Cretaceous sandstone that gives mineralized artesian water; areas of Cretaceous shale have little water. In addition there are glacial deposits in the north and the famous Roswell artesian basin in New Mexico, which is situated in Permian limestone.

966. What is the Western mountain region like? About one-third of the United States belongs to the Western mountain ground-water region. The aridity of most of it makes water resources of especially great significance to the population, which is thin except along the Pacific Coast. The Northwest, however, has the heaviest precipitation in the country. The chief water-bearing beds—especially fine in California—are the sand and gravel in Pleistocene or Tertiary valley fill. Volcanic rocks in the Northwest feed much water to springs and wells.

967. Why is ice considered a rock? Water is no less a mineral when frozen than when liquid, and a large body of any mineral constitutes a rock. Ice is the most abundant rock exposed over large parts of the earth's surface, especially in Antarctica and Greenland. Ice caps are prominent in Iceland, where they represent the fragments of greater masses once entirely covering that country. The present glaciers of Alaska, the Canadian Rockies, and New Zealand, though only remnants of their former selves, are nevertheless still imposing in their bulk. The Seward Glacier in Alaska, for instance, is 50 miles long.

XVI. MINERAL COLLECTING AS A HOBBY

Introduction. The mineral hobby is growing at a rapid pace because it offers so wide a variety of activities and interests, enough to appeal to nearly every conceivable taste. It can be carried on outdoors or at home, and in both places—finding specimens in the field, studying and displaying them inside. The lure of pretty minerals is aesthetic; the lore of minerals and rocks may be historical and intellectual, thereby combining a useful science and a pleasing hobby. The shut-in may contemplate the wonders of nature in his own hands, while the physically vigorous climbs the high places in search of suitable materials; the in-betweens wander through forest and plains idly picking up likely specimens at one spot, at another spot testing their worth by "knapping the chunky staines to pieces," as Sir Walter Scott put it. The craftsman likewise fits into this happy hobby by cutting and polishing gem stones, with surprising simplicity turning simple stones into works of art, which he may then mount in jewelry to adorn himself, his family, and his friends. There is indeed something for everybody in mineral collecting, as the following questions and answers will bring out.

968. Where are minerals on exhibit? Mineral collections are open for inspection in every part of the country, in nearly every nation in the world. Mineralogy is an old and honorable science! Apart from the major museums (see Question 969), exhibits are often found in colleges and universities, local libraries and historical displays, county court houses (especially in the Western states and in mining regions elsewhere), chambers of commerce, assay offices, and many store windows, again, especially in mining districts. These, it should be emphasized, are by no means confined to the West, for some of the largest mines in the United States are in New York, New Jersey (Franklin is within 40 miles of New York City), Michigan, Wisconsin, Minnesota, Florida, Alabama, and Arkansas, as well as the huge quarries in Vermont, Indiana, Tennessee, Virginia, Georgia, and other Eastern states. Not only are minerals to be found nearly everywhere in the earth, but they have been brought together and put on display in many towns and crossroad settlements around the country.

969. Which are the great mineral museums? Perhaps the outstanding mineral exhibits in North America are those of the United States National Museum (Smithsonian Institution) in Washington, D.C., the American Museum of Natural History in New York, the Harvard University Mineralogical Museum in Cambridge, Massachusetts, the Chicago Museum of Natural History, and the Royal Ontario Museum in Toronto, Canada. Superbly presented, also, are the exceptionally fine collections in the Cranbrook Institute in Broomfield Hills, Michigan, the Denver Museum of Natural History and the Colorado School of Mines in Golden, and the California Academy of Science in San Francisco. Los Angeles and Philadelphia have excellent collections, as do numerous colleges and universities, including New Haven, Connecticut; Houghton, Michigan; and elsewhere. Your librarian can show you lists of museums in any section of the country you may live or visit, and all the standard guidebooks to foreign travel emphasize museums and their collections. With the expanding interest in minerals, new collections are being opened to the public and old collections refurbished for enhanced enjoyment. The new Lizzadro Museum of Lapidary Art in Elmhurst, Illinois, promises to become one of the finest in the country.

970. What is a micromount? Miniature crystals, revealing a fairyland of form and color within their tiny world of enchantment, are known to collectors as micromounts. These can be broken off of larger specimens, and in fact are frequently the small particles left behind when a specimen is trimmed for display. Cemented onto a cork or piece of balsa wood inside a small paper or plastic box, typically ⅞ inch square, from which the cover can be removed, these crystals must be observed under a low-power binocular or monocular microscope, although an inexpensive one is entirely satisfactory, and a good hand lens can be used temporarily. Because the smaller crystals and clusters are more perfectly developed than larger ones, micromounts show a quality that is scarcely believable to collectors who are acquainted only with hand-size specimens. Micromounts are fast becoming popular today, although there was considerable interest in them among the expert collectors of several decades ago, before the mineral hobby acquired its present momentum. Philadelphia, Colorado Springs, and Phoenix—through the enthusiasm generated by local specialists such as George W. Fiss, Lazard Cahn, and Arthur L. Flagg, respectively, are particularly acute centers of micromount collecting.

971. What is a thumbnail specimen?   In size between the micromount (see Question 970) and the usual small specimen is the so-called thumbnail—the name indicates the size. Fitted into compartmented boxes having hinged or removable lids, these specimens are an almost ideal way of maintaining a comprehensive collection within a small space, and equally so of carrying a display to show away from home. No extra equipment is needed to observe them, yet if well chosen they can show all the necessary features of any mineral specimen for purposes of instruction.

Somewhat larger than these are the 1 x 1 or 1½ x 1½ or 1 x 2 specimens often used in study sets. Enough of these can be acquired to serve all the functions of a mineral collection except the elaborate exhibits of public museums.

972. Where can specimens be purchased?   A few years ago the regular mineral store was a rarity; the few that existed were principally part-time or retirement businesses or were operated as an adjunct to a roadside vegetable stand or chicken ranch. With the increasing interest in mineral collecting everywhere in the United States and Canada, however, more and more dealers are opening full-fledged "rock shops" in cities and towns, along main highways, and in odd corners of both countries. Many of them, and dozens of other dealers as well, advertise in the mineral magazines described in Question 976. Many issue catalogs from which specimens and equipment may be bought. Sets of correctly identified specimens are especially recommended for the collector who wishes to become acquainted with the common minerals as readily as possible.

973. How much equipment does a mineral collector need?   None, actually. Simple collecting can be done in many places without tools or other equipment. A mineral hammer is handy, and so is a knapsack in which to carry specimens. Paper to wrap them in, and a pencil and paper to write labels would be all that most collectors will ever want. Beyond that level of bare-bones collecting, a gradual accumulation of useful tools will prove helpful when working with more difficult rocks and in a wider variety of localities. These might include more than one type of hammer—chisel edge and pick edge—some cold chisels, sledge hammer, crow bar, and pair of nippers. To these may be added a magnifying glass, eye shield (for rock breaking), compass, camera, field glasses, first-aid kit, and whatever you personally like in the way of camping and outing paraphernalia. A Geiger counter and ultraviolet lamp belong more in the category of prospecting equipment, but they have become familiar items in today's collecting activities.

974. What is the value of a label? Nearly any mineral that is not adequately labeled may be considered as "just a rock" and has slight value or interest to the serious collector. A substantial diamond crystal or gold nugget may be an exception, but even such a specimen would be worth considerably more if it were accompanied by a label. The essential information on a label is not the scientific identification —this can be furnished at will by a mineral expert. It is not the date of discovery, the price paid, or the previous owner—although these may have historical significance and can scarcely hurt. The one indispensable piece of knowledge about a mineral or rock specimen is the locality, as complete and accurate as it can be given. Then we have something worth while, to which all other facts are subordinate. Some collectors like to save the older labels that may come with a specimen, for their association value, and this whim is to be encouraged as part of the hobby.

975. Where can minerals be identified? Every state has one or more agencies where minerals can be sent for free identification. In some states, it is the state bureau (or department, division, etc.) of mines, usually situated in the state capital or wherever the school of mines is located. In other states, the appropriate office is the state geologic survey, situated at the capital or state university. In some states, the mining school or college performs this service itself. In others, the department of geology at the state university is the likeliest place to obtain such information. When in doubt where to send specimens, it is best to first address a postal card to any one of these agencies in your own state—and, similarly, to the provinces in Canada—because they are not apt to forward packages. Assays and detailed analyses are not undertaken in competition with private chemists or assayers, whose names can be obtained from these same agencies or from the telephone book. Radioactive samples of uranium and thorium minerals may be sent for free examination to the U. S. Geological Survey, Geochemistry and Petrology Branch, Building 213, Naval Gun Factory, Washington 25, D.C.

976. What are the mineral magazines? Three magazines are written, edited, and published on a national scale for the mineral hobbyist. In spite of their different names, which suggest an emphasis on different aspects of the hobby, they cover much the same subjects and have the same advertisers and similar kinds of readers. They carry articles about collecting methods and localities, amateur gem cutting and jewelry making, and information about collectors and clubs. Still, each of these magazines has its own personality because they are all individually edited and none is the creation of a large, impersonal publishing company. The mineral collector is encouraged to send for a sample copy of each and decide for himself which appeals to him the most. The names, addresses, and subscription prices follow:

Geotimes, American Geological Institute, 4220 King Street, Alexandria, VA 22303. $24.95 per year, sample copy $4.00

Lapidary Journal, Lapidary Journal, Inc., 60 Chestnut St., Suite 201, Devon, PA 19333. $26.00 per year, sample copy $6.50

Rocks and Minerals, Heldref Publications, 1319 18th Street, N.W., Washington, DC 20036. $38.00 per year, sample copy $6.50

977. What are the activities of mineral clubs? More than 1,100 mineral clubs in the United States and Canada offer exceptionally good opportunities to join with other hobbyists in the fun and satisfaction of collecting, studying, and cutting gems, minerals, and rocks.

The exhibits of specimens and lapidary work and the exchange of ideas constitute perhaps the most important function of such an organization, so that the members benefit beyond the limits of what they can learn in a magazine or book. Most clubs have programs at which talks by leaders in mineral work may be heard. Field trips to collecting spots are often the outstanding events of the year.

Most of the many local clubs are affiliated with one of the six regional federations—Eastern, Midwest, Rocky Mountain, Texas, California, and Northwest. These are joined together in the American Federation of Mineralogical Societies, which does not have individual members except by virtue of their belonging to one of the local clubs. A principal feature of these regional and national federations is their sponsorship of mineral conventions, which combine all the activities mentioned above in a grand conclave which attracts hobbyists from all parts of the continent.

978. What is fluorescence? The ability of a mineral to absorb radiation and to emit it again is the basis of the interesting effect known as fluorescence. If the energy is held over and the reaction sets in after the radiation has ceased—as when the lamp is turned off—the property is termed *phosphorescence*. Other types of *luminescence,* as the general range of phenomena is known, result from heat or friction, and these are very interesting though not nearly so common and well known. Sphalerite from certain localities, for instance, glows like white fire when merely scratched in the dark.

979. How can fluorescence be shown? A variety of sources of illumination can be purchased to demonstrate fluorescence and phosphorescence. First, it is essential to know that ultraviolet light— which is by far the most suitable means of showing these startling effects—is divided into two convenient groups known as long wave and short wave. Each reacts with a different selection of minerals, though some minerals perform in both ranges of wavelength, perhaps giving different colors. Thus, some outstanding Texas calcite is pink in long-wave ultraviolet light but blue in short-wave, in which it also phosphoresces.

An *argon bulb,* which costs less than a dollar and can be screwed into any ordinary light socket, produces weak long-wave rays. So does an inexpensive *hot bulb,* which, however, is rather dangerous to use because it generates so much heat. Most of the museum and portable (battery-operated) units are of the short-wave type, though some of the newer ones combine both lengths of waves so that they can be used alternately.

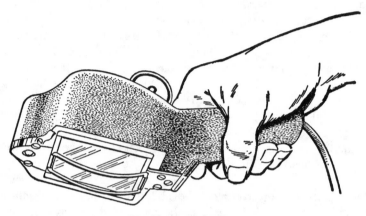

Portable ultraviolet lamp

980. Which are the fluorescent minerals? It is impossible to know in advance which minerals will fluoresce or phosphoresce. In most specimens it seems to be the result of some minor chemical impurity, which may be absent in specimens of the same mineral from other localities. Fluorite, though it gave its name to this property, is one of the least dependable. The bright blue appearance of fluorite from Weardale, England, is missing in the otherwise equally attractive material from Rosiclare, Illinois. Altogether, the minerals from Franklin, New Jersey, hold first rank in the world of luminescence. The pink to red calcite and brilliant green willemite—some of which phosphoresces for a prolonged interval—make a handsome combination, especially when the daylight colors of snow-white calcite, yellowish-green or brown willemite, orange-red zincite, and black franklinite are observed without any artificial aid.

981. Why is the collector concerned with the stability of minerals? Every mineral collector wants to keep his specimens as nearly as possible in their original condition. At least as much thought should be given to caring for minerals once they are acquired as is devoted to obtaining them in the first place. Such effort would of course be unnecessary if all minerals were imperishable. On the contrary, it is probable that every mineral alters somewhat with the passage of time, although the change is too slight to be noticeable in the majority of minerals while they are confined in a collection during a human lifetime. Unfortunately, however, certain minerals undergo more or less serious alteration, which may range all the way from a slight lessening of their native beauty to ultimate ruin. The loss in value of such specimens may be considerable. Some species of minerals owe their rarity in museums and private collections to the fact that they have not been protected adequately against the hazards to which they have actually been exposed while resting in the apparent safety of a mineral cabinet.

The very act of removing minerals from the earth, which is their natural home, has brought them into a foreign environment. Minerals, like living organisms, are responsive to their environment. They are in general stable under the conditions existing at the time that they were created, but they become unstable in different surroundings. A few less-sensitive minerals, such as diamond, quartz, and cassiterite, maintain themselves indefinitely during changed conditions.

982. What are examples of unstable minerals? Feldspar, the most abundant mineral in the familiar igneous rocks (see Chapter II), weathers readily to clay at the surface of the earth. If this clay is later buried beneath a thick load of sediments, the increased temperature and pressure cause it to change into muscovite mica or some other metamorphic mineral that is more stable at that depth.

The cosmic conditions that existed when meteorites were formed is not known with certainty, but they must have been different from those at the earth's surface (see Chapter 3). Meteorites that hurtle through space and strike our planet, only to begin crumbling into powder within a few years after they have been added to a museum collection, bear witness to this difference in environment.

Likewise a piece of molten iron, if thrown from a blast furnace, quickly succumbs to the oxygen and moisture in the air and rusts to iron oxide, which is more stable in the air. The mineral pyrite does somewhat the same thing. Hence sulfides, formed mostly within the earth where there is a deficiency of oxygen, are the least stable of the major chemical classes of minerals. Oxides, already containing the oxygen that is so abundant in the atmosphere, are the most stable.

Secondary minerals, which have altered from primary minerals under surface or near-surface conditions, are usually the most colorful (see Question 85), and these fortunately are the specimens that are least likely to trouble or disappoint the collector.

983. Can light injure minerals?   It might seem unlikely that exposure to light would affect a mineral unfavorably, but this is not true, for there are a number of *photosensitive minerals*. A few of these are damaged within a relatively short time after they have been taken from the earth and put on display in museums or private collections.

Among the minerals that are decomposed by light, the silver compounds—such as cerargyrite, bromyrite, embolite—are especially striking, for it is upon the silver halides that the whole process of photography is based. Other minerals are decomposed by the combined action of light and oxygen. Of these minerals the most important ones that become tarnished rather easily include argentite, chalcocite, cinnabar, crocoite, cuprite, proustite, pyrargyrite, realgar, and stibnite. Realgar is perhaps the best known in its decomposition; this red arsenic sulfide mineral gradually falls to a powder consisting of a mixture of yellow orpiment and the substance arsenic trioxide.

984. Which minerals change color?   Certain minerals that undergo a natural change in color can scarcely be regarded as injured. Often, though not always, the color is actually an improvement. Brown and brownish yellow topaz from Japan, for instance, turns blue in daylight, although the originally blue crystals become colorless—as happens also with the sherry-colored topaz from the Thomas Range in Utah and the wonderful crystals from the Urulga River at Nerchinsk in Transbaikal, Soviet Union. English miners at Weardale, in County Durham, used to expose specimens of green fluorite to the sun in order to change it to purple. The fading of rose quartz in sunlight is a familiar change.

985. Which mineral has a reversible color?   The most remarkable example of the effect of light on color in the whole mineral kingdom is the reversible photosensitivity of several members of the sodalite group. Hackmanite, especially, from Bancroft, Ontario, is amazing. In daylight or direct sunlight the colorless hackmanite assumes a pale pink hue and then goes on to raspberry or deep violet shade. The color disappears rapidly and almost completely when the specimens are held before a strong electric light.

986. What is efflorescence? Minerals that lose water and fall to pieces upon exposure to the atmosphere are said to effloresce or be efflorescent. Certain crystalline hydrates, especially borates, sulfates, and carbonates, may be destroyed by this effect. Borax, trona, kernite, epsomite, and chalchanthite belong in this group, along with a number of less common minerals. Turquois is susceptible to change upon exposure to dry air, specimens from some localities slowly turning greener as they lose moisture. Opal is one of the more troublesome minerals in respect to loss of moisture. Specimens from certain places, including the noted locality of Virgin Valley, Humboldt County, Nevada, are often translucent and deep green when first mined, but they soon lose much of their water content in the desert air, becoming semi-opaque and turning yellowish green.

Efflorescent minerals can be protected by sealing them in glass jars, keeping them cool or moist, dipping them in alcohol, or lacquering them—one treatment or another will serve the purpose.

987. What is deliquescence? Minerals that become moist on exposure to damp air and eventually dissolve in their own moisture are said to deliquesce or be deliquescent. The result, of course, will be disastrous to specimens in a collection. Such minerals include soda niter, halite, carnallite, kainite, kierserite, melanterite, sylvite, and others less well known. Several of them are not deliquescent when pure but only when they contain deliquescent magnesium minerals or other impurities, especially in specimens from the famous German locality of Stassfurt. The preventive action to be taken includes lacquering the specimens, keeping them near a tray of quicklime or silica gel, or sealing them in a dry jar.

988. What is the case of the Cranbourne meteorite? This, the largest meteorite in any European collection, is a classic and extreme example of disintegration of a meteorite, and it illustrates a process of oxidation more complex than mere rusting. Although known earlier to the natives of Australia, it was found by white settlers in 1853 or 1854 in Mornington County, Victoria. Part of it protruded above the soil and some of the iron seemed to have flaked away after rusting. The buried part was embedded about 4 feet; the surrounding subsoil and sandstone rock presumably protected it rather well. However, after the meteorite had been excavated in 1862, shipped to England in 1865, and put on display on a large turntable at the British Museum at Bloomsbury in 1866, it began to rust. One of its constituent minerals, lawrencite (ferrous chloride), became oxidized to ferric chloride and was exuded in the form of drops, which permeated through the cleavages of the nickel-iron alloy. The metallic iron in turn reduced the ferric chloride back to ferrous chloride and became oxidized itself. The cycle was continuous as oxygen and water vapor were absorbed from the air.

Lester J. Spencer and F. A. Bannister have related interesting accounts of the problems involved in trying to preserve this 8,227-pound Cranbourne meteorite. The surface was first varnished to exclude air. Then it was coated with red wax. When the specimen was transferred to its present location in the Mineral Gallery of the British Museum of Natural History at South Kensington in 1881, it was enclosed in a glass cabinet provided with trays for quicklime which was replenished monthly. Nevertheless, the meteorite continued to oxidize and decompose to such an extent that 40 pounds of loose rust was brushed off after 10 years. The difficulty of removing all the surface crust from so large and irregular a mass makes it impossible to seal in the specimen by coating it. Finally, the present method of caring for the Cranbourne meteorite was adopted. It is now housed in a gas-tight case filled with nitrogen, and dry nitrogen is passed through at a slow rate. The troublesome drops of iron chloride disappeared quickly from the surface of the meteorite, and when the small amount of loose surface rust dried, it flaked away.

989. How may dirt be removed from minerals?   Ordinary house dirt is a mixture of dry pulverized mineral matter and organic matter, such as textile lint. Soot is a deposit of carbon from burning coal and gas. Cooking grease in the home tends to cause these to stick to any solid substance upon which they settle. Common dust and soot are usually only a minor nuisance to the mineral collector because they can be blown, brushed, or washed off. Sometimes, however, the mineral is too fragile for even the most gentle of these mechanical methods, as may be the situation with delicate needlelike or hairlike crystals. Dust and soot then become a serious hazard to the beauty and value of such specimens, which will steadily decline in appearance and worth until they have no appeal to anyone.

Blowing dust from minerals can be done with the breath, though an atomizer or a metal hand-blower, such as is used by window dressers for keeping store window displays clean, is convenient to use. Live steam under pressure has been recommended to remove clay and dirt. A camel's hair brush will remove dust only, and a stiff quill or wire brush will clean sturdier minerals more thoroughly. The technique to be used for washing specimens depends upon the nature of the mineral. Water-soluble minerals may occasionally be washed in a dry-cleaning fluid. Marcasite is a common mineral that should be kept away from water, and there are a few others that decompose easily in water. Other minerals—and this includes most of them— can be cleaned in soapy water or, preferably, with a synthetic detergent. Sometimes alcohol, acids, or ammonia are suitable for removing obstinate stains from certain minerals.

990. How can organic incrustations be removed from specimens?
A coating of lichens often spoils the appearance of mineral or rock specimens. Dilute ammonia will usually soften lichens sufficiently so that they can be removed mechanically. Especially tenacious ones may require the dissolving action of sulfuric or nitric acid. Care should be taken with these acids and the specimens should be thoroughly rinsed in water for a prolonged period.

991. What is the lapidary art? The lapidary phases of the mineral hobby have become hugely popular in America, where they number tens of thousands of adherents. Gem cutting is more than a craft, though that would be enough to recommend it. In the process of turning ordinary looking stones into real gems, which can be set into jewelry and used in many ornamental ways, the lapidary learns the full physical nature of his material—its texture, its exact hardness, its resistance and its yielding. Except for the tendency that many amateurs have of buying too poor a grade of rough stone, literally wasting their time on it, the amateur cutter has the great advantage over the professional in that his time is his own and he can experiment with odd gem cuts and promising techniques until his skill yields a finished product often greatly superior to the work of the commercial shop.

992. Why is agate the favorite gem of amateur lapidaries? Agates—the chalcedony gems in general—are favored by amateur cutters above all others because of their infinite variety of patterns and colors. An agate can be cut so that it is distinctive, even unique, yet such material in the rough costs virtually nothing. Agate, furthermore, has just the right degree of hardness to make lapidary work satisfying—soft enough to fashion readily, hard enough to offer some challenge and to hold together while being shaped. The amateur lapidary hobby gained its first secure foothold in the Western United States, where agates are plentiful.

993. How are gems cut? Diamond cutting (see Question 714) is very different from the rest of the lapidary arts—partly because of the enormous difference in hardness between diamond and any other gem, and partly because diamond is the only gem that can be cut and polished in the same operation. All the other gems are amenable to the skill of the amateur lapidary, even the hardest of colored stones—ruby and sapphire and their synthetic counterparts. The beginner usually starts with one of the rounded or cabochon cuts, and progresses later to the flat-surfaced or faceted cuts, in which the tiny faces have a definite geometric relation to one another. For these more difficult cuts, a holding device known as a faceting head is used, whereas cabochons are usually done free-hand. The two techniques are different in other ways, also, and they utilize unlike kinds of raw material—opaque stones for cabochons, transparent stones for faceting.

994. What are the steps in cutting cabochons? Five steps are generally required in completing a cabochon-cut gem, though some can be omitted by buying the rough material already sliced or even by buying so-called pre-forms which are rather closely cut to shape. These steps are *slabbing, trimming, grinding, sanding,* and *polishing.*

995. How is slabbing done? Slabbing consists of preparing thin slices (mostly $\frac{3}{16}$ to $\frac{1}{4}$ inch thick) on a diamond saw, which is a diamond-set blade, usually 12 to 16 inches in diameter, moistened with an oil or kerosine coolant. This is run by a ¼- to ½-horsepower motor at a speed of 850 to 1,000 revolutions per minute.

996. How is trimming done? Trimming consists of outlining with a saw the gemmy area to be used, gauging it with a template, which has holes representing standard sizes and shapes of finished stones. Except that it is smaller (6 to 10 inches in diameter) and moves faster (1,725 RPM), the trim saw is like the slabbing saw (see Question 995).

997. How is grinding done? Grinding consists of shaping the stone, first to its outline and then to its final dimensions, using a wet carborundum wheel, or two wheels, one for coarse work (100 grit) and the other for fine work (220 grit). An inward slope is given the top of the stone to enable it to be set in a mounting.

998. How is sanding done? Sanding consists of smoothing the rough spots and removing grinding marks on a carborundum cloth mounted on a belt, disc, or drum, conveniently about 8 inches across and running at 850 RPM. This operation may be done either dry or preferably wet, and two grits of cloth may be desired.

999. How is polishing done? Polishing consists of putting the final gloss on the stone. Leather, felt, canvas, or muslin is used for the buff, and cerium oxide, tin oxide, and other metallic oxides are used as the abrasive. Each lapidary has his own choices for various kinds of gems.

1000. What is dopping? The polishing and sanding, sometimes even the grinding, are accomplished with the stone held on the end of a hardwood "dop stick" about 5 inches long, on which it is gripped in heated wax.

1001. How are gems tumbled? The irregularly rounded gems so popular today in informal jewelry are fashioned by a process known as tumbling. This duplicates in a man-made device the smoothing action of streams and beaches that nature has employed for a long while. The stones themselves are often called *baroques*. The machine is a round or hexagonal drum or barrel made of metal or wood, kept slowly rotating so that an abrasive is always in contact with the rough specimens, which grind and polish one another. Water is added to the mixture, and sometimes such things as sawdust or nut shells serve to carry the cutting powder. Successively finer grit is added when the batch is changed. The tumbling process is not standardized and many privately developed techniques are in everyday use.

BIBLIOGRAPHY

The following list of recommended books for further reading and study is confined to standard books readily available in print in the United States and Canada. These represent various levels of difficulty, from the popular but scientifically accurate book for the layman, to a few technical volumes largely useful for reference. They are arranged alphabetically by author beneath each subject heading.

Literature Reference

American Geological Institute. *Glossary of Geology and Related Sciences.* 1957. Supplement 1960.

Pangborn, Mark W., Jr. *Earth for the Layman.* American Geological Institute. 1957.

Mineralogy

Berry, Leonard, and Mason, Brian. *Mineralogy* . . . Freeman. 1959.

Dana, Edward Salisbury, and Ford, William E. *A Textbook of Mineralogy* . . . Wiley. 1932.

Dennen, William H. *Principles of Mineralogy.* Ronald. 1959.

Hurlbut, Cornelius S., Jr. *Dana's Manual of Mineralogy.* Wiley. 1959.

Kraus, Edward Henry; Hunt, Walter Fred; and Ramsdell, Lewis Stephen. *Mineralogy* . . . McGraw-Hill. 1959.

Palache, Charles; Berman, Harry; and Frondel, Clifford. *The System of Mineralogy* . . . Vol. 1, 1944; Vol. 2, 1951; Vol. 3, 1962. Wiley.

Wade, F. Alton, and Mattox, Richard B. *Elements of Crystallography and Mineralogy.* Harper. 1960.

Rocks

Kemp, James Furman, and Grout, Frank F. *A Handbook of Rocks* . . . Van Nostrand. 1940.

Pirsson, Louis V., and Knopf, Adolph. *Rocks and Rock Minerals.* Wiley. 1947.

Spock, L. E. *Guide to the Study of Rocks.* Harper. 1962.

Meteorites

Mason, Brian. *Meteorites*. Wiley. 1962.
Nininger, H. H. *Out of the Sky*. . . . Dover. 1959.
Watson, Fletcher G. *Between the Planets*. Harvard University. 1956.

Economic Minerals

American Institute of Mining, Metallurgical, and Petroleum Engineers. *Industrial Minerals and Rocks*. 1960.
Bateman, Alan M. *Economic Mineral Deposits*. Wiley. 1950.
Bateman, Alan M. *The Formation of Mineral Deposits*. Wiley. 1951.
Bates, Robert L. *Geology of the Industrial Rocks and Minerals*. Harper. 1960.
Lindgren, Waldemar. *Mineral Deposits*. McGraw-Hill. 1933.
Park, Charles F., Jr., and MacDiarmid, Roy A. *Ore Deposits*. Freeman. 1964.
Riley, Charles M. *Our Mineral Resources*. Wiley. 1959.

Radioactive Minerals

Heinrich, E. William. *Mineralogy and Geology of Radioactive Raw Materials*. McGraw-Hill. 1958.
Nininger, Robert D. *Exploration for Nuclear Raw Materials*. Van Nostrand. 1956.

Gems

Kraus, Edward H., and Slawson, Chester B. *Gems and Gem Materials*. McGraw-Hill. 1947.
Pearl, Richard M. *American Gem Trails*. McGraw-Hill. 1964.
Pearl, Richard M. *Popular Gemology*. Wiley. 1965.
Smith, G. F. Herbert, and Phillips, F. C. *Gemstones*. Pitman. 1958.
Spencer, L. J. *A Key to Precious Stones*. Emerson. 1947.
Whitlock, Herbert P. *The Story of the Gems*. Emerson. 1941.

Petroleum

Ball, Max. *This Fascinating Oil Business*. Bobbs-Merrill. 1940.
Lalicker, Cecil G. *Principles of Petroleum Geology*. Appleton-Century-Crofts. 1949.

Landes, Kenneth K. *Petroleum Geology.* Wiley. 1959.
Levorsen, A. I. *Geology of Petroleum.* Freeman. 1967.
Russell, William L. *Principles of Petroleum Geology.* McGraw-Hill. 1960.

Mining

Hoover, Herbert C. *Principles of Mining.* McGraw-Hill. 1909.
Lewis, Robert S. and Clark, G. B. *Elements of Mining.* Wiley. 1964.

Water Resources

Kazmann, Raphael G. *Modern Hydrology.* Harper. 1965.
Meinzer, O. E. *Hydrology.* Dover. 1942.
Tolman, C. F. *Ground Water.* McGraw-Hill. 1937.

Mineral Collecting

Dana, Edward S., and Hurlbut, Cornelius S., Jr. *Minerals and How to Study Them.* Wiley. 1949.
English, George L., and Jensen, David E. *Getting Acquainted with Minerals.* McGraw-Hill. 1958.
Gleason, Sterling. *Ultraviolet Guide to Minerals.* Van Nostrand. 1960.
MacFall, Russell P. *Gem Hunters Guide.* Crowell. 1963.
Pearl, Richard M. *Gems, Minerals, Crystals, Ores* . . . Odyssey. 1964.
Pearl, Richard M. *How to Know the Minerals and Rocks.* McGraw-Hill. 1955.
Pearl, Richard M. *Rocks and Minerals.* Barnes & Noble. 1956.

INDEX

A CATALOG OF SELECTED
DOVER BOOKS
IN ALL FIELDS OF INTEREST

A CATALOG OF SELECTED DOVER
BOOKS IN ALL FIELDS OF INTEREST

CONCERNING THE SPIRITUAL IN ART, Wassily Kandinsky. Pioneering work by father of abstract art. Thoughts on color theory, nature of art. Analysis of earlier masters. 12 illustrations. 80pp. of text. 5⅜ × 8½.   23411-8 Pa. $3.95

ANIMALS: 1,419 Copyright-Free Illustrations of Mammals, Birds, Fish, Insects, etc., Jim Harter (ed.). Clear wood engravings present, in extremely lifelike poses, over 1,000 species of animals. One of the most extensive pictorial sourcebooks of its kind. Captions. Index. 284pp. 9 × 12.   23766-4 Pa. $11.95

CELTIC ART: The Methods of Construction, George Bain. Simple geometric techniques for making Celtic interlacements, spirals, Kells-type initials, animals, humans, etc. Over 500 illustrations. 160pp. 9 × 12. (USO)   22923-8 Pa. $8.95

AN ATLAS OF ANATOMY FOR ARTISTS, Fritz Schider. Most thorough reference work on art anatomy in the world. Hundreds of illustrations, including selections from works by Vesalius, Leonardo, Goya, Ingres, Michelangelo, others. 593 illustrations. 192pp. 7⅛ × 10¼.   20241-0 Pa. $8.95

CELTIC HAND STROKE-BY-STROKE (Irish Half-Uncial from "The Book of Kells"): An Arthur Baker Calligraphy Manual, Arthur Baker. Complete guide to creating each letter of the alphabet in distinctive Celtic manner. Covers hand position, strokes, pens, inks, paper, more. Illustrated. 48pp. 8¼ × 11.

24336-2 Pa. $3.95

EASY ORIGAMI, John Montroll. Charming collection of 32 projects (hat, cup, pelican, piano, swan, many more) specially designed for the novice origami hobbyist. Clearly illustrated easy-to-follow instructions insure that even beginning papercrafters will achieve successful results. 48pp. 8¼ × 11.   27298-2 Pa. $2.95

THE COMPLETE BOOK OF BIRDHOUSE CONSTRUCTION FOR WOOD-WORKERS, Scott D. Campbell. Detailed instructions, illustrations, tables. Also data on bird habitat and instinct patterns. Bibliography. 3 tables. 63 illustrations in 15 figures. 48pp. 5¼ × 8½.   24407-5 Pa. $1.95

BLOOMINGDALE'S ILLUSTRATED 1886 CATALOG: Fashions, Dry Goods and Housewares, Bloomingdale Brothers. Famed merchants' extremely rare catalog depicting about 1,700 products: clothing, housewares, firearms, dry goods, jewelry, more. Invaluable for dating, identifying vintage items. Also, copyright-free graphics for artists, designers. Co-published with Henry Ford Museum & Greenfield Village. 160pp. 8¼ × 11.   25780-0 Pa. $9.95

HISTORIC COSTUME IN PICTURES, Braun & Schneider. Over 1,450 costumed figures in clearly detailed engravings—from dawn of civilization to end of 19th century. Captions. Many folk costumes. 256pp. 8⅜ × 11¾.   23150-X Pa. $10.95

THE WIT AND HUMOR OF OSCAR WILDE, Alvin Redman (ed.). More than 1,000 ripostes, paradoxes, wisecracks: Work is the curse of the drinking classes; I can resist everything except temptation; etc. 258pp. 5⅜ × 8½.   20602-5 Pa. $4.95

SHAKESPEARE LEXICON AND QUOTATION DICTIONARY, Alexander Schmidt. Full definitions, locations, shades of meaning in every word in plays and poems. More than 50,000 exact quotations. 1,485pp. 6½ × 9¼. 2-vol. set.
Vol. 1: 22726-X Pa. $15.95
Vol. 2: 22727-8 Pa. $15.95

SELECTED POEMS, Emily Dickinson. Over 100 best-known, best-loved poems by one of America's foremost poets, reprinted from authoritative early editions. No comparable edition at this price. Index of first lines. 64pp. 5³⁄₁₆ × 8¼.
26466-1 Pa. $1.00

CELEBRATED CASES OF JUDGE DEE (DEE GOONG AN), translated by Robert van Gulik. Authentic 18th-century Chinese detective novel; Dee and associates solve three interlocked cases. Led to van Gulik's own stories with same characters. Extensive introduction. 9 illustrations. 237pp. 5⅜ × 8½.
23337-5 Pa. $5.95

THE MALLEUS MALEFICARUM OF KRAMER AND SPRENGER, translated by Montague Summers. Full text of most important witchhunter's "bible," used by both Catholics and Protestants. 278pp. 6⅝ × 10.   22802-9 Pa. $10.95

SPANISH STORIES/CUENTOS ESPAÑOLES: A Dual-Language Book, Angel Flores (ed.). Unique format offers 13 great stories in Spanish by Cervantes, Borges, others. Faithful English translations on facing pages. 352pp. 5⅜ × 8½.
25399-6 Pa. $8.95

THE CHICAGO WORLD'S FAIR OF 1893: A Photographic Record, Stanley Appelbaum (ed.). 128 rare photos show 200 buildings, Beaux-Arts architecture, Midway, original Ferris Wheel, Edison's kinetoscope, more. Architectural emphasis; full text. 116pp. 8¼ × 11.   23990-X Pa. $9.95

OLD QUEENS, N.Y., IN EARLY PHOTOGRAPHS, Vincent F. Seyfried and William Asadorian. Over 160 rare photographs of Maspeth, Jamaica, Jackson Heights, and other areas. Vintage views of DeWitt Clinton mansion, 1939 World's Fair and more. Captions. 192pp. 8⅞ × 11.   26358-4 Pa. $12.95

CAPTURED BY THE INDIANS: 15 Firsthand Accounts, 1750–1870, Frederick Drimmer. Astounding true historical accounts of grisly torture, bloody conflicts, relentless pursuits, miraculous escapes and more, by people who lived to tell the tale. 384pp. 5⅜ × 8½.   24901-8 Pa. $7.95

THE WORLD'S GREAT SPEECHES, Lewis Copeland and Lawrence W. Lamm (eds.). Vast collection of 278 speeches of Greeks to 1970. Powerful and effective models; unique look at history. 842pp. 5⅜ × 8½.   20468-5 Pa. $13.95

THE BOOK OF THE SWORD, Sir Richard F. Burton. Great Victorian scholar/adventurer's eloquent, erudite history of the "queen of weapons"—from prehistory to early Roman Empire. Evolution and development of early swords, variations (sabre, broadsword, cutlass, scimitar, etc.), much more. 336pp. 6⅛ × 9¼. 25434-8 Pa. $8.95

FRANK LLOYD WRIGHT'S HOLLYHOCK HOUSE, Donald Hoffmann. Lavishly illustrated, carefully documented study of one of Wright's most controversial residential designs. Over 120 photographs, floor plans, elevations, etc. Detailed perceptive text by noted Wright scholar. Index. 128pp. 9¼ × 10¾.
27133-1 Pa. $11.95

THE MALE AND FEMALE FIGURE IN MOTION: 60 Classic Photographic Sequences, Eadweard Muybridge. 60 true-action photographs of men and women walking, running, climbing, bending, turning, etc., reproduced from rare 19th-century masterpiece. vi + 121pp. 9 × 12.
24745-7 Pa. $10.95

1001 QUESTIONS ANSWERED ABOUT THE SEASHORE, N. J. Berrill and Jacquelyn Berrill. Queries answered about dolphins, sea snails, sponges, starfish, fishes, shore birds, many others. Covers appearance, breeding, growth, feeding, much more. 305pp. 5¼ × 8¼.
23366-9 Pa. $7.95

GUIDE TO OWL WATCHING IN NORTH AMERICA, Donald S. Heintzelman. Superb guide offers complete data and descriptions of 19 species: barn owl, screech owl, snowy owl, many more. Expert coverage of owl-watching equipment, conservation, migrations and invasions, etc. Guide to observing sites. 84 illustrations. xiii + 193pp. 5⅜ × 8½.
27344-X Pa. $7.95

MEDICINAL AND OTHER USES OF NORTH AMERICAN PLANTS: A Historical Survey with Special Reference to the Eastern Indian Tribes, Charlotte Erichsen-Brown. Chronological historical citations document 500 years of usage of plants, trees, shrubs native to eastern Canada, northeastern U.S. Also complete identifying information. 343 illustrations. 544pp. 6½ × 9¼.
25951-X Pa. $12.95

STORYBOOK MAZES, Dave Phillips. 23 stories and mazes on two-page spreads: Wizard of Oz, Treasure Island, Robin Hood, etc. Solutions. 64pp. 8¼ × 11.
23628-5 Pa. $2.95

NEGRO FOLK MUSIC, U.S.A., Harold Courlander. Noted folklorist's scholarly yet readable analysis of rich and varied musical tradition. Includes authentic versions of over 40 folk songs. Valuable bibliography and discography. xi + 324pp. 5⅜ × 8½.
27350-4 Pa. $7.95

MOVIE-STAR PORTRAITS OF THE FORTIES, John Kobal (ed.). 163 glamor, studio photos of 106 stars of the 1940s: Rita Hayworth, Ava Gardner, Marlon Brando, Clark Gable, many more. 176pp. 8⅜ × 11¼.
23546-7 Pa. $10.95

BENCHLEY LOST AND FOUND, Robert Benchley. Finest humor from early 30s, about pet peeves, child psychologists, post office and others. Mostly unavailable elsewhere. 73 illustrations by Peter Arno and others. 183pp. 5⅜ × 8½.
22410-4 Pa. $5.95

YEKL and THE IMPORTED BRIDEGROOM AND OTHER STORIES OF YIDDISH NEW YORK, Abraham Cahan. Film Hester Street based on Yekl (1896). Novel, other stories among first about Jewish immigrants on N.Y.'s East Side. 240pp. 5⅜ × 8½.
22427-9 Pa. $5.95

SELECTED POEMS, Walt Whitman. Generous sampling from *Leaves of Grass*. Twenty-four poems include "I Hear America Singing," "Song of the Open Road," "I Sing the Body Electric," "When Lilacs Last in the Dooryard Bloom'd," "O Captain! My Captain!"—all reprinted from an authoritative edition. Lists of titles and first lines. 128pp. 5³⁄₁₆ × 8¼.
26878-0 Pa. $1.00

MY BONDAGE AND MY FREEDOM, Frederick Douglass. Born a slave, Douglass became outspoken force in antislavery movement. The best of Douglass' autobiographies. Graphic description of slave life. 464pp. 5⅜ × 8½. 22457-0 Pa. $8.95

FOLLOWING THE EQUATOR: A Journey Around the World, Mark Twain. Fascinating humorous account of 1897 voyage to Hawaii, Australia, India, New Zealand, etc. Ironic, bemused reports on peoples, customs, climate, flora and fauna, politics, much more. 197 illustrations. 720pp. 5⅜ × 8½. 26113-1 Pa. $15.95

THE PEOPLE CALLED SHAKERS, Edward D. Andrews. Definitive study of Shakers: origins, beliefs, practices, dances, social organization, furniture and crafts, etc. 33 illustrations. 351pp. 5⅜ × 8½. 21081-2 Pa. $7.95

THE MYTHS OF GREECE AND ROME, H. A. Guerber. A classic of mythology, generously illustrated, long prized for its simple, graphic, accurate retelling of the principal myths of Greece and Rome, and for its commentary on their origins and significance. With 64 illustrations by Michelangelo, Raphael, Titian, Rubens, Canova, Bernini and others. 480pp. 5⅜ × 8½. 27584-1 Pa. $9.95

PSYCHOLOGY OF MUSIC, Carl E. Seashore. Classic work discusses music as a medium from psychological viewpoint. Clear treatment of physical acoustics, auditory apparatus, sound perception, development of musical skills, nature of musical feeling, host of other topics. 88 figures. 408pp. 5⅜ × 8½. 21851-1 Pa. $9.95

THE PHILOSOPHY OF HISTORY, Georg W. Hegel. Great classic of Western thought develops concept that history is not chance but rational process, the evolution of freedom. 457pp. 5⅜ × 8½. 20112-0 Pa. $8.95

THE BOOK OF TEA, Kakuzo Okakura. Minor classic of the Orient: entertaining, charming explanation, interpretation of traditional Japanese culture in terms of tea ceremony. 94pp. 5⅜ × 8½. 20070-1 Pa. $2.95

LIFE IN ANCIENT EGYPT, Adolf Erman. Fullest, most thorough, detailed older account with much not in more recent books, domestic life, religion, magic, medicine, commerce, much more. Many illustrations reproduce tomb paintings, carvings, hieroglyphs, etc. 597pp. 5⅜ × 8½. 22632-8 Pa. $9.95

SUNDIALS, Their Theory and Construction, Albert Waugh. Far and away the best, most thorough coverage of ideas, mathematics concerned, types, construction, adjusting anywhere. Simple, nontechnical treatment allows even children to build several of these dials. Over 100 illustrations. 230pp. 5⅜ × 8½. 22947-5 Pa. $5.95

DYNAMICS OF FLUIDS IN POROUS MEDIA, Jacob Bear. For advanced students of ground water hydrology, soil mechanics and physics, drainage and irrigation engineering, and more. 335 illustrations. Exercises, with answers. 784pp. 6⅛ × 9¼. 65675-6 Pa. $19.95

SONGS OF EXPERIENCE: Facsimile Reproduction with 26 Plates in Full Color, William Blake. 26 full-color plates from a rare 1826 edition. Includes "The Tyger," "London," "Holy Thursday," and other poems. Printed text of poems. 48pp. 5¼ × 7. 24636-1 Pa. $3.95

OLD-TIME VIGNETTES IN FULL COLOR, Carol Belanger Grafton (ed.). Over 390 charming, often sentimental illustrations, selected from archives of Victorian graphics—pretty women posing, children playing, food, flowers, kittens and puppies, smiling cherubs, birds and butterflies, much more. All copyright-free. 48pp. 9¼ × 12¼. 27269-9 Pa. $5.95

PERSPECTIVE FOR ARTISTS, Rex Vicat Cole. Depth, perspective of sky and sea, shadows, much more, not usually covered. 391 diagrams, 81 reproductions of drawings and paintings. 279pp. 5⅜ × 8½. 22487-2 Pa. $6.95

DRAWING THE LIVING FIGURE, Joseph Sheppard. Innovative approach to artistic anatomy focuses on specifics of surface anatomy, rather than muscles and bones. Over 170 drawings of live models in front, back and side views, and in widely varying poses. Accompanying diagrams. 177 illustrations. Introduction. Index. 144pp. 8⅜ × 11¼. 26723-7 Pa. $7.95

GOTHIC AND OLD ENGLISH ALPHABETS: 100 Complete Fonts, Dan X. Solo. Add power, elegance to posters, signs, other graphics with 100 stunning copyright-free alphabets: Blackstone, Dolbey, Germania, 97 more—including many lower-case, numerals, punctuation marks. 104pp. 8⅛ × 11. 24695-7 Pa. $7.95

HOW TO DO BEADWORK, Mary White. Fundamental book on craft from simple projects to five-bead chains and woven works. 106 illustrations. 142pp. 5⅜ × 8. 20697-1 Pa. $4.95

THE BOOK OF WOOD CARVING, Charles Marshall Sayers. Finest book for beginners discusses fundamentals and offers 34 designs. "Absolutely first rate . . . well thought out and well executed."—E. J. Tangerman. 118pp. 7¾ × 10⅝. 23654-4 Pa. $5.95

ILLUSTRATED CATALOG OF CIVIL WAR MILITARY GOODS: Union Army Weapons, Insignia, Uniform Accessories, and Other Equipment, Schuyler, Hartley, and Graham. Rare, profusely illustrated 1846 catalog includes Union Army uniform and dress regulations, arms and ammunition, coats, insignia, flags, swords, rifles, etc. 226 illustrations. 160pp. 9 × 12. 24939-5 Pa. $10.95

WOMEN'S FASHIONS OF THE EARLY 1900s: An Unabridged Republication of "New York Fashions, 1909," National Cloak & Suit Co. Rare catalog of mail-order fashions documents women's and children's clothing styles shortly after the turn of the century. Captions offer full descriptions, prices. Invaluable resource for fashion, costume historians. Approximately 725 illustrations. 128pp. 8⅜ × 11¼. 27276-1 Pa. $10.95

THE 1912 AND 1915 GUSTAV STICKLEY FURNITURE CATALOGS, Gustav Stickley. With over 200 detailed illustrations and descriptions, these two catalogs are essential reading and reference materials and identification guides for Stickley furniture. Captions cite materials, dimensions and prices. 112pp. 6½ × 9¼. 26676-1 Pa. $9.95

EARLY AMERICAN LOCOMOTIVES, John H. White, Jr. Finest locomotive engravings from early 19th century: historical (1804–74), main-line (after 1870), special, foreign, etc. 147 plates. 142pp. 11⅜ × 8¼. 22772-3 Pa. $8.95

THE TALL SHIPS OF TODAY IN PHOTOGRAPHS, Frank O. Braynard. Lavishly illustrated tribute to nearly 100 majestic contemporary sailing vessels: Amerigo Vespucci, Clearwater, Constitution, Eagle, Mayflower, Sea Cloud, Victory, many more. Authoritative captions provide statistics, background on each ship. 190 black-and-white photographs and illustrations. Introduction. 128pp. 8⅞ × 11¾. 27163-3 Pa. $12.95

EARLY NINETEENTH-CENTURY CRAFTS AND TRADES, Peter Stockham (ed.). Extremely rare 1807 volume describes to youngsters the crafts and trades of the day: brickmaker, weaver, dressmaker, bookbinder, ropemaker, saddler, many more. Quaint prose, charming illustrations for each craft. 20 black-and-white line illustrations. 192pp. 4⅝ × 6. 27293-1 Pa. $4.95

VICTORIAN FASHIONS AND COSTUMES FROM HARPER'S BAZAR, 1867-1898, Stella Blum (ed.). Day costumes, evening wear, sports clothes, shoes, hats, other accessories in over 1,000 detailed engravings. 320pp. 9⅜ × 12¼. 22990-4 Pa. $13.95

GUSTAV STICKLEY, THE CRAFTSMAN, Mary Ann Smith. Superb study surveys broad scope of Stickley's achievement, especially in architecture. Design philosophy, rise and fall of the Craftsman empire, descriptions and floor plans for many Craftsman houses, more. 86 black-and-white halftones. 31 line illustrations. Introduction. 208pp. 6½ × 9¼. 27210-9 Pa. $9.95

THE LONG ISLAND RAIL ROAD IN EARLY PHOTOGRAPHS, Ron Ziel. Over 220 rare photos, informative text document origin (1844) and development of rail service on Long Island. Vintage views of early trains, locomotives, stations, passengers, crews, much more. Captions. 8⅞ × 11¾. 26301-0 Pa. $13.95

THE BOOK OF OLD SHIPS: From Egyptian Galleys to Clipper Ships, Henry B. Culver. Superb, authoritative history of sailing vessels, with 80 magnificent line illustrations. Galley, bark, caravel, longship, whaler, many more. Detailed, informative text on each vessel by noted naval historian. Introduction. 256pp. 5⅜ × 8½. 27332-6 Pa. $6.95

TEN BOOKS ON ARCHITECTURE, Vitruvius. The most important book ever written on architecture. Early Roman aesthetics, technology, classical orders, site selection, all other aspects. Morgan translation. 331pp. 5⅜ × 8½. 20645-9 Pa. $8.95

THE HUMAN FIGURE IN MOTION, Eadweard Muybridge. More than 4,500 stopped-action photos, in action series, showing undraped men, women, children jumping, lying down, throwing, sitting, wrestling, carrying, etc. 390pp. 7⅞ × 10⅝. 20204-6 Clothbd. $24.95

TREES OF THE EASTERN AND CENTRAL UNITED STATES AND CANADA, William M. Harlow. Best one-volume guide to 140 trees. Full descriptions, woodlore, range, etc. Over 600 illustrations. Handy size. 288pp. 4½ × 6⅜. 20395-6 Pa. $5.95

SONGS OF WESTERN BIRDS, Dr. Donald J. Borror. Complete song and call repertoire of 60 western species, including flycatchers, juncoes, cactus wrens, many more—includes fully illustrated booklet. Cassette and manual 99913-0 $8.95

GROWING AND USING HERBS AND SPICES, Milo Miloradovich. Versatile handbook provides all the information needed for cultivation and use of all the herbs and spices available in North America. 4 illustrations. Index. Glossary. 236pp. 5⅜ × 8½. 25058-X Pa. $5.95

BIG BOOK OF MAZES AND LABYRINTHS, Walter Shepherd. 50 mazes and labyrinths in all—classical, solid, ripple, and more—in one great volume. Perfect inexpensive puzzler for clever youngsters. Full solutions. 112pp. 8⅛ × 11. 22951-3 Pa. $3.95

PIANO TUNING, J. Cree Fischer. Clearest, best book for beginner, amateur. Simple repairs, raising dropped notes, tuning by easy method of flattened fifths. No previous skills needed. 4 illustrations. 201pp. 5⅜ × 8½. 23267-0 Pa. $5.95

A SOURCE BOOK IN THEATRICAL HISTORY, A. M. Nagler. Contemporary observers on acting, directing, make-up, costuming, stage props, machinery, scene design, from Ancient Greece to Chekhov. 611pp. 5⅜ × 8½. 20515-0 Pa. $11.95

THE COMPLETE NONSENSE OF EDWARD LEAR, Edward Lear. All nonsense limericks, zany alphabets, Owl and Pussycat, songs, nonsense botany, etc., illustrated by Lear. Total of 320pp. 5⅜ × 8½. (USO) 20167-8 Pa. $5.95

VICTORIAN PARLOUR POETRY: An Annotated Anthology, Michael R. Turner. 117 gems by Longfellow, Tennyson, Browning, many lesser-known poets. "The Village Blacksmith," "Curfew Must Not Ring Tonight," "Only a Baby Small," dozens more, often difficult to find elsewhere. Index of poets, titles, first lines. xxiii + 325pp. 5⅜ × 8¼. 27044-0 Pa. $8.95

DUBLINERS, James Joyce. Fifteen stories offer vivid, tightly focused observations of the lives of Dublin's poorer classes. At least one, "The Dead," is considered a masterpiece. Reprinted complete and unabridged from standard edition. 160pp. 5³⁄₁₆ × 8¼. 26870-5 Pa. $1.00

THE HAUNTED MONASTERY and THE CHINESE MAZE MURDERS, Robert van Gulik. Two full novels by van Gulik, set in 7th-century China, continue adventures of Judge Dee and his companions. An evil Taoist monastery, seemingly supernatural events; overgrown topiary maze hides strange crimes. 27 illustrations. 328pp. 5⅜ × 8½. 23502-5 Pa. $7.95

THE BOOK OF THE SACRED MAGIC OF ABRAMELIN THE MAGE, translated by S. MacGregor Mathers. Medieval manuscript of ceremonial magic. Basic document in Aleister Crowley, Golden Dawn groups. 268pp. 5⅜ × 8½. 23211-5 Pa. $7.95

NEW RUSSIAN-ENGLISH AND ENGLISH-RUSSIAN DICTIONARY, M. A. O'Brien. This is a remarkably handy Russian dictionary, containing a surprising amount of information, including over 70,000 entries. 366pp. 4½ × 6⅛. 20208-9 Pa. $8.95

HISTORIC HOMES OF THE AMERICAN PRESIDENTS, Second, Revised Edition, Irvin Haas. A traveler's guide to American Presidential homes, most open to the public, depicting and describing homes occupied by every American President from George Washington to George Bush. With visiting hours, admission charges, travel routes. 175 photographs. Index. 160pp. 8¼ × 11. 26751-2 Pa. $10.95

NEW YORK IN THE FORTIES, Andreas Feininger. 162 brilliant photographs by the well-known photographer, formerly with *Life* magazine. Commuters, shoppers, Times Square at night, much else from city at its peak. Captions by John von Hartz. 181pp. 9¼ × 10¾. 23585-8 Pa. $12.95

INDIAN SIGN LANGUAGE, William Tomkins. Over 525 signs developed by Sioux and other tribes. Written instructions and diagrams. Also 290 pictographs. 111pp. 6⅛ × 9¼. 22029-X Pa. $3.50

THE BEST TALES OF HOFFMANN, E. T. A. Hoffmann. 10 of Hoffmann's most important stories: "Nutcracker and the King of Mice," "The Golden Flowerpot," etc. 458pp. 5⅜ × 8½. 21793-0 Pa. $8.95

FROM FETISH TO GOD IN ANCIENT EGYPT, E. A. Wallis Budge. Rich detailed survey of Egyptian conception of "God" and gods, magic, cult of animals, Osiris, more. Also, superb English translations of hymns and legends. 240 illustrations. 545pp. 5⅜ × 8½. 25803-3 Pa. $11.95

FRENCH STORIES/CONTES FRANÇAIS: A Dual-Language Book, Wallace Fowlie. Ten stories by French masters, Voltaire to Camus: "Micromegas" by Voltaire; "The Atheist's Mass" by Balzac; "Minuet" by de Maupassant; "The Guest" by Camus, six more. Excellent English translations on facing pages. Also French-English vocabulary list, exercises, more. 352pp. 5⅜ × 8½. 26443-2 Pa. $8.95

CHICAGO AT THE TURN OF THE CENTURY IN PHOTOGRAPHS: 122 Historic Views from the Collections of the Chicago Historical Society, Larry A. Viskochil. Rare large-format prints offer detailed views of City Hall, State Street, the Loop, Hull House, Union Station, many other landmarks, circa 1904–1913. Introduction. Captions. Maps. 144pp. 9⅜ × 12¼. 24656-6 Pa. $12.95

OLD BROOKLYN IN EARLY PHOTOGRAPHS, 1865–1929, William Lee Younger. Luna Park, Gravesend race track, construction of Grand Army Plaza, moving of Hotel Brighton, etc. 157 previously unpublished photographs. 165pp. 8⅞ × 11¾. 23587-4 Pa. $12.95

THE MYTHS OF THE NORTH AMERICAN INDIANS, Lewis Spence. Rich anthology of the myths and legends of the Algonquins, Iroquois, Pawnees and Sioux, prefaced by an extensive historical and ethnological commentary. 36 illustrations. 480pp. 5⅜ × 8½. 25967-6 Pa. $8.95

AN ENCYCLOPEDIA OF BATTLES: Accounts of Over 1,560 Battles from 1479 B.C. to the Present, David Eggenberger. Essential details of every major battle in recorded history from the first battle of Megiddo in 1479 B.C. to Grenada in 1984. List of Battle Maps. New Appendix covering the years 1967–1984. Index. 99 illustrations. 544pp. 6½ × 9¼. 24913-1 Pa. $14.95

SAILING ALONE AROUND THE WORLD, Captain Joshua Slocum. First man to sail around the world, alone, in small boat. One of great feats of seamanship told in delightful manner. 67 illustrations. 294pp. 5⅜ × 8½. 20326-3 Pa. $5.95

ANARCHISM AND OTHER ESSAYS, Emma Goldman. Powerful, penetrating, prophetic essays on direct action, role of minorities, prison reform, puritan hypocrisy, violence, etc. 271pp. 5⅜ × 8½. 22484-8 Pa. $5.95

MYTHS OF THE HINDUS AND BUDDHISTS, Ananda K. Coomaraswamy and Sister Nivedita. Great stories of the epics; deeds of Krishna, Shiva, taken from puranas, Vedas, folk tales; etc. 32 illustrations. 400pp. 5⅜ × 8½. 21759-0 Pa. $9.95

BEYOND PSYCHOLOGY, Otto Rank. Fear of death, desire of immortality, nature of sexuality, social organization, creativity, according to Rankian system. 291pp. 5⅜ × 8½. 20485-5 Pa. $7.95

A THEOLOGICO-POLITICAL TREATISE, Benedict Spinoza. Also contains unfinished Political Treatise. Great classic on religious liberty, theory of government on common consent. R. Elwes translation. Total of 421pp. 5⅜ × 8½. 20249-6 Pa. $7.95

PHOTOGRAPHIC SKETCHBOOK OF THE CIVIL WAR, Alexander Gardner. 100 photos taken on field during the Civil War. Famous shots of Manassas, Harper's Ferry, Lincoln, Richmond, slave pens, etc. 244pp. 10⅝ × 8¼.
22731-6 Pa. $9.95

FIVE ACRES AND INDEPENDENCE, Maurice G. Kains. Great back-to-the-land classic explains basics of self-sufficient farming. The one book to get. 95 illustrations. 397pp. 5⅜ × 8½.
20974-1 Pa. $6.95

SONGS OF EASTERN BIRDS, Dr. Donald J. Borror. Songs and calls of 60 species most common to eastern U.S.: warblers, woodpeckers, flycatchers, thrushes, larks, many more in high-quality recording.
Cassette and manual 99912-2 $8.95

A MODERN HERBAL, Margaret Grieve. Much the fullest, most exact, most useful compilation of herbal material. Gigantic alphabetical encyclopedia, from aconite to zedoary, gives botanical information, medical properties, folklore, economic uses, much else. Indispensable to serious reader. 161 illustrations. 888pp. 6½ × 9¼. 2-vol. set. (USO)
Vol. I: 22798-7 Pa. $9.95
Vol. II: 22799-5 Pa. $9.95

HIDDEN TREASURE MAZE BOOK, Dave Phillips. Solve 34 challenging mazes accompanied by heroic tales of adventure. Evil dragons, people-eating plants, bloodthirsty giants, many more dangerous adversaries lurk at every twist and turn. 34 mazes, stories, solutions. 48pp. 8¼ × 11.
24566-7 Pa. $2.95

LETTERS OF W. A. MOZART, Wolfgang A. Mozart. Remarkable letters show bawdy wit, humor, imagination, musical insights, contemporary musical world; includes some letters from Leopold Mozart. 276pp. 5⅜ × 8½.
22859-2 Pa. $6.95

BASIC PRINCIPLES OF CLASSICAL BALLET, Agrippina Vaganova. Great Russian theoretician, teacher explains methods for teaching classical ballet. 118 illustrations. 175pp. 5⅜ × 8½.
22036-2 Pa. $4.95

THE JUMPING FROG, Mark Twain. Revenge edition. The original story of The Celebrated Jumping Frog of Calaveras County, a hapless French translation, and Twain's hilarious "retranslation" from the French. 12 illustrations. 66pp. 5⅜ × 8½.
22686-7 Pa. $3.50

BEST REMEMBERED POEMS, Martin Gardner (ed.). The 126 poems in this superb collection of 19th- and 20th-century British and American verse range from Shelley's "To a Skylark" to the impassioned "Renascence" of Edna St. Vincent Millay and to Edward Lear's whimsical "The Owl and the Pussycat." 224pp. 5⅜ × 8½.
27165-X Pa. $4.95

COMPLETE SONNETS, William Shakespeare. Over 150 exquisite poems deal with love, friendship, the tyranny of time, beauty's evanescence, death and other themes in language of remarkable power, precision and beauty. Glossary of archaic terms. 80pp. 5³⁄₁₆ × 8¼.
26686-9 Pa. $1.00

BODIES IN A BOOKSHOP, R. T. Campbell. Challenging mystery of blackmail and murder with ingenious plot and superbly drawn characters. In the best tradition of British suspense fiction. 192pp. 5⅜ × 8½.
24720-1 Pa. $5.95

AUTOBIOGRAPHY: The Story of My Experiments with Truth, Mohandas K. Gandhi. Boyhood, legal studies, purification, the growth of the Satyagraha (nonviolent protest) movement. Critical, inspiring work of the man responsible for the freedom of India. 480pp. 5⅜ × 8½. (USO) 24593-4 Pa. $7.95

CELTIC MYTHS AND LEGENDS, T. W. Rolleston. Masterful retelling of Irish and Welsh stories and tales. Cuchulain, King Arthur, Deirdre, the Grail, many more. First paperback edition. 58 full-page illustrations. 512pp. 5⅜ × 8½.
26507-2 Pa. $9.95

THE PRINCIPLES OF PSYCHOLOGY, William James. Famous long course complete, unabridged. Stream of thought, time perception, memory, experimental methods; great work decades ahead of its time. 94 figures. 1,391pp. 5⅜ × 8½. 2-vol. set.
Vol. I: 20381-6 Pa. $12.95
Vol. II: 20382-4 Pa. $12.95

THE WORLD AS WILL AND REPRESENTATION, Arthur Schopenhauer. Definitive English translation of Schopenhauer's life work, correcting more than 1,000 errors, omissions in earlier translations. Translated by E. F. J. Payne. Total of 1,269pp. 5⅜ × 8½. 2-vol. set. Vol. 1: 21761-2 Pa. $10.95
Vol. 2: 21762-0 Pa. $11.95

MAGIC AND MYSTERY IN TIBET, Madame Alexandra David-Neel. Experiences among lamas, magicians, sages, sorcerers, Bonpa wizards. A true psychic discovery. 32 illustrations. 321pp. 5⅜ × 8½. (USO) 22682-4 Pa. $8.95

THE EGYPTIAN BOOK OF THE DEAD, E. A. Wallis Budge. Complete reproduction of Ani's papyrus, finest ever found. Full hieroglyphic text, interlinear transliteration, word-for-word translation, smooth translation. 533pp. 6½ × 9¼.
21866-X Pa. $9.95

MATHEMATICS FOR THE NONMATHEMATICIAN, Morris Kline. Detailed, college-level treatment of mathematics in cultural and historical context, with numerous exercises. Recommended Reading Lists. Tables. Numerous figures. 641pp. 5⅜ × 8½. 24823-2 Pa. $11.95

THEORY OF WING SECTIONS: Including a Summary of Airfoil Data, Ira H. Abbott and A. E. von Doenhoff. Concise compilation of subsonic aerodynamic characteristics of NACA wing sections, plus description of theory. 350pp. of tables. 693pp. 5⅜ × 8½. 60586-8 Pa. $13.95

THE RIME OF THE ANCIENT MARINER, Gustave Doré, S. T. Coleridge. Doré's finest work; 34 plates capture moods, subtleties of poem. Flawless full-size reproductions printed on facing pages with authoritative text of poem. "Beautiful. Simply beautiful."—*Publisher's Weekly.* 77pp. 9¼ × 12. 22305-1 Pa. $5.95

NORTH AMERICAN INDIAN DESIGNS FOR ARTISTS AND CRAFTS-PEOPLE, Eva Wilson. Over 360 authentic copyright-free designs adapted from Navajo blankets, Hopi pottery, Sioux buffalo hides, more. Geometrics, symbolic figures, plant and animal motifs, etc. 128pp. 8⅜ × 11. (EUK) 25341-4 Pa. $7.95

SCULPTURE: Principles and Practice, Louis Slobodkin. Step-by-step approach to clay, plaster, metals, stone; classical and modern. 253 drawings, photos. 255pp. 8⅛ × 11. 22960-2 Pa. $9.95

ANATOMY: A Complete Guide for Artists, Joseph Sheppard. A master of figure drawing shows artists how to render human anatomy convincingly. Over 460 illustrations. 224pp. 8⅜ × 11¼. 27279-6 Pa. $9.95

MEDIEVAL CALLIGRAPHY: Its History and Technique, Marc Drogin. Spirited history, comprehensive instruction manual covers 13 styles (ca. 4th century thru 15th). Excellent photographs; directions for duplicating medieval techniques with modern tools. 224pp. 8⅜ × 11¼. 26142-5 Pa. $11.95

DRIED FLOWERS: How to Prepare Them, Sarah Whitlock and Martha Rankin. Complete instructions on how to use silica gel, meal and borax, perlite aggregate, sand and borax, glycerine and water to create attractive permanent flower arrangements. 12 illustrations. 32pp. 5⅜ × 8½. 21802-3 Pa. $1.00

EASY-TO-MAKE BIRD FEEDERS FOR WOODWORKERS, Scott D. Campbell. Detailed, simple-to-use guide for designing, constructing, caring for and using feeders. Text, illustrations for 12 classic and contemporary designs. 96pp. 5⅜ × 8½. 25847-5 Pa. $2.95

OLD-TIME CRAFTS AND TRADES, Peter Stockham. An 1807 book created to teach children about crafts and trades open to them as future careers. It describes in detailed, nontechnical terms 24 different occupations, among them coachmaker, gardener, hairdresser, lacemaker, shoemaker, wheelwright, copper-plate printer, milliner, trunkmaker, merchant and brewer. Finely detailed engravings illustrate each occupation. 192pp. 4⅝ × 6. 27398-9 Pa. $4.95

THE HISTORY OF UNDERCLOTHES, C. Willett Cunnington and Phyllis Cunnington. Fascinating, well-documented survey covering six centuries of English undergarments, enhanced with over 100 illustrations: 12th-century laced-up bodice, footed long drawers (1795), 19th-century bustles, 19th-century corsets for men, Victorian "bust improvers," much more. 272pp. 5⅜ × 8¼. 27124-2 Pa. $9.95

ARTS AND CRAFTS FURNITURE: The Complete Brooks Catalog of 1912, Brooks Manufacturing Co. Photos and detailed descriptions of more than 150 now very collectible furniture designs from the Arts and Crafts movement depict davenports, settees, buffets, desks, tables, chairs, bedsteads, dressers and more, all built of solid, quarter-sawed oak. Invaluable for students and enthusiasts of antiques, Americana and the decorative arts. 80pp. 6½ × 9¼. 27471-3 Pa. $7.95

HOW WE INVENTED THE AIRPLANE: An Illustrated History, Orville Wright. Fascinating firsthand account covers early experiments, construction of planes and motors, first flights, much more. Introduction and commentary by Fred C. Kelly. 76 photographs. 96pp. 8¼ × 11. 25662-6 Pa. $7.95

THE ARTS OF THE SAILOR: Knotting, Splicing and Ropework, Hervey Garrett Smith. Indispensable shipboard reference covers tools, basic knots and useful hitches; handsewing and canvas work, more. Over 100 illustrations. Delightful reading for sea lovers. 256pp. 5⅜ × 8½. 26440-8 Pa. $7.95

FRANK LLOYD WRIGHT'S FALLINGWATER: The House and Its History, Second, Revised Edition, Donald Hoffmann. A total revision—both in text and illustrations—of the standard document on Fallingwater, the boldest, most personal architectural statement of Wright's mature years, updated with valuable new material from the recently opened Frank Lloyd Wright Archives. "Fascinating"—The New York Times. 116 illustrations. 128pp. 9¼ × 10¾. 27430-6 Pa. $10.95

THE INFLUENCE OF SEA POWER UPON HISTORY, 1660–1783, A. T. Mahan. Influential classic of naval history and tactics still used as text in war colleges. First paperback edition. 4 maps. 24 battle plans. 640pp. 5⅜ × 8½.
25509-3 Pa. $12.95

THE STORY OF THE TITANIC AS TOLD BY ITS SURVIVORS, Jack Winocour (ed.). What it was really like. Panic, despair, shocking inefficiency, and a little heroism. More thrilling than any fictional account. 26 illustrations. 320pp. 5⅜ × 8½.
20610-6 Pa. $7.95

FAIRY AND FOLK TALES OF THE IRISH PEASANTRY, William Butler Yeats (ed.). Treasury of 64 tales from the twilight world of Celtic myth and legend: "The Soul Cages," "The Kildare Pooka," "King O'Toole and his Goose," many more. Introduction and Notes by W. B. Yeats. 352pp. 5⅜ × 8½.
26941-8 Pa. $7.95

BUDDHIST MAHAYANA TEXTS, E. B. Cowell and Others (eds.). Superb, accurate translations of basic documents in Mahayana Buddhism, highly important in history of religions. The Buddha-karita of Asvaghosha, Larger Sukhavativyuha, more. 448pp. 5⅜ × 8½. ,
25552-2 Pa. $9.95

ONE TWO THREE . . . INFINITY: Facts and Speculations of Science, George Gamow. Great physicist's fascinating, readable overview of contemporary science: number theory, relativity, fourth dimension, entropy, genes, atomic structure, much more. 128 illustrations. Index. 352pp. 5⅜ × 8½.
25664-2 Pa. $8.95

ENGINEERING IN HISTORY, Richard Shelton Kirby, et al. Broad, nontechnical survey of history's major technological advances: birth of Greek science, industrial revolution, electricity and applied science, 20th-century automation, much more. 181 illustrations. ". . . excellent . . ."—Isis. Bibliography. vii + 530pp. 5⅜ × 8¼.
26412-2 Pa. $14.95

Prices subject to change without notice.
Available at your book dealer or write for free catalog to Dept. GI, Dover Publications, Inc., 31 East 2nd St., Mineola, N.Y. 11501. Dover publishes more than 500 books each year on science, elementary and advanced mathematics, biology, music, art, literary history, social sciences and other areas.